Translating Southwestern Landscapes

Translating Southwestern Landscapes

The Making of an Anglo Literary Region

AUDREY GOODMAN

The University of Arizona Press   Tucson

The University of Arizona Press

© 2002 The Arizona Board of Regents

First printing

⊛ This book is printed on acid-free, archival-quality paper.

Manufactured in the United States of America

07   06   05   04   03   02   6   5   4   3   2   1

Library of Congress Cataloging-in-Publication Data

Goodman, Audrey, 1966–

Translating southwestern landscapes : the making of an Anglo literary
region / Audrey Goodman.

p. cm.

Includes bibliographical references and index.

ISBN 0-8165-2187-5

1. American literature—Southwestern States—History and criticism. 2.
Photography—Southwestern States—History.

3. Landscape photography—Southwestern States. 4. Southwestern States—
Intellectual life. 5. Southwestern States—In literature.

6. Landscape in literature. I. Title.

PS277 .G66 2002

810.9′979′09034—dc21

2002000712

British Library Cataloguing-in-Publication Data

A catalogue record for this book is available from the British Library.

Publication of this book is made possible in part by the proceeds of a
permanent endowment created with the assistance of a Challenge Grant
from the National Endowment for the Humanities, a federal agency.

FOR DAVID

Contents

Figures

Acknowledgments

MANY PEOPLE AIDED ME in the conception, research, and writing of this book. The project began at Columbia University, where my fellow Americanists shared their time and energies with someone just beginning to know what to write. Without Robert Ferguson's steady, rigorous, and repeated readings of the manuscript, I would never have realized my ambitions for the book. Ann Douglas, Andrew Delbanco, Karl Kroeber, and David Simpson provided me with models of intellectual passion, and posed critical questions that helped me to clarify my subject. At Georgia State, my colleagues in the English Department, especially Robert Sattelmeyer, Matthew Roudané, Virginia Spencer Carr, and Janet Gabler-Hover, encouraged me in the final stages of research and revision. Adam Wood assisted me with research for chapter 1. Patti Hartmann, my editor at the University of Arizona Press, combined good judgment and enthusiasm from the start; my anonymous readers made suggestions that improved the final manuscript.

Particular thanks are due to the many archivists, colleagues, and friends who generously extended their knowledge and their resources. Richard Rudisill and Arthur Olivas at the Museum of New Mexico Photo Archives supplied me with both essential images and the beginnings of my own Southwestern education. Laura Holt at the Laboratory of Anthropology in Santa Fe, Carolyn Garner at the Pasadena Public Library, and Leslie Calmes and Tony Celestino at the Center for Creative Photography opened their collections to me and guided me through them.

The following foundation directors, archivists, and librarians kindly gave me permission to reprint materials from their collections: Anthony Montoya at the Paul Strand Archive and Aperture Foundation; Agapita Judy Lopez at the Georgia O'Keeffe Foundation; Claudia Kishler at the Ansel Adams Publishing Rights Trust; John Cahoon at the Seaver Center for Western History Research, Los Angeles County Museum of Natural History; Stella De Sa Rego at the Center for Southwest Research, University of New Mexico; Kim Walters at the Braun Research Library, Southwest Museum; Ngadi

Kponou at the Beinecke Rare Book and Manuscript Library, Yale University; Maggie Kimball at the Cecil H. Green Library, Stanford University; Shan Sutton at the University of Arizona Library; and Joe McGregor at the USGS Photography Library. Alex Harris allowed me to reproduce his wonderful photographs, and Keith Lummis gave me license to quote extensively from his father's manuscripts.

For encouragement to investigate Navajo verbal and textile arts, I thank Grant Luckhardt. For introductions to the terrible beauty of Mexican culture and history, I am indebted to Enriqueta Rodriguez Carrington and Seth Fein. Teri Reynolds and Franco Moretti allowed me to complete the manuscript in Rome, and thus to feel anew the lure of a foreign landscape and the culture of everyday life.

I am grateful to the many institutions that sustained my research and provided audiences for my work. The Mellon Foundation, the Charles Redd Center for Western Studies, and Georgia State University all awarded grants essential for my archival work. Members of the Western Literature Association welcomed me despite my state of institutional origin and listened carefully as I tested my ideas. My thanks also go to the following journals for allowing me to publish here revised versions of articles which first appeared in their pages: "The Immeasurable Possession of Air: Willa Cather and Southwestern Romance," *Arizona Quarterly* 55, no. 4 (Winter 1999): 49–78; and "The Tasks of Southwestern Translation: Charles Lummis at Isleta Pueblo, 1888–92," *Journal of the Southwest* 43, no. 3 (Autumn 2001): 343–378.

Finally, I thank my family, and my husband David Payne most of all, for helping me to act on the conviction that culture deserves our best work and yields the greatest rewards.

Introduction

In LESLIE MARMON SILKO'S novel *Gardens in the Dunes* (1999), members of various Indian groups and a few Mormons gather to summon the Messiah along the western border of the Arizona Territory. First seen by the Paiute visionary Wovoka in 1890 and subsequently summoned by Ghost Dancers in the Plains and the Southwest, the Messiah was thought to respond to the devotional call of each people, in their own language. In his presence, however, "there was only one language spoken—the language of love—which all people understood" (34). The dream of a unifying language and a redemptive vision lures the novel's Indian and white heroines across late nineteenth-century America, through Europe, and back toward their original and adopted homelands. Learning foreign terms for familiar things, as Silko's Sand Lizard heroine Indigo does throughout her travels, only deepens the longing for her lost homeland's physical presence; to her, the promise of the infinitely comprehensible Messiah means both the possibility of an inter-tribal community and the hope that native peoples will be reunited with their places of origin. To have more than one name, to live in more than one place: Silko shows us that these dislocating effects of modernity require multiple acts of translation, acts of writing across cultures and histories that aim to communicate particular experiences of space and time but may not succeed in doing so.

Like Silko's narrative, this book reimagines the Southwest at the turn of the twentieth century as a space shaped by the antinomies of American modernity, a site of competing landscapes and translation practices. These antinomies include the forces of capitalist expansion that lowered spatial barriers only to create a demand for diverse places; the rise of corporate, scientific, and artistic specialization as well as a psychology of individuation, reinvention, and escape; and formulations of American "high culture" in response to the domination of mass audiences in every cultural field. As Russell Berman explains, "To be modern is to find ourselves in an environment that promises adventure, power, joy, growth, transformation of ourselves and the world—

and at the same time, that threatens to destroy everything we have, everything we know, everything we are."[1] In late nineteenth and early twentieth century America, the Southwest emerged as a modern battleground between dreams of self-transformation and fears of irreversible assimilation. For white Americans, the Southwest was all the more alluring because its history was unknown, its landscape exotic, and its cultures unfamiliar.

Beginning in the 1880s, Anglo-American writers and photographers projected themselves into the Southwest's many landscapes and documented the meeting of promised and actual experience. Their simultaneous dependence on the region's economic development and rhetorical resistance to it have correctly been deemed hypocritical and identified as imperialist nostalgia. Antimodernist ideology and colonial comforts unquestionably reinforced one another; as a result, the incorporation of the Southwest into the United States has consistently been articulated through discourses of loss. But we might also interpret this rhetorical resistance to the region's modernization as a sign that Anglos feared a homogeneous future. Southwestern spaces seemed to promise knowledge of native cultures; if these spaces were destroyed, such knowledge would pass away. Rather than univocally confirming a dominant imperial ideology or producing easily commodified regional images, Southwestern texts and images articulate the struggle between the intensity of an outsider's individual perception and his or her historical and cultural awareness. These struggles also speak to modernism's problematic "recovery" of the histories of native peoples even as modernization created a horizon of public tedium and private sameness. Southwestern writers tended to idealize cultural differences as they attempted cultural exchange by imagining "primitive" cultures to be purer and more powerful than their own. This study provides an archaeological description of these Anglo discourses of modernization and loss, discourses which still dominate North America's newest and most traditional region.

Region, Borderland, or Transnational Space?

The identity of regions has always been at issue in American literature, although it was only after the Civil War that writers began to delimit the region as a site of access to universal truths and to make "local color" writing into a dominant genre. Richard Brodhead explains the reasons for regionalism's late nineteenth-century popularity as a function of its complex public role, which "was not just to mourn lost cultures but to purvey a certain story of contemporary cultures and of the relations among them: to tell local cultures into a history of their supersession by a modern order now risen to national dominance."[2] Another way to explain local color's popularity at this time is to consider it as a particularly felicitous fit between the needs of expanding classes of writers and readers. Distinguished by its setting in a backward zone where locally variant folkways still prevailed, its ethnologically colorful characters, and its simulation of vernacular speech, regional fiction demanded local experience rather than an extensive literary education. As a result, it enabled writers with particular kinds of cultural knowledge to enter into a literary marketplace once dominated by the cultural elite, providing what Brodhead calls an "extension of literary franchise."

At the turn of the last century, the cultural construction of region seemed to serve the same purpose as the resurgence of national identity: it provided an imagined escape from racial, class, and gender conflicts, and an apparent recovery of society's cohesive forces. It is not surprising, then, to find similarities in the nostalgic rhetorics of regionalism and nationalism.[3] The antimodern turn to the concept of region was a protective response against much larger economic systems, as well as specifically national ones. By 1930 a region had become an aesthetic space where premodern traditions resisted social and technological change, culture took precedence over economics, local relationships were more important than national policies and international treaties, and concern for the natural environment outweighed the forces of development. Such aesthetic regionalism was nostalgic to the extent that it specified—and longed for—an older social organization, but it also provided a means of imagining local alternatives to the systemic expansion of the capitalist order.

The practices of regional representation in the early twentieth century are best understood as strategies of negotiation between the conceptual oppositions of city and country, center and periphery, insider and outsider, and authenticity and invention. Many American theorists in this period proposed the concept of region as a means of integrating culture and environment and mediating ideological extremes. Frederick Jackson Turner introduced not only the notion that the frontier closed in 1890 but also a conception of region as the nation's organic foundation. For Lewis Mumford and for Howard Odum and Harry Estill Moore, regional planning was a scientific strategy for managing social change. Mumford deployed an aesthetic regionalism in *The Golden Day* (1926) to counter the disintegration of American culture, and a "regional framework" in *The Culture of Cities* (1938) to halt the progression of world civilization from Metropolis to Megalopolis,

Tyrannopolis, and Nekropolis. He conceived region as an organic whole, and regional survey as "the bridge by which the specialist whose face is turned toward the library and the laboratory, and the active worker in the field, whose face is turned toward the city and region in which he lives, may come into contact."[4] Odum and Moore's *American Regionalism: A Cultural-Historical Approach to National Integration* (1938) envisioned a "folk-regional society" that would balance man, nature, and culture, and called attention to the multiple, interdependent definitions of region; facing the first page is a list of twenty-eight possibilities. And Donald Davidson, writing from the position of the Southern Agrarians, saw regionalism as a protest against "false nationalism" and "the condition under which the national American litera-ture exists as a literature: that is, its constant tendency to decentralize rather than centralize; or to correct overcentralization by conscious decentraliza-tion."[5] Such hopes of mediation run through the history of American re-gionalism, and through the literature of the Anglo Southwest.

To define a region is to draw boundaries that contain social relations. Because the Southwest is a space whose geographic boundaries are highly contested, I am less concerned with defining its physical parameters than with describing its competing symbolic forms, mapping its liminal spatial imaginaries, and speculating on its social meanings. Even geographical stud-ies arrive at territories of varying dimensions: Wilbur Zelinsky's *The Cul-tural Geography of the United States* finds southeastern Arizona, New Mexico, Texas, and Oklahoma to comprise the center of the "Southwest," while Daniel Meinig's *Southwest* defines the "basic" regional area as Arizona and New Mexico, with "an ambiguous border zone on the north and a distinct separation on the east and west" (8). Against these geographical definitions and the Southwest's imperial history, Richard Francaviglia argues for "as broad a definition as possible," and in this matter I take his lead. The area he terms the "Greater Southwest" spans the Anglo Southwest and *el norte*. Geographically, culturally, and politically, the Southwest is best understood as an area where "three major cultures—Native American, Hispanic, and Anglo American—have interacted, and been in considerable conflict, for more than five hundred years," an area that spans both sides of the U.S.–Mexican border.[6]

The Literary and Photographic Southwest
The chapters that follow analyze how Anglo writers and photographers struggled to construct the Southwest as a region, a cultural borderland, and

an emerging field of artistic production with its own rules for claiming authority and authenticity. In each case, extended experience in the Southwest challenged existing spatial classifications, political relations, and representational forms. Most writers and photographers initially imagined the Southwest through rhetorical modes traditionally engaged to impose colonial authority: tropes of sublime landscapes and empty spaces, images of picturesque and eroticized natives, and assertions of communal harmony.[7] Yet through hybrid forms of transcription, imagined scenes of brotherhood and sisterhood between Anglos and Indians, images of vernacular landscapes, and moments of ecological understanding, they translated their cross-cultural experience into new aesthetic forms and began to dream of transcending such colonial relations. Many writers brought the American literary tradition of regional realism to the Southwest, only to transform that tradition by mixing it with the utopian possibilities of romance. Distinguished by generic mobility and an overt ambivalence toward both subject and audience, Southwestern writing proved that no literary language and no single form of representation could adequately represent an entire set of cultures.

A study of the Anglo Southwest in the period might well proceed by genre: landscape photography, travel narrative, the novel, the naturalist essay, poetry, ethnographic translation, and Native American autobiography all have specific histories within the region. Such an approach would emphasize the way that region inflects aesthetic conventions, and would situate regional representation within larger literary categories. I have chosen instead to organize the book around the trajectories of five major figures and to focus on how the collaborative—and often imagined—relation between native inhabitant and regionalist writer seemed to demand of each writer perpetual shifts in genre or transformations of literary form.[8] My key figures are Charles Fletcher Lummis, who wrote tourist guides and popular story translations at a dizzying pace; Zane Grey, who concocted the first Western romances; Paul Strand, who applied modernist photographic technique to Southwestern landscapes; Mary Austin, who theorized and practiced ecocriticism and anti-imperial translation; and Willa Cather, who refined the destination of late imperial romance from a feeling of place to an experience of air. Each figure occupied a different position in the cultural field, and I show how each used the experience of Southwestern spaces and history either to blur formal and generic boundaries or to invent new literary categories.

Charles Lummis claimed, for better or worse, to have been the first to call the region the Southwest and thus to unify it for tourist consumption. He opens my study because his writing and his critical reception reveal the complicity between aesthetic production and capitalist expansion in the Southwest. But to call Lummis a self-serving, graceless promoter is to miss the meanings of his early career, when he lived at Isleta pueblo and aimed to translate his enthusiasm for Pueblo culture through a medium and a literary genre just beginning to reach popular audiences: photography and transcriptions of oral tales. His unpublished images, diaries, and correspondence provide further insight into his effort to negotiate between Pueblo and Anglo cultures, and to succeed in the literary marketplace through various forms of translation. Just as Frank Cushing's writings at Zuni illustrate what Curtis Hinsley has called a "heterodox poetics," so Lummis's hybrid writings at Isleta from the 1890s show the combined effects of participant-observer ethnography, romantic identification, and commercial pressure. His late career, however, proved less successful: with the growth of academic specialization in anthropology and folklore, the expansion of the literary marketplace and the museum industry, and the large-scale corporate advertisement of the Southwest through railroad promotion and World's Fairs and Expositions, a lone generalist like Lummis could not hold his own.

In the second chapter, I analyze the symbolic production of space in the earliest examples of the Western romance, the Southwest's major fictional genre and one that continues to sustain the contradictions and intimate the utopian possibilities of America's most distinctive landscape. Zane Grey's first formula Westerns, *The Heritage of the Desert* (1910), *Riders of the Purple Sage* (1912), *Desert Gold* (1913), and *The Rainbow Trail* (1915), all map the modern West through differentiating frontiers or borderlands into contradictory spaces of belief and economic necessity, feminine empowerment and masculine renewal, historical awareness and utopian imagining, desire and repression. I argue that Grey's ability to spatialize these contradictions enabled him to develop the flexible structure essential for a formulaic enterprise. I also speculate that the Western's ability to produce new meanings from previously claimed spaces accounts for the genre's unprecedented popularity. The Western's simultaneous construction of imperial innocence and pursuit of an inner spirituality makes it a modernist quest and encourages us to read it as an extension of the aesthetics and ideology more commonly associated with high culture—that is, to "read high and mass culture as objectively related and dialectically interdependent phenomena, as twin and inseparable forms of the fission of aesthetic production under capitalism."[9]

Chapter 3 pauses to display the transition from the late nineteenth to the early twentieth century in Southwestern photographs. My exhibit tells "A Little History of Southwestern Photography," beginning with the sublime wilderness depicted by Carleton Watkins and William Henry Jackson, proceeding through portraits of Indians taken by members of the "Pasadena Eight" and Edward S. Curtis, and concluding with photographs of canyons, mountains, skies, and churches taken by two modernist masters, Paul Strand and Ansel Adams. These frequently reproduced images remind us of the Southwest we probably already envision, and of the problem of reimagining a place that is now impossible to see for the first time. Following the historical and philosophical arguments about the medium proposed by Walter Benjamin, I suggest that photographic reproductions of the Southwest refuse to dispel the region's timeless aura; to revise our habits of returning automatically to the region's artificial emptiness, I propose that we reconsider J. B. Jackson's understanding of "a sense of place" as something we create over time, through a mixture of experience and received images.

Chapter 4 approaches Mary Austin's career as a case study in the convergence of ecological, literary, and ethnographic interest in the early twentieth-century Southwest. My discussion ranges from the contextualization of naturalist essays in Eastern periodicals to the formation of Mabel Dodge Luhan's Taos salon and the literary experiments of Boasian anthropologists, for Austin's work intersects and builds on each of these developments. *The Land of Little Rain* (1903) and *Lost Borders* (1909), collections of essays comparable to John Muir's studies of the Sierra, depict an intricate system of natural and native lives in the Mojave Desert that resist appropriation by an outsider. I explain how Austin's books appealed to the emerging passion for wilderness conservation and to modernism's localizing aesthetics, and how they redefined regional realism as the literary expression of ecological principles. Then I turn to *The American Rhythm,* Austin's landscape-centered theory of cross-cultural poetics first published in 1923, to historicize a mystical approach to translation that continues to attract contemporary poets. I argue that Austin's vision of a cross-cultural art blurs when applied to the greater Southwest, imposing a reciprocity that whites only dreamed could exist.

My final chapter meditates on how Willa Cather uses the real and imagined Southwest to explore the relation between place and consciousness. While the Nebraska novels initiate a poetics of place that provides access to local knowledge without claiming full possession, *The Song of the Lark* (1915), *The Professor's House* (1925), and *Death Comes for the Archbishop* (1927) further test the experience of the present (figured in the language of the body or in images) against an awareness of the past (figured as abandoned artifacts or geological formations). Each of Cather's novels thus engages in an anti-modern quest to re-enchant American spaces. I locate the generic origins of Cather's novels in Hawthorne's American romances and Jameson's theory of "late imperial romance," and then sketch the affinities between Cather's poetics and the pragmatism of William James, the poetry of Wallace Stevens, and the Navajo Creation Story. Cather not only articulates the difficulty of constructing a poetics of place in a period of rapid modernization but, as a writer hostile to the industry of literary criticism, poses the problem of reconciling popularity among readers with unpopularity in the modernist canon as well. I draw a critical connection between the two issues, proving that Cather's romance with American places has always been intertwined with her narrative experiments, her popularity, and her critical status.

The similarities among my chosen figures run deep: all came from middle-class families in the East or Midwest, discovered the Southwest as outsiders at a crucial point in their careers, and used the region as a means of both repudiating their own bourgeois pasts and defining their position with respect to the Eastern establishment. For male writers like Lummis and Grey, taking on the Southwest meant affirming masculine independence and asserting power in a marketplace increasingly constituted by popular demand; for Austin and Cather, as for many women regionalists, assuming responsibility for exploring, cultivating, and preserving the region meant breaking away from the conventions of marriage and family into a vocation. Each writer's experience in the Southwest enabled the construction of literary authority, although each often felt his or her position to be embattled.

Despite these similarities, however, my study emphasizes the differences between the writers in terms of class position and gender, and the differences between their work in terms of genre and media, so as to resist a misleadingly consistent definition of what a "Southwestern writer" might be. Compared with the major urban sites of modernist cultural production, and even with other artists' communities, the Southwest attracted few artists, fewer writers, and only a handful of major literary figures. The potential subjects for a study of Southwestern cultural production in the modernist period are thus to a great extent already self-selected. Within this limited field I have made strategic choices in order to focus on a series of mediations or translations between Anglo and non-Anglo culture—that is, between two distinct, and to some extent incompatible, modes of cultural expression.

Translation as Critical Practice

My choice of "translation" as the study's organizing trope speaks to my conviction that discourses of resistance and ambivalence have always accompanied triumphalist claims of conquest. It also expresses my understanding of what it is to be modern: to be perpetually between historical periods, cultures, and places. These two premises apply in particular to the cultural work that Anglo-American representations of the Southwest performed at the turn of the last century, but they also extend back to the Southwest's earliest formations. In *The Conquest of America,* Tzvetan Todorov takes Cabeza de Vaca's failed experience of conquest in the sixteenth century as the personification of "a tendency characteristic of our society: a being who has lost his country without thereby acquiring another, who lives in a double exteriority" (249). Translation is the linguistic equivalent of such double exteriority, the process that carries meaning across physical and symbolic boundaries, for it mediates the foreign and the familiar, abstract knowledge and local expression. Lawrence Venuti calls translation "domestic inscription," a rewriting of the foreign text "in domestic dialects and discourse, registers and styles." His approach to translation emphasizes a central feature of my approach here: the "textual effects" of translation, like the effects of Anglo writing, "signify only in the history of the domestic language and culture."[10]

As I read texts and images that attempt to translate the Southwest's verbal art and visual landscapes for English-speaking, largely Anglo-American readers and viewers, I analyze their significance in terms of this "domestic" and historically limited audience.[11] Because written translations are produced after an original text or experience, they are always also belated and nonsynchronous, oscillating between periods as well as between cultures. They mediate often incompatible experiences of time and space, whether or not they achieve symbolic resolution.

By focusing on translation as well as representation, crossings as well as boundaries, this book elaborates on the spatial metaphors of culture that have come to inform a range of interdisciplinary studies. Scholars and poets Lawrence Herzog, Oscar Martínez, José David Saldívar, José Limón, and Gloria Anzaldúa, who study the intercultural area of the *frontera,* or borderlands, between Mexico and the United States, argue for the conception of a "transfrontier social space" (Herzog). The "*transfrontera* contact zone," as Saldívar calls geopolitical border areas, "is the social space of subaltern encounters."[12] Limón considers how "the play of desire and eroticism" between Mexicans and Anglos complicates our understanding of relations between Greater

Mexico and the United States, and "allows us to envision and experience alternative, if perhaps utopian, models" of this relationship.[13] While the imaginary space of the border zone derives from a geopolitical formation, each of these writers shows that its hybrid culture resonates beyond any single site of origin. "The borderlands thus transform the traditional notion of the frontier from the primitive margins of civilization to a decentered cosmpolitanism."[14]

Scholars of ethnography and Native American literature have likewise used spatial metaphors to make visible the politics and poetics of writing culture. Perhaps the most influential anthropologist in this respect is Victor Turner, who developed the notion of a threshold or "liminal" state between everyday and fantastic experience in the context of theatrical rituals, and then extended its meaning to any set of cultural symbols that sustain creative possibility and ambiguity. Whereas rationality dominates ordinary life, "a fructile chaos, a storehouse of possibilities, not a random assemblage but a striving after new forms and structures, a gestation process" defines liminality. Though Turner's "liminal" state does not necessarily result from cross-cultural contact, it suggestively spatializes a mood of cultural and imaginative possibility.[15] While in *Imperial Eyes* (1992) Mary Louise Pratt elaborates on the concepts of "transculturation" and "contact zones" in the Americas, in *Routes* (1997) James Clifford calls attention to how we cross cultural boundaries, identifying the process of travel itself as a "translation term." A comparative concept "built from imperfect equivalences," travel requires that we "become aware, always belatedly, of limits, sedimented meanings, tendencies to gloss over differences" (23). Recognizing the extreme situatedness of all knowledge, including knowledge produced en route, means giving up the fantasy of a complete transcription. "[G]iven the historical contingency of translations, there is no single location from which a full comparative account could be produced," Clifford concludes.[16] Meanwhile, Arnold Krupat's *Ethnocriticism* (1992) has brought such cross-cultural reflexivity into the field of literature by focusing on the hybridity of Native American texts. Krupat imagines a criticism that "will only be achieved by means of complex interactions between a variety of Western discursive and analytic models and a variety of non-Western modes of knowing and understanding" (43–44), and seeks a critical mode of "anti-imperial translation" that might undo translation's "largely imperial history" (198). Each of these critical approaches—borderland studies, American studies, postmodern ethnography, and ethnocriticism—builds on critical tensions in postcolonial theory between dominance and opposition, essentialism and hybridity, the colonizer's text and the subaltern's voice. Each addresses the active and contested relations *between* cultures in ways that have stimulated my thinking about the problems of producing and interpreting place-specific texts.

The paradox of translation as cultural study that this book aims to articulate and historicize has been clearly posed by Clifford Geertz, among others. We may never be able to "apprehend another people's or another period's imagination neatly, as though it were our own," but this lack of identity between people and periods, which is also an inability to unify competing voices, does not mean that we should abandon the effort. We apprehend others, Geertz argues, "not by looking *behind* the interfering glosses that connect us to it but *through* them."[17] Marginal explanation can constitute a primary text for understanding the differences between others and ourselves; likewise, liminal regions like the Southwest can provide critical materials for understanding America's diverse and contested cultural history.

As we continue to pursue firsthand or imagined contact with the complexity of the world's environment and cultures, we now face the necessity of ordering our apprehension of simultaneity and complexity. Because we recognize that cultural differences cannot always be translated, we may try to contain those differences in a single language or a single theory. Ácoma poet Simon Ortiz has said that "acceptance and recognition," along with respect, are more important for tribal peoples than the single liberal ideal of "understanding."[18] Recognizing the limits of translation—what we cannot know about each other—is a first step toward such acceptance, recognition, and respect. If "all is translation / And every bit of us is lost in it," as poet James Merrill claims, we must all engage in translation's delicate art and strenuous work.

Imperial Dreams and Southwestern Development

Though this study concentrates on a relatively narrow period, from the "close" of the frontier to the onset of the Great Depression, it draws on scholarship that shows the American Southwest to have been continuously produced through what I call "dreams of translation": fantasies of collaborative and cross-cultural communication. Translation and transculturation in the Americas have always been inextricable from property relations and the expansion of a dominating culture, and this imperial history made the dream of communication all the more compelling. From the moment of conquest, Spanish and American conquerors imposed material dreams onto the territory Mexicans now call *el norte* and Americans now call the "Southwest," and the narratives of their invasions filter the experience of conflict through lenses ground at home and tinted with the desire of what the conquerors hoped to find. To view *el norte*/the Southwest through Euro-American writing is to look at it through what Pratt calls "imperial eyes."

The first Southwestern translator might be Cabeza de Vaca, the shipwrecked explorer-turned-faith healer who reached New Mexico in 1535 and claimed perfect understanding between his party and the natives of the region, despite barriers of language and custom. "We passed from one strange tongue to another, but God our Lord always enabled each new people to understand us and we them. You would have thought, from the questions and answers in signs, that they spoke our language, and we theirs," he wrote in 1542.[19] His intermediary, Estevanico, surely felt most of the difficulties of translation, since he was the one "constantly in conversation" with those who spoke unfamiliar languages. The conclusion to this first Southwestern invasion is well known: despite his good intentions, de Vaca's party failed to protect the Indians from a group of more barbarous Spanish invaders, and his resistance to official Spanish policy earned him exile in Algeria and a prohibition from ever returning to America.

As a peripheral area for the Spanish empire centered in Mexico City and later for the United States centered in Eastern cities, the space that Mexicans call *el norte* and North Americans call the Southwest long remained too distant from either center of power to be incorporated easily into the larger colonial or national unit. Instead, its undetermined resources became the subject of missionary and colonial fantasy. Bernard Fontana argues that the Spanish first marketed the Southwest in the late eighteenth century when King Charles III created a distinct region called Provincias Internas, or Interior Provinces, in response to Father Eusebio Kino's glowing accounts of the fertility of the Sonoran Desert. To support his divinely inspired mission, Kino wrote letters to the Viceroy of New Spain and the Father General of the Society of Jesus. Kino predicted he could convert the natives with ease and, more important for the colonizing missions that followed, reported on the veins of gold and silver, the abundance of fig trees, and the Castilian roses in the new lands of the Pimería Alta. Beside Kino's promotional letters were counterreports characterizing the land as a "miserable kingdom" and its people as living by "animal instincts," but Fontana notes ironically that realistic descriptions only increased the land's mystique: dreams of wealth and redeemed savagery already constituted the region's romantic image. To a great extent, this pattern of willfully realized fantasy held through the twentieth century. "A key element in our invention of the American Southwest/Mexican north," Fontana concludes, "is that of historical continuity. Whatever ideas have shaped our conception of ourselves and the conceptions of us by outsiders were planted in the days of Church and Crown."[20]

The cultural history of the Greater Southwest is best approached through its "cycles of conquest," as Edward Spicer characterizes the successive stages of regional domination from the sixteenth century through the 1960s. This model unsettles premises of geographical and cultural fixity and locates regional continuity in the histories of its transcultural relations; it exposes "the wider global world of intercultural import-export in which the ethnographic encounter is always already enmeshed."[21] Because most travelers and settlers in the Southwest produced local authority through importing legal and cultural discourses into the region, the wider, transnational world has always been inscribed in Southwestern writing.

The material foundations of the Southwest's late nineteenth-century cycle of conquest can be found in—and on—the ground itself: in the silver, copper, and gold deposits that made mining the region's major source of employment (and its most lucrative and dangerous industry); in the stands of surviving timber; in the grazing land of ranches and the farmland increasingly under corporate control; and on the railroad tracks that provided easy access to the region for the first time.[22] In addition to transporting goods, the railroad transported new migrants, especially to California, and tourists.[23] Between 1890 and 1910, the populations of Colorado, New Mexico, and California roughly doubled through immigration; Arizona's more than tripled in the same period.[24] A key indication of New Mexico's growth was the increase in the number of banks serving the territory—from two in 1879, when the Santa Fe Railroad first arrived, to fifty in 1900.[25]

However, the economy of the Greater Southwest, including the northern Mexican states of Chihuahua and Sonora, continued to depend on extensive capital investment from outside the region. This dependence made its economic relation to the rest of the United States in this period a colonial one; the emergence of a popular Southwestern culture that could be easily exported to tourists reinforced this relation. Following the colonial model, Hispanic communities in New Mexico and Native American groups throughout the region either remained peripheral or became subservient to an economy increasingly shaped by outside investors, imported skills, and national and international markets. In northern New Mexico, for instance, communal lands that Congress refused to recognize legally were seized by large cattle companies while many men left their villages to work for large companies.[26] Mines, corporate ranches, large-scale farms, and railroads came to depend on the labor of Hispanos, Mexicans, and other immigrants even as they threatened local economies and social structures. Each of these forms of capitalist expansion was part "of an expanding world economy that neither Indian or Hispanic Villagers, traditional rancheros, nor the Mormon church were able to stand against," Richard White explains. "Inexorably and relentlessly, resources once ignored or consumed within the West began to flow out of the area; manufactured goods began to flow into it" (242).

Propelled by an expanding (and volatile) national economy and funded by Eastern and European capitalists, Anglo-American development in the Arizona and New Mexico territories proceeded with the blind confidence of the Gilded Age and produced the extractive economy that defined the late nineteenth-century American West. William Robbins calls the late nineteenth and early twentieth-century West "the great natural-resource reservoir and the investment arena" for outside capital; economically, the West "was part of the wider subordination of colonial sectors to the requirements of metropolitan-based economies."[27] In David Harvey's theoretical terms, the barriers that had limited the free flow of capital to the West were lowered in this period, producing a "strong emphasis upon the particular qualities of the spaces to which that capital might be attracted."[28] By differentiating itself culturally, the Southwest could compete in the national and transnational economies, and cultural production and tourism soon became the Southwest's "localized competitive strategy."

For tourists and investors in the tourist industry, the Southwest had to remain the undeveloped periphery of either Los Angeles or Eastern capitals. Tourism in the Southwest coincided with—and propelled—the region's economic development. A new Pullman sleeping car for tourists was introduced in the late 1880s, followed by convenient branch rail lines to the Grand Canyon and Yosemite Valley, new sites of the American sublime. The Southwest's Indian groups, along with its natural scenery, soon became tourist destinations. According to Earl Pomeroy, the status of "the Indian as a major tourist attraction, as featured advertising copy, as a human equivalent to the geographical curiosities of earlier generations, belongs to the twentieth century."[29] Proof came with the construction of imitation Mesa Verde cliff dwellings near Manitou, Colorado, in 1905, a project engineered by a group of businessmen to make the cultural wonders of the Southwest easier to visit. Luxury hotels like El Tovar, opened at the Grand Canyon in 1905, were decorated with Indian art and promoted with Indian motifs; at the Hopi House nearby, visitors could watch Navajo and Pueblo performers demonstrate weaving and fashion pottery and jewelry. At the same time, Americans were cultivating an appreciation for managed wilderness. In 1919 the Grand Canyon was declared a national park, and between 1919 and 1929 tourist traffic per year increased from 44,000 to 200,000.[30]

Beginning in the 1920s, the automobile made visiting the Southwest an option for middle-class tourists. The typical regional "explorer" became a Harvey Detour "dude," a tourist whisked from a Santa Fe railcar to Mesa Verde in a "Tesuque" brown Packard, accompanied by a guide dressed as an "Indian maid" in Navajo costume.[31] As Charles Lummis would write in 1925, "The unknown corners and lonely trails I pried into and unraveled with plodding bronco in the Eighties are now buzzed upon with automobiles—many of them taking the transcontinental tour and turning aside here and again to view the 'Strange Corners' which are still strange enough, though no longer unknown."[32]

If "the very existence of capitalism presupposes the sustaining presence and vital instrumentality of geographically uneven development," as Edward Soja argues, undeveloped regions like the Southwest allowed capitalism to flourish.[33] The oppositions between developed center and undeveloped periphery, modern and "primitive," took geological and temporal form in the tourist literature through figures of surface and depth and tropes of "timelessness." To a great extent, the dominant, commercial identity of the Southwest was constructed out of rhetoric promoting the "Southwestern Wonderland" rather than land grants, imagined scenes from the ancient past rather than practical settlement in the present, and testimony of cultural contact rather than signatures of surrender. Like nearly every Western "tradition," this process of defining the Southwest from an Anglo perspective constituted a late nineteenth-century "invention" because it fabricated symbolic regional meanings from materials appropriated from a non-Anglo past.[34]

The period between 1890 and 1920 is most significant in the transition from a producer-based to a consumer-based economy because it saw the greatest conflict between traditional rural and metropolitan modes of production.[35] I am particularly interested in this transitional period, when the symbolic, cultural, and commodified relations between metropolitan centers and Southwestern peripheries were taking shape. Although we can distinguish between early phases of Anglo development based on natural resources and later phases based on cultural resources, the dynamics of Anglo cultural domination and native resistance, of communication and misunderstanding, do not fit so neatly into distinct periods. Material and cultural development continued to overlap and transform one another, alternately encouraged and impeded by relations between Anglos and natives in the region. The stage of development Fredric Jameson calls "late" capitalism is in fact defined by the "coexistence of realities from radically different moments of history—handicrafts alongside the great cartels, peasant fields with the Krupp factories or the Ford plant in the distance."[36] In the Southwest, we find Native American women selling pottery at railroad stations at the turn of the twentieth century, an exit for Los Alamos on the highway leading to "historic" Taos pueblo by midcentury, and a glittering casino between trailer parks and Tucson's missionary church San Xavier del Bac at century's end. Many subsequent events confirm the incorporation of the Southwest into national politics, international relations, and global economies in this conflicted state: the admission of Arizona and New Mexico as states in 1912; atomic detonation at White Sands, New Mexico, in 1945; the national popularity of the "Santa Fe style" and the sales of souvenirs like dream catchers and kachinas; the construction of a postindustrial landscape in Rio Rancho, Intel's headquarters just outside Albuquerque. Each of these moments crystallizes processes of political, economic, and cultural incorporation initiated in the late nineteenth century, but still at work today.

I have suggested that the incorporation of the Southwest into the United States has been consistently articulated through discourses of loss: imperialist nostalgia, regionalism, ecocriticism. At the same time, the interpenetration of global and local histories demands that newcomers and natives perform the work of mediating incompatible economies, worldviews, and practices of everyday life. Geographers like Harvey and Soja, anthropologists like Geertz and Arjun Appadurai, and journalist Thomas Friedman all claim that globalization has *not* resulted in the homogenization foretold by the self-proclaimed "regionalists" of the first part of the twentieth century.[37] The restructurings of the past century have sustained spatial differentiations through intensifying uneven development, a situation most visible in Native American communities and in the West's small towns, and through commodifying regional cultures. Meanwhile, as the necessity of perpetual displacement has come to dominate American work and private life, the longing for a feeling of place becomes even stronger. The art historian

Lucy Lippard has called this longing "the lure of the local," which she explains as "the undertow of modern life that connects it to the past we know so little and the future we are aimlessly concocting."[38] This book explores the material and symbolic history of one exemplary case of this apparently endless process.

Translating Southwestern Landscapes

I

Charles Lummis's Tasks of Translation

BETWEEN 1890 AND 1900, the Yankee Charles Fletcher Lummis published seven books about the Southwest in at least three genres: an autobiographical account, *A Tramp across the Continent* (1892); the romantic tour books *Some Strange Corners of Our Country: The Wonderland of the Southwest* (1892) and *The Land of Poco Tiempo* (1893); and four books of folklore—*A New Mexico David and Other Stories and Sketches of the Southwest* (1891), *The Man Who Married the Moon and Other Pueblo Indian Folk-Stories* (1894), *The Enchanted Burro* (1897), and *The King of the Broncos and Other Stories of New Mexico* (1897). These texts collect scenes and stories to produce regional versions of what Earl Pomeroy has called "romantic stories of pioneer times," stories typical of the Far West that satisfied economic needs and collective desires simultaneously.[1] By rendering the Southwest exotic but unthreatening, such stories of underdevelopment made the region alluring for investors, potential settlers, and armchair travelers alike. In 1893 Lummis became the editor of *Land of Sunshine,* begun as a twenty-four-page folio to promote southern California. Again he mixed genres, expanding the publication to include history, personal narrative, public affairs, literature, and art. John Muir soon wrote admiringly of the "plucky little magazine" under Lummis's direction: it has "the ring & look of true literary material."[2]

Anglo writing in the late nineteenth-century Southwest mixed genres to include a variety of cultural materials within a single text and to reach the widest possible readership, but it never relinquished the poetry and romance of this last American region. The official Western frontier may have vanished by 1893, but the cultural frontiers of the Southwest remained unexplored territory. Lummis was the first writer in the postfrontier era to wrestle the diversity of the region into literary form, and his popular guidebooks register the mixture of amazement and anxiety, desire and loss that would character-ize Anglo writing in the region. Like his predecessor Frank Cushing and his successor Zane Grey, Lummis self-consciously positioned himself between a genteel culture that he left behind and the native cultures he encountered in his adopted region, paradoxically claiming the authority of firsthand experi-ence as the foundation of a true postfrontier romance. Critics have recently stressed the impurity of his story translations and the complicity between Lummis's rhetoric and the Southwest's commercial promotion in the early twentieth century. Indeed, the hybrid nature of Southwestern translation, the edgy exuberance of its descriptive writing, and the growth of South-western tourism must be considered as mutually reinforcing developments that define not only the form and mood of the region's modern literature but its patterns of consumption as well. In this chapter, I re-evaluate Lummis's self-definition as a regional explorer, translator, and mythmaker through his relation to the emerging fields that together shaped the modern Anglo Southwest: ethnography, literature, and tourism.

Lummis's writing requires further consideration because critics have overemphasized his powerful romanticizing rhetoric at the expense of his more subtle and still unfinished work as a translator and cultural preserva-tionist. The few who argue for his broad range of enthusiasms are outnum-bered by his many detractors, who see him primarily as an agent of imperial-ism. Among the few is Kevin Starr, who admits the "unevenness of his talents" and "the egocentricity of his methods" but still claims that Lummis made a "lasting contribution" to reconciling Spanish and North American cultures.[3] Richard Etulain's survey of frontier, regional, and postregional periods in the West also identifies Lummis as a "forerunner of the regional-ists" who "clearly moved from viewing the West as a strange frontier to seeing it as a region whose cultures needed to be understood and appreci-ated" (85). And Martin Padget's analysis of Lummis's "creation" of the Southwest, while proving that "racialist and class-biased assumptions were always at work in Lummis's promotional activity," cautions that "this is not the whole story." Though Lummis worked with a received cultural hier-archy, Padget argues that he "contributed to Anglo audiences a simulta-neously popular yet more complex understanding of Native American and Mexicano cultures in the Southwest."[4]

Most critics, including the New Western Historians, object that Lum-mis's inventions of California and the Southwest are prime examples of Anglo bias and imperialist nostalgia that enabled a commercial regionalism to distort and destroy Hispanic and Native American cultures. Characterized as a writer intent on promoting the Southwest's romance, Lummis has been faulted for paying little attention to "the technological and demographic realities which dominated the economic and political nature of the region."[5] Because he aimed to preserve the Spanish missions in California and reproduce mission architecture, he has been held responsible for eliding the region's history of Anglo conquest and its continued dependence on Hispanic labor. Legends of Coronado that Lummis retold concealed the reality of forced land acquisition by Anglos, while the decorative restoration of missions that Lummis encouraged diverted attention from the tough work Hispanics and Native Americans put in on the railroads and in the mines.

The result, argues Patricia Limerick in *The Legacy of Conquest,* was a selective grafting of history onto a present whose symbols were unappealing, incoherent, or not yet visible to Anglos on their way west. "The distant past was colorful and appealing; the immediate past and the present were pedestrian matters of agricultural production, labor supply, and border regulation. Hispanic history came in two parts, and the parts did not connect" (256). Mike Davis notes that while the influence of the Arroyo Set waned in the 1920s, the preference it expressed for Mediterranean and "Spanish colonial" styles based on an "ersatz history" left its permanent mark on Los Angeles architecture and advanced an ideology of white superiority.[6] In New Mexico, the superiority of pure-blood Spanish over mixed-blood Mexicans or mestizos—a fiction Lummis endorsed—long sustained the dominance of the Mexicano elite. In short, historians argue that the alliance between race, elite culture, and capital that Lummis alternately exploited and concealed set a racial and class-based model for Western development that is still difficult to recast.

Lummis has received credit and blame not only for producing a powerfully distorted regional image but also for establishing a romanticizing pattern in popular literature that corporate enterprises, especially the Santa Fe Railway, could easily co-opt to sell fantasies of escape and exoticism. I think it is important to locate the origins of Lummis's romantic rhetoric in his New England origins, as I do at the beginning of the chapter, and to identify the defensive return of nostalgia late in his career, as I do at the chapter's end. I concentrate, however, on the conditions of his literary and photographic production in the early 1890s to argue that Lummis's importance to Southwestern writing and iconology lies in his interdisciplinary experiments and his ambivalent juxtaposition of Anglo and Native American poetics. Both his writings and his photographs evince tension between a textualized and com-modified West and an understanding of local cultures that expressed them-selves primarily through oral traditions and artifacts. Whereas the West of myth and commercial development could be simplified, the native South-west resisted a common mode of textualization. Lummis struggled to trans-late the intensity of his own regional contact into collective expressions of longing for rugged cross-cultural experience, and as he did so, he sustained the tension between history and fantasy that defines modern experience and the literature of the Anglo Southwest.

From New England Poet to a "Kind of Worker"

A New England childhood and college years at Harvard determined the social and aesthetic structures that would direct Lummis's writing and field-work in the Southwest, though Lummis would always denigrate his formal "instruction" at Harvard in favor of real "education" on the road. Identifying himself as an "emancipated Yankee," he wrote in his autobiography, "I have always been grateful I was born in New England. It is a great heritage. I am doubly grateful that I escaped in Time." A member of the group Richard Hofstadter identified as "Mugwumps," Lummis came from a family of mod-erate means who began to feel its loss of influence in the 1870s and, in re-sponse, sought new sources of moral idealism in "regional romanticism." At the end of the century, such families "looked southwestward for an unspoiled American region where they could satisfy their desire for a reactionary agrar-ian alternative to growing American urban-industrial capitalism."[7] Along with other white upper- and middle-class men who felt themselves to be losing power, Lummis struggled to restore the lost vitality of genteel culture through his own program of physical training and, eventually, through his contact with the Southwest. With his newfound regional identification, he protested against a culture that had failed to empower him; with claims to unbounded vigor, spiritual health, and cultural expertise, he epitomized both the "antimodernist" and the simple, healthy man Emerson and Whitman called the native American poet.[8]

Lummis may have already envisioned himself as the next Whitman while a student at Harvard, for his first publication was a slim collection of romantic nature poems printed in minuscule type on slippery pieces of birch bark. Perhaps because the format was a novelty, the response to his verses was underwhelming. T. W. Higginson pronounced the volume "very curious," and expressed the hope that Lummis "could put [his] text in larger type."[9]

Oliver Wendell Holmes, Sr., wrote dryly that he had "long known the birch as a stimulus of scholarship" and was "pleased to find it a source of inspiration" but proclaimed the poems merely "pleasing."[10] Though Whitman eventually wrote to express his thanks for the "fragrant little Birch Bark Poems," he withheld any impressions of the aspiring poet's work.[11] For success as a writer, Lummis learned that he would have to turn to journalism, which relied more on the right choice of subject than on expressive technique. The booster journalism he practiced in Los Angeles would reward the "truth" of real Southwestern experience, he thought, as long as it was generously embellished.

What Lummis shared with Whitman was less a poetic sensibility than a genius for self-fashioning. Seeking the salutary effects of the open road, Lummis set off for the West alone on 11 September, 1884, to walk from Ohio to California "without any press-agenting, or wagers, or time-limits, or anything else to fetter or chafe" him.[12] Like Whitman, he sought the promise of mobility. But first he had to dress the part. He stripped down to knickers, stockings, and low-cut shoes. Wearing a felt hat and a money belt filled with gold coins, and carrying a revolver, equipment for writing and fishing, a pouch of tobacco, and presumably some food, Lummis endured a host of physical hardships in his 3,507 miles—scorching heat, snowstorms, robbery attempts, a sprained ankle, and a broken arm—as well as unexpected doses of New Mexican chile. Newly laid railroad tracks literally hastened his journey, for Lummis would often follow their leveled path, and he trained himself to step only on every third tie.[13] Sending weekly reports on his progress to the Chillicothe, Ohio, *Leader* and the *Los Angeles Times* (which paid him five dollars per installment), Lummis arrived on the west coast 143 days later, a local celebrity.

In a gallery of late nineteenth-century men, portraits of Lummis outfitted for his tramp, relaxing at Isleta Pueblo (fig. 1.1), or surrounded by a group of Pueblo Indians at the Coronado Hotel in San Diego (fig. 1.2) belong next to the famous daguerreotype that Whitman used as the frontispiece for *Leaves of Grass.* As Miles Orvell describes Whitman's daguerreotype in *The Real Thing,* so could we describe photographs of Lummis: "It is an image of informality, of casualness, of man outdoors; we are looking at a kind of worker, perhaps; certainly not a man in a study" (12). Indeed, of the many images of Lummis I have seen, only one shows him at his desk—and even then, souvenirs of a life in the field surround him. He could usually be found in his trademark corduroy suit, a practical uniform for this new kind

Figure 1.1. Yankee-turned-Southwesterner Charles Fletcher Lummis and his second wife, Eve Douglas, relax at Isleta Pueblo after honeymooning on horseback. In New Mexico, Lummis cultivated a hybrid persona as both cultural worker and rugged outdoorsman. (Courtesy Center for Southwest Research, General Library, University of New Mexico; neg. no. 990-009-0002)

Figure 1.2. Lummis with his extended Pueblo family at the Coronado Hotel in San Diego. Whether recruited to work on Lummis's Los Angeles house, El Alisal, or to perform at the Panama-Pacific Exposition of 1915, Lummis's Isleta friends frequently traveled from New Mexico to the Southland. (Courtesy Center for Southwest Research, General Library, University of New Mexico; neg. no. 990-009-0108)

of Southwestern worker that took him from the pueblos to the White House (fig. 1.3).[14]

The year of the tramp, 1884, has been called a "watershed" year for the invention of the Southwest.[15] It was one year after Buffalo Bill launched his Wild West Show and Frank Cushing published "My Adventures in Zuñi" in *Century Illustrated* magazine, and the same year that Mark Twain published *Huckleberry Finn* and Helen Hunt Jackson published *Ramona* to protest Anglo treatment of mission Indians. In 1884 a coalition of Eastern and Western physicians established the American Climatological Association to discuss the uses of climate to cure such ailments as rheumatism, dyspepsia, mental exhaustion, and "female diseases."[16] It seems fitting, then, that Lummis's narrative would claim a rugged authenticity, disclaim pretension and refinement, and locate the source of personal transformation outside of culture, in the atmosphere. "I would have this unpretentious book taken only for what it is—the wayside notes of a happy vagabonding," he announces in *A Tramp*

Figure 1.3. Lummis in the trademark corduroy suit he even wore to lunch with Theodore Roosevelt at the White House. On the letterhead of his California-based magazine *Out West*, Lummis quoted—without permission—Roosevelt's praise: "I always read it, for I am heartily in sympathy with so many of the things for which it works." (Courtesy Center for Southwest Research, General Library, University of New Mexico; neg. no. 990-031-0002)

across the Continent. "It was written in hurried moments by the coal-oil lamps of country hotels, the tallow dips of section-house and ranch, the smoky pine-knots of the cowboy's or the hunter's cabin, the crackling *fogon* of a Mexican adobe, or the snapping greasewood of my lonely campfire upon the plains; and from that vagrant body and spirit I have not tried to over-civilize it." Lummis recovered solitude and the simple life of the open air, and he claims that if the experience is real, romance is not needed. "It is merely a truthful record of some of the experiences and impressions of a walk across the continent—the diary of a man who got outside the fences of civilization and was glad of it. It is the simple story of joy on legs" (vii). His narrative enacts what would become the dominant paradigm in Southwestern writing: a journey from the felt unreality of bourgeois life to the imagined authenticity of tourist experience.

Lummis's aesthetic education would have given him a view of the West as both frontier and sublime landscape, and *A Tramp across the Continent* accordingly stages a wondrous view from Pike's Peak: "Such a vista could only be where the greatest mountains elbow the infinite plains. Eastward they stretch in an infinite sea of brown. . . . Time seems hardly to exist up there. Alive, one is yet out of the world. The impression could hardly be stronger if one stood upon a planet sole in all space" (47–49). From this vantage point, the viewer can see all and suspend the passage of time.[17] In a scene Lummis describes elsewhere as "the grandest sight of all—the sublimest I ever saw," he invites us to watch with him as the sun sets and the darkness moves swiftly in all directions.[18] He probably knew that the Grand Canyon had already acquired the status of the Southwestern sublime, but he still insisted on locating and expressing his own sense of wonder.[19] Stephen Greenblatt describes the object that arouses wonder as "so new that for a moment at least it is alone, unsystematized, an utterly detached object of rapt attention"; explorers of the New World frequently encountered such objects. The articulation of wonder, then, "stands for all that cannot be understood, that can scarcely be believed"—but also all that the writer has actually witnessed.[20] By emphasizing wonder in his writings, Lummis belatedly proclaims himself a true explorer and constructs the Southwest as the last unknown "corner" of the New World.

Such a late Victorian sensibility structured Lummis's own conception of the Southwest so thoroughly that, in some cases, he felt no need to rewrite existing accounts. For a description of the Grand Canyon, *Some Strange Corners of Our Country* (1892) relies entirely on an article by Charles Dudley Warner published in *Harper's* in 1891. The article recommends the entire desert region for "the unlimited freedom of it, its infinite expansion, its air like wine to the senses, the floods of sunshine, the waves of color, the translucent atmosphere that aids the imagination."[21] Not only did Lummis lift Warner's description of the Canyon directly into his book, he echoed the tone and point of view of the article throughout *Some Strange Corners* as well. Throughout his career Lummis displayed such admiration for a few select writers and scientists working in the Southwest that enthusiastic agreement often blurred into duplication, initiating a pattern of repetition and reinvention that would persist in Anglo descriptions of Southwestern places.

While exposure to romantic aesthetics shaped Lummis's initial impressions, his contact with anthropologists in the field provided more lasting models for rugged and sustained cultural study. As he explored the territories of New Mexico and Arizona, he met and came to idolize the Swiss anthropologist Adolph Bandelier for his physical and intellectual vigor. During their joint exploration of Rito de los Frijoles in 1888, the two men faced physical challenges that Lummis had been training for since his college days (which overlapped with those of Roosevelt, the period's most popular figure of rugged Western masculinity). The two men "travailed" with "no blankets, no overcoats, or other shelter; and the only commissary a few cakes of sweet chocolate, and small sack of parched popcorn meal." For Lummis, such hardship defined pioneer scholarship and made intellectual discoveries "unforgettable glory." He recalled that Bandelier persisted in nightly notetaking, "even when I had to crouch over him and the precious paper with my water-proof focusing cloth."[22] He also noted the anthropologist's ability to learn languages and dialects, and communicate across classes and cultures, proclaiming that "he could find common ground with *anyone,*" from presidents to Irish section hands to "Mexican peons." For Lummis, the pursuit of anthropology brought into alignment everyday work, spiritual longing, ideals of cross-cultural understanding, and a homosociality missing from typical Victorian domestic arrangements. In *Routes,* James Clifford describes ethnographic "fieldwork" as "a distinctive cluster of academic research practices, traditions, and representational rules" (66); for Lummis and other Anglo explorers and anthropologists, the Southwest as a "field" became an imaginary replacement for the habitus they had inherited.

The completion of the railroad across New Mexico and Arizona both enabled and threatened such fieldwork. When in 1880 the Santa Fe Railroad built tracks south from Albuquerque to El Paso, and when the Atlantic and Pacific built west from Albuquerque to Los Angeles, the pueblos of Laguna, Isleta, and Zuni suddenly found themselves on the two major travel routes through New Mexico.[23] The railroad accelerated "the flow of people, goods, and influence in and out of the pueblo[s]."[24] Alarm at subsequent signs of local change was recorded first by Anglo anthropologists and folklorists; Matilda Coxe Stevenson's writings provide a typical example. Stevenson accompanied her husband on geological surveys before joining him as a "volunteer" for Powell's 1879 research expedition to Zuni and training herself as an anthropologist. She wrote in an 1894 report, "The Sia," that the railroad was the last of several forces of cultural destruction brought by Anglo settlers: "Thus the railroad, the merchant, and the cowboy, without this purpose in view, are effecting a change which is slowly closing, leaf by leaf, the record of the religious beliefs and practices of the pueblo Indian" (15). Finding the detrimental effects of cultural contact particularly acute at Laguna, where communal dwellings were abandoned because of their proximity to the tracks and ceremonial practices were disrupted because men needed to watch their cattle more vigilantly, Stevenson dramatically projected her fear of cultural change onto her subjects: "aged men cried out in horror that their children were forgetting the religion of their forefathers" (14).

To put this kind of imperialist nostalgia in perspective, we can compare Stevenson's writing with that of Elsie Clews Parsons, a student of Franz Boas who published ninety articles and monographs on Pueblo cultures between 1916 and 1941.[25] Whereas Stevenson feared the loss of Southwestern culture, Parsons embraced the ongoing process of cultural contact and conflict in the region. Conditions had changed somewhat in Isleta by Parsons's arrival there in the early 1920s, for by then the pueblo had become a standard tourist stop. Postcards displayed the interior of the mission church, with its mixture of Spanish and native cultures, just as cards of other pueblos emphasized rituals that originated in Catholic worship. But these images, according to Parsons, merely made visible a long process of adaptation. She came to identify the defining feature of Pueblo culture as just this capacity for change and renewal: its "facility, so notable throughout the tribes, for keeping definite tribal patterns in mobile combination,—a facility which, from an aesthetic point of view, results in style, and from the standpoint of general culture, in vitality and durability."[26] Her own observations led her to follow Boas's advice to collect modern and traditional stories; she also began to experiment with new forms of ethnographic writing.[27] Alfonso Ortiz lists the many historical moments in which Pueblo peoples have adapted and revitalized themselves in response to physical hardship and invasion, from their abandonment of villages at Chaco Canyon and Mesa Verde in search of water in the thirteenth century to the Pueblo Revolt of 1680, the smallpox epidemic of 1781–82, and Anglo threats to Pueblo land and sovereignty beginning in the nineteenth century. "Those numerous revitalization efforts have simply not attracted much attention among scholars," Ortiz maintains, "because most of their efforts have proceeded quietly and without fanfare."[28]

Explorers and anthropologists in the 1880s and 1890s, however, produced prolific reports in a desperate attempt to document the "vanishing" cultures they observed. The Bureau of American Ethnology and the Smithsonian Institution, the *Journal of American Folklore,* and magazines like *Harper's* and *Scribner's* all published textual versions of oral narratives and ritual practices in the name of preserving native traditions. Scholars have interpreted this textual production and cultural study as a means of "institutionalizing" anthropology and folklore as academic disciplines and legitimating modernity's claim to cultural "progress."[29] Professional journals presented transcriptions of stories and rituals for scientists eager to study evidence of the differences between cultures that would refute evolutionist theories. For Boas, especially, folklore served "to define the crucial aspect of culture on all levels of human development and in all its manifestations."[30]

But how were nonscholarly readers to interpret these texts? Museums supplemented what Steven Conn calls the "object-based epistemology" of the Victorian era with comprehensible frameworks for understanding artifacts; though not obvious on first glance, "meanings held within objects would yield themselves up to anyone who studied and observed the objects enough."[31] The meanings of Native American texts, though, seemed less accessible, so publications aimed at a general readership faced the challenge of constructing an interpretive apparatus. Most whites did not expect to find complex artistry among cultures they viewed as less developed than their own; "[t]he notion that Native American discourse at best amounted to a pre-literature characterized the views of most Euroamericans throughout the nineteenth century and well into the twentieth."[32] A literary translation was neither an open book that could yield its stories, like an artifact, nor a piece of evidence to be fitted into a systematic study of culture. It aimed to produce pleasure, but first it had to construct the conditions for such aesthetic reception. Because of Anglo biases, the translator of Native American verbal art faced the task of cultural education first. And without recognizing that stories and songs were art, Anglo audiences could not begin to respond to aesthetic strategies of translation.

Surprisingly, a common problem that Southwestern translators faced was an excess of material. Lummis's ideal storyteller in *Pueblo Indian Folk-Stories,* Tata Lorenso, "never saw the inside of a book," but if he "could write out all the fairy stories he knows, Webster's Unabridged Dictionary would hardly hold them" (11). The Navajo translator Washington Matthews shrewdly pointed to a Navajo elder as an ideal literary source, claiming that "a whole library of dime novels might be written from his dictation."[33] Such dictation would be a wildly efficient mode of literary production, provided that one chose the collaborator and the genre well; as we will see, writers of the Western romance novel in the early twentieth century made just these choices. Finding an audience for writings about Native American culture in the 1880s and 1890s, however, proved to be more difficult. While anthropologists like Bandelier and Boas wrote for a specialized group of scientists, self-trained cultural workers like Cushing, Lummis, and Matthews struggled with their methods of gathering materials and with forms of translation that might reach a wider readership.

Anglo translators also had to gain access to native communities and develop working relationships with collaborators. Whereas the process of translating one text into another often leads to a theoretical meditation on the relation between languages, the collaborative translation of Native American poetry into texts requires access to storytelling performances and an understanding of the relation between living cultures. When Walter Benjamin asks whether "a translation [is] meant for readers who do not understand the original" and asserts that "no poem is intended for the reader, no picture for the beholder, no symphony for the listener," he is not thinking of Native American art.[34] When he insists on the autonomy of art and locates art's importance in "the unfathomable, the mysterious, the 'poetic,'" he discounts the work's genesis in relation to its audience. Benjamin's modernist poetics, in which the translator alone struggles with "the foreignness of languages," is the very opposite of the hybrid poetics of Southwestern translation.

Translation Production at Zuni and Isleta

I now turn to a critical experience in Lummis's career: his residence at Isleta between 1892 and 1894. In this period Lummis followed the examples of Washington Matthews and Frank Cushing; he also experimented with photography and many forms of writing in order to translate his cultural knowledge for a national audience and to project a professional persona. In histories of the late nineteenth-century Southwest, Lummis and Cushing tend to play the role of the translator "tainted" by romantic conceptions of Indians; Matthews tends to be cast as more "pure," though limited at times by notions of Victorian propriety. Not surprisingly, among Anglo readers the "tainted" translations were more popular than the "pure" ones, which initially found professional audiences. Matthews especially feared that he would not find an audience for his most significant project, a transcription of the Night Chant ceremonial. Though the former Army surgeon confessed that "it afforded me pleasure to write it" and was convinced that it would be "the most complete single work on one ceremony that has yet appeared," he still complained, "Of course, nobody will ever read it."[35]

It was such public indifference to Matthews's "noble and conclusive" work that Lummis saw as symptomatic of the simultaneous erosion of "humanistic" science and the rise of consumer culture. He wrote to Matthews: "I presume you can guess something of the uphill fight it is to run a magazine in the West which prefers Matthews to a "write-up' or "boom article.' I have faith in the outcome, certainly, or I wouldn't waste my time. But ad interim, it's a climb."[36] Though Matthews tried to make his popular articles less technical and to "squeeze" his material to the expected word count for a magazine like *Land of Sunshine,* he remained "ahead of his times" and never attracted the popular audience enjoyed by Cushing and Lummis.[37] Only in the late twentieth century did Paul Zolbrod's *Diné bahane'* (1984) incorporate Matthews's work into a full literary form for nonacademic readers.[38] The act of translation itself signals a lack of synchronicity, a break between the development of the original culture and the culture of the translator; as Benjamin points out in "The Task of the Translator," a translation "comes later than the original" and marks a "stage of continued life" (16). For every translation that sustains such an "afterlife," there are many failures that attract a wide readership for reasons that have little to do with accuracy or "purity." Cushing's *Zuñi Folk Tales* and Lummis's *Pueblo Indian Folk-Stories* are two such failures.

Asked by John Wesley Powell of the newly founded Bureau of Ethnology to study "our North American Indians in their primitive conditions," Cushing arrived at Zuni in 1879. He soon moved into the village, and eventually into the house of the governor. He also adopted native dress, accepted the name Te-na-tsa-li, and gained membership in a sacred society called the Priesthood of the Bow.[39] Yet, despite his unprecedented access to the inner circles of Zuni society, he worried whether the Bureau would keep him on, and if not, how he would support himself. In search of funding for independent research, Cushing appeared at a meeting of the Harvard Athletic Association in 1882 and promoted his intellectual pursuits with his exotic persona. An impression of Cushing as a modern-day "cavalier" had already been given by journalist Sylvester Baxter in *Harper's*. Others who encountered Cushing and his work couldn't decide whether he was a romantic hero or a pioneering scientist. Lummis would remember him on this occasion as a "white Indian," "a slender young man with long yellow hair and an almost unearthly ambidexterity of utterance."[40] The two sides of his speech were presumably Indian and white—and just as the ability to use both hands refuses allegiance to one side, so Cushing's hybrid speech seemed "unearthly," or not properly situated.

Remembering the occasion in 1900, Lummis proclaimed Cushing "epidemic in the culture circles of New England, that year of 1882," noting that "[h]is personal magnetism, his witchcraft of speech, his ardor, his wisdom in the unknowabilities, the undoubted romance of his life of research among 'wild Indians of the frontier' . . . and the impressive dignity and poise of his Indian comrades—all were contagious" (11). *Land of Sunshine* published two complementary portraits with Lummis's description of this "white Indian." One was a posed portrait with animal skins on the ground, Indian blankets in the background, and the subject displaying his "Zuni garb": a headdress, long earrings hanging nearly to the shoulders, necklaces, a wool tunic, a long knife in a holder, trousers studded with silver medallions, decorated chaps— all worn by Cushing as he gazed dreamily into the distance. The other was a highly respectable studio portrait, a three-quarter view of Cushing seated in a black wooden chair, wearing a vest, white cuffed shirt, tie, and gleaming watch chain.

The published impressions and images of Cushing, deployed to publicize and legitimate his experience among the Zuni, emphasized romance over science and scholarship. Alfred Kroeber, Matilda Stevenson, and Frederick Webb Hodge expressed serious reservations about the scientific value of his work, and even Lummis concluded, in "The White Indian," that "Cushing was too much—let us say, poet. The same acute imagination which enabled him to discover occult things, went on to the discovery of things which weren't there" (15). In *Playing Indian,* Philip Deloria agrees that Cushing "moved from anthropology to Indian play while doing fieldwork at Zuni," offering as proof his ubiquitous costume and his New York apartment "decorated to simulate a Zuni kiva" (119). But Cushing's self-fashioning as a mystical Southwestern hero paid off: his charisma attracted popular readership for his personal narrative *My Adventures in Zuñi,* published serially in *Century Illustrated* in 1882–83, and the support of philanthropist Mary

Hemenway in the form of a research grant of $25,000 per year. Though for reasons of poor health Cushing never completed a final report on the Hemenway Southwestern Archaeological Expedition (Harvard-trained Jesse Fewkes replaced him as expedition leader), he succeeded in creating a precedent for fieldwork and an audience for imaginative writing in the region.

Curtis Hinsley has continued to investigate how Cushing's "heterodox" poetics reveals a "double dilemma of epistemology and expression," and his extended study of Cushing also provides a model for my analysis of Lummis.[41] Lummis's unpublished journals, photographs, and correspondence further demonstrate the improvised nature of fieldwork, and the struggle between a desire for personal immersion in native ways of life and the necessity of shaping such experience into written form. His texts and images work to construct local knowledge and develop a critical awareness of the difference between Anglos and natives in the Southwest.

Unlike Cushing, Lummis had no official sanction for his residence in Isleta. Though Col. Harrison Gray Otis had provided Lummis the opportunity to walk west with the promise of employment at the *Los Angeles Times,* the Yankee's body seemed to rebel against work that required submission to a higher authority. In 1888 "he suffered the first of several strokes, which partially paralyzed his left arm, affected his gait and speech and helped him decide to return to New Mexico."[42] Seeking personal recovery more than professional acclaim, he used his friendship with the family of Amadeo Chavez, who had befriended him on his cross-country "tramp," to secure access to Isleta.

We have only a partial record of how he was received at Isleta, although his children Turbesé Lummis Fiske and Keith Lummis drop some "hints" suggesting "that white Americans were not particularly welcome" (49). Because he was paralyzed, Lummis fell under suspicion of witchcraft, a dangerous charge for an outsider; though the Pueblo eventually concluded that Anglos, including Lummis, were too ignorant to be witches, he surely tested their tolerance. Still, he became friendly with the prominent, educated family of Juan Rey Abeita, a situation that probably provided some access to ritual practices and perhaps a privileged status within the pueblo's "progressive" faction.[43] According to Parsons, who published the results of her own field-work at Isleta in 1932, Lummis was the only other student who had lived in this particularly "secretive" pueblo, and he had been "well liked." Given the name Paxöla, meaning "Star," Lummis christened his daughter Turbesé, "Sun." When he moved back to Los Angeles, a group from Isleta came to help build his house, and others came yearly to perform in the Fiesta de Los Angeles. Yet Parsons also notes that whites and Mexicans were excluded from all Pueblo ceremonials, and recounts a council convened in 1927 to discuss Lummis's *Pueblo Indian Folk-Stories*. The meeting was apparently the first time that the book had been brought to the attention of the pueblo, and it raised the question of whether Isleta's "white Indian" had betrayed private or sacred knowledge.[44] Lummis's extended residence in Isleta reveals a nagging suspicion on both sides.

Journal entries made during this residence document Lummis's relentless efforts to support himself and succeed in a variety of markets. Much of his time was spent learning Tiwa language and folklore, writing, sending off manuscripts, taking and printing photographs; for productive relaxation, he hunted rabbits, made jam, and fried doughnuts. On many days the diary records the number of hours spent listening to a storyteller (whom Lummis paid for his time), the number of words written, or the number of cyanotypes turned out.[45] Aside from the photographs he supplied for his book illustrators and magazine editors, it is impossible to tell which of the images he succeeded in selling, and to whom. Still, it is clear that by maintaining his publishing contacts in Los Angeles, forging new ones in New York, and selling his portraits and landscape photographs as prints or postcards, Lummis eked out a living without institutional support.[46] Much of his income came from magazine publishing, though on at least one occasion he risked his professional status by submitting nearly identical work to *St. Nicolas* and *Drake's*.[47]

By this time, Lummis photographed regularly as part of his effort to document the Southwest, though no one seems sure how he first learned how. A decisive influence seems to have been the "nervy" work of one Camillus Fly, a photographer who sneaked into Geronimo's camp the day before his surrender to General George Crook. Lummis was in Tombstone at the time, covering the Apache Wars for the *Los Angeles Times*. A figure verging on myth, Fly seems to have inspired Lummis's first serious photographic project, and his riskiest: the 1888 New Mexican Penitente series.[48] Lummis subsequently exposed over ten thousand glass-plate negatives in his career, and the number suggests that for him photography functioned as another mode of regional translation rather than as an artistic practice. The two printing processes he used, the cyanotype and the salted-paper print, required basic supplies and running water for developing; they were simple and fast techniques. Though innovations of the 1890s like handheld cameras and flexible film made travel easier, camera work more rapid, and printing less risky, given his penchant for physical hardship it is not surprising that Lummis would shun the new portable camera. Printing at Isleta presented additional difficulties, which he tried to turn to his advantage in recollection. "If there is anything that is something of a test, it is to develop two 5 x 8 glass negatives at a time in an adobe room with a big basin bowl for a sink, no outlet except the outside door, no running water, nor other water except what was brought in *tinajas* (Indian pottery jars) and without any other facility whatsoever." When he cut himself on the glass, his "chief concern was that the blood spoiled the negatives." Lummis would value his photographs primarily as records of a vanishing way of life: "There are very many that are unique and can never be made again—of types that are dead, buildings that are destroyed, ceremonials that are no more."[49]

Despite the nostalgic rhetoric, many of the photographs are candid portraits of everyday life and work that depict both tension and accommodation between natives and Anglos in the Southwest. At Isleta, especially, Lummis focused on the daily and ceremonial activities occurring around him: women winnowing beans, sweeping, spinning, caring for children, and offering corn and squash for the dead (fig. 1.4); lounging young men with their hands placed affectionately on each other's shoulders (fig. 1.5); and children playing around the *horno* (oven). One image of winemaking shows men and women working together, the men blurry with the actions of trampling skins and tasting the first drops. The man in the center smiles at the photographer, including him in this communal scene (fig. 1.6). These are not the kinds of images that made their way onto Fred Harvey postcards, but they document patterns of Pueblo life—and Lummis's inclusion in them—more completely than the staged portraits and picturesque scenes that dominated commercial images of the Southwest by the turn of the century. Lummis, of course, also produced many stereotypical images of Indian femininity and desert pastoral.[50] It is just as important, however, to recognize the mixture of moods and subjects in his images and to consider how history has selected among them, a matter we will return to in chapter 3.

The results of his writing were equally mixed. It seems that Lummis could never quite find the fit between material and genre in any form other than episodic tour book or variety magazine. Even William Dean Howells's request that he write "a novel of the contemporary life of that part of America which you know better than any body else," or "something very *actual*" was not sufficient motivation to pursue ethnographic fiction.[51] With

Figure 1.4. "Offering for the Dead, Isleta Pueblo," by Charles Lummis. Lummis's photographs, rarely posed, typically document domestic rituals and scenes from daily life at Isleta. (Courtesy Center for Southwest Research, General Library, University of New Mexico; neg. no. 990-009-0068)

Figure 1.5. "Pueblo Boys, Isleta," by Charles Lummis. The ease that these men display with each other includes Lummis, the photographer. (Courtesy Center for Southwest Research, General Library, University of New Mexico; neg. no. 990-009-0085)

such encouragement, we might ask why Lummis did not pursue the path of novel writing. Though certainly adept at spinning myths, as many critics have pointed out, he may have lacked the skill to develop a sustained narrative. His hyperbolic and repetitive style might serve an adventure plot well, but this style would not lend itself to contemplative prose. Lummis was too curious and restless to write a novel, preferring the immediate adventures the Southwest offered him to the distant possibility of literary prestige—and too deeply invested in what he saw as the truth of his experience to transform it consciously into fiction.

Interpreting Coyote Tales

The popular success of Cushing's and Lummis's translations illustrate how a reading community for Native American poetry began to be constituted. In search of the audience that initially eluded Matthews, these cultural workers grafted new ethnographic content onto familiar literary genres: the travel narrative, the tour book, and the collection of folk tales. More than a traditional ethnography, this heterogeneous mixture resembles older forms of travel writing that aimed to evoke in readers at home a desire to encounter

Figure 1.6. "A Pueblo Wine-making, Isleta," by Charles Lummis. With this image Lummis captures the motion of seasonal work in the pueblo and lays claim to his own inclusion in Isletan rituals. (Courtesy Center for Southwest Research, General Library, University of New Mexico; neg. no. 990-009-0085)

the Indian's Southwest. "Before the separation of genres associated with the emergence of modern fieldwork," Clifford points out in *Routes,* "travel and travel writing covered a broad spectrum" (66), from adventure and evangelism to natural science and philosophy. The hybrid forms of Lummis's and Cushing's translations build on this older tradition as they aim to satisfy both a modern middle-class Anglo readership and emerging professional fields. Their texts mark a rare moment of convergence between literature and anthropology, two modes of writing most often "out of phase."[52] By struggling to reconcile a partial understanding of Pueblo culture with the competing expectations of scientific colleagues and general readers, they expose the conflicting tasks of cultural translation and regional literary production in the period: advancing scientific knowledge, educating and entertaining general readers, and constructing a literary representation of Native American verbal art.

The common necessity of compromise becomes clear when we consider their versions of a structurally similar coyote story: Cushing's "The Coyote and the Locust," collected in *Zuñi Folk Tales* (1901), and Lummis's "The Coyote and the Thunderknife," included in *The Man Who Married the Moon and Other Pueblo Indian Folk-Stories* (1894) and reprinted in *Pueblo Indian Folk-Stories* (1910). The story tells how Coyote meets a locust (or, in some variants, another singing animal) and wants to learn the song the locust sings. Each of three times Coyote thinks he has learned the song, something happens to distract him, and he returns for a new lesson. The third time the locust plays a trick on Coyote that injures him. In the Zuni version, Locust leaves her husk with a stone inside, and when it fails to respond to Coyote's request, the trickster bites husk and stone in frustration, breaking his teeth. In the Isleta version, Locust fills the husk with sand; Coyote first swallows it to have the song inside him, then cuts through his breast with an obsidian knife trying to release the locust, and finally dies.

Cushing's telling in *Zuñi Folk Tales* provides a minimal narrative frame (merely a geographic note at the beginning and a brief interpretation at the end) to allow the reader to listen directly to the tales, just as he presumably did. The story opens with a displacement into the unspecified past common in European folk tales, but quickly explains the local significance of the place where the story occurs: "In the days of the ancients, there lived south of Zuñi, beyond the headland of the rocks, at a place called Suski-ashokton ('Rock Hollow of the Coyotes'), an old Coyote. And this side of the headland of rocks, in the bank of a steep arroyo, lived an old Locust, near where stood a piñon tree, crooked and so bereft of needles that it was sunny" (255). Dennis Tedlock, the Zuni and Mayan translator, has criticized Cushing for just such explanatory glosses.[53] In his view, they are utterly insensitive to the story's performative situation: native listeners would likely know exactly where the rock hollow and the crooked piñon tree were, and would need no explanation. Tedlock's own translation of "Coyote and Junco" renounces such inauthentic additions and aims instead to reconstruct a story performance by including nonverbal gestures and paralinguistic elements.[54] To indicate the pace of the performance, its pauses, and its variations in volume and emphasis, Tedlock deploys different sizes of type, capitals, indentations, and white space; he also preserves sounds (in this case, of Junco's song) without attempting to give the sounds meaning. By recording these expressive details, Tedlock seeks to sustain the "openness" of the story.[55] For Cushing's nonnative readers, however, such a gloss was necessary to convey the rootedness of the story in the natural environment.

Diné poet Luci Tapahonso has spoken to this need to situate stories, even when retelling them for native audiences. She explains that many of the stories in her 1997 collection *Blue Horses Rush In* "were originally told in

Diné, taking no longer than ten minutes in the telling. Yet in re-creating them, it is necessary to describe the land, the sky, the light, and other details of time and place." To "create and convey the setting for the oral text," she says, "I revisit the place or places concerned and try to bring the reader to them, thereby enabling myself and other Navajos to sojourn mentally and emotionally to our home, Dinetah" (xiv). To be effective as both a means of cultural instruction and a record of local history, the tale must be imagined in its geographical context; Cushing's frames attempt to convey that context.[56]

Furthermore, though Cushing's formal diction seems to sacrifice the immediacy of dialogue and suppress the performative nature of the story, his choice of tone might well represent the manner in which the story was traditionally told. When Coyote first comes across Locust, he calls out, "Delight of my senses, how finely you play your flute." When Locust asks, "Do you think so?" Coyote replies, "Goodness, yes!" Then he says, "What a song it is! Pray, teach it to me" (256). This language seems stiff, and possibly too formal. However, if we compare Cushing's translation with both Parsons's 1925 translation of a similar Tewa tale and more recent versions produced by native speakers, we begin to hear the appropriateness of Cushing's tone. Parsons's "Forgetting the Song" tells of a Coyote woman who compliments a fly's song and politely asks the fly to teach it to her: "You are singing a very pretty song. I like to hear it," Coyote woman says. "I would like to learn it. I have some children, I would like to sing it to them."[57] The fly invites her to jump down in the wash and teaches her the song, but Coyote woman keeps forgetting it and has to return; finally the fly tires, sings the song one last time, and flies away—prompting Coyote to jump after him, fall into the wash, and break her neck. Throughout the story, both the fly and Coyote woman continue to treat each other with reserve and seeming respect, allowing the audience's anticipation of Coyote woman's downfall to build.[58] Like Cushing's, this translation refrains from expressing emotion through conversation, leaving the response to the story as a whole open to its readers.

Lummis, too, works between his own experience in listening to performances of the tales and his readers' literary expectations. Framing his version of the Coyote story with a general description (the story will present yet another "sad misadventure of the Coyote") and a discussion of local variants, Lummis presents "The Coyote and the Thunderknife" as typical of the genre and a case study in folkloric transformation. Though he begins with "Once upon a time," the mark of a European folktale, he otherwise presents the story directly and mediates little. Significant words and names, like *oo-ún* (children) and *Cheech-wée-deh* (locust), remain untranslated; the Tiwa name for ducks, "Afraids-of-the-Water," appears in the text with an explanatory footnote. The song Coyote sings as he searches for Locust is set off as verse, indicating a break between the prose in which the story is told and the poetic, presumably tuneful performance of the song. With this story, Lummis experiments with retaining a few original elements as he situates it within an interpretive framework familiar to his readers.

The inconsistencies of Lummis's presentation indicate his tenuous control over narrative form, his haphazard mode of collecting at least some of the tales, and his difficulty in finding an audience. To reproduce the immediacy of a storytelling performance, Lummis unifies *Pueblo Indian Folk-Tales* into a common structure: Pueblo elders pass the responsibility for recitation among themselves on successive winter nights, with a group of children gathered around them. By the end of the third night, however, Lummis has taken over the role of the narrator from the native speakers, and begins to comment on the origins of the folklore (noting similarities between legends from Laguna and Isleta), the status of the stories (as truth or legend), and his own position. In Robert Gish's description, "the respective narrators fuse into composites," creating "a kind of Pueblo chorus."[59] Lummis probably sat in on some storytelling sessions, but to transcribe the tales he relied on paid collaborators who spoke in a mixture of Tiwa, Spanish, and English—and whose presence the published text effaces. The prominence of the narrative framework, at least at the beginning of the stories, might be seen to compensate for the fragmentary nature of the fieldwork, while the presentation of the tales as children's stories or folktales (which some reviewers compared with Joel Chandler Harris's Uncle Remus stories) reveals a calculated appeal to a middle-class audience.

In the 1890s, short stories collected into book form were a hard sell. In reference to his collection *A New Mexico David,* Charles Scribner cautioned Lummis, "It is only when the literary qualities of such a collection overcome our objections on business grounds that we are induced to make it"; Scribner also urged a change in title from Lummis's original "How I Lost My Shadow" because "the success of the book depends largely upon the way it is put on the market."[60] When *The Man Who Married the Moon* was reprinted in 1910, Lummis's editor at the Century Company likewise suggested that they change the collection's name to *Pueblo Indian Folk-Stories.* Lummis proposed many titles that included the description "fairy tales," clearly knowing his translations would be received as children's fare.[61]

Throughout the collection, Lummis indicates the mixture of ethnographic observation, literary ambition, and personal affinity that informs his hybrid mode of translation. The last set of translations of "P'á-í-shia," or "Grandmother Spider," confirms the rhetorical location of the text between ethnography and literature. Announcing at the start that he is imitating Mark Twain's play with French translations of "The Celebrated Jumping Frog of Calaveras County," Lummis transcribes the story in Tiwa from a native storyteller; transfers it into English word by word; produces a Spanish version judged a "good translation of the original" by an Indian narrator; and finally translates the Spanish version into an English story. We can be skeptical of Lummis's rhetoric of translation and still analyze—and admire—the results of his work.

First, consider the beginning of the interlinear translation:

> In a house, they say, Cane-Black-Old-Man and Ear-of-Corn-with-Husks-Woman, Corn-Yellow-Girl, (and) Blue Dawn (proper name) (and) their little son, lived they. Cane-Black-Old-Man rain worked for (to call).
>
> Corn-Old-Woman was without eyes (blind). Then [Na-chur-ú-chu] (proper name) came at dawn whib-stick used to run. Then Corn-Yellow-Girl she used to grind. Then Ear-of-Corn-Old-Woman she used to the child take care of. On the belt she used to tie. Far when gone far, thought she thought, the belt she pulled back. Then (the) eagle the child had eyed. Then one day the eagle came. Then child he stole. (241–42)

This word-for-word translation may exaggerate the "grotesque" foreignness of the original version by maintaining Tiwa syntax, but it still allows the reader to decipher the meaning. Now compare it with Lummis's version of the tale that follows it:

> Once upon a time, they say, Old-Man-with-a-Black-Cane and his wife Ear-of-Corn-Woman lived with their children—with their daughter Yellow-Corn-Girl, and her baby, and their little son Na-chur-ú-chu (whose name means Boy-of-the-Blue-of-Dawn).
>
> Old-Man-with-a-Black-Cane was the Rain-Maker of the pueblo,

and worked to bring the rains. His wife was without eyes (blind). The little boy Na-chur-ú-chu used to play *whib* in the morning. Then his sister Yellow-Corn-Girl used to grind corn on the metate. The old mother used to take care of the baby and to work, weaving a belt. She used to tie the baby at the end of the belt, so that he could play while she worked.

One day she thought about the belt and pulled it back, and there was no boy tied to it. An eagle had watched the child. That one day the eagle came and stole the child; and when his grandmother pulled the belt there was no child tied to it. (252–53)

From the interlinear to the interpretive translation, Lummis keeps the index of the story's communal origin ("they say"), the proper names, and the sequence of events. More important, he maintains the syntactic structure of the source text: nearly every sentence in his own tale corresponds to a single unit, or sentence, in the original version. Contemporary translators might consider each of these units to be lines of verse; as an example of what Zolbrod calls "colloquial poetry," the story "might fill each line from the left margin to the right, with no need for the kind of spacing that delineates measured linear or stanzaic units."[62] Yet, because this is a story, its transcription as poetry might be misleading. As Robert Parker has argued, translators like Tedlock and Dell Hymes who write stories with line breaks are actually transforming them into poetry; according to Parker, this strategic shift in genre works to legitimate the aesthetic value of the translation (poetry is more prestigious than prose) and, more generally, to increase the cultural capital of Native American oral narratives.[63] Lummis treats the units as compressed sentences, or poetic prose, to be expanded with each retelling. Meanwhile, his few embellishments sketch the context for each action: "Old-Woman she used to the child take care of" becomes "the old mother used to take care of the baby and to work, weaving a belt," completing the description of habitual activity that sets the stage for the events to follow. Comparing the translations makes Lummis's own version seem less fanciful than his rhetoric leads us to expect, for in fact he takes few liberties; he simply rearranges the order within the sentences to make them sensible and provides a few explanatory notes.

The ostensible purpose of this exercise in translation is to teach an "object-lesson as to the difference in 'habits,' so to speak, between the two languages" and to prove a literal, non-idiomatic translation "unintelligible"

(240). A secondary purpose is surely to flaunt the author's ability to play the native language against Anglo literary convention. Judging Twain's English version of French to be "grotesque," Lummis locates the source of distortion in the translation strategy itself, not in the particular language under study. Where Twain aims for laughter, though, Lummis seeks merely to "interest" his reader—and to justify his own claim that only a nonliteral retelling can convey "the exact Indian *spirit*" (6), or "exactly the same sense" in which "the Indian boys and girls understood it when it was told them in the soft and musical Tée-wahn" (252). The choice of Twain as a model is an interesting one, because through it Lummis aligns himself with the powerful tradition of the Western tall tale. But now, as the frontier begins to close, the meaning of the West starts to be located in its real cultures, not in their mock-heroic or exaggerated representations. Whereas Twain's tales reveal the hard times and disappointments that Anglo settlers and speculators experienced on the frontier, Lummis's stories and translations begin to invent a new, postfrontier West that is both authentic and enchanted.[64]

Contemporary critics praised Lummis for literary judgment and for his ability to combine science and amusement. Later readers, however, have found his texts to be unacceptable compromises. On the surface, their traditional form as prose stories seems to repress cultural difference, whereas the typographic experiments of ethnopoetic texts heighten such difference. As I have argued, however, close scrutiny of both the conditions of Lummis's textual production and the surface itself yields a more complex and ambivalent result. In order to reconstruct the regional, cultural, and discursive boundaries Lummis's writing crossed, we need first to consider the conditions in which he gathered and constructed his texts—that is, to follow David Murray's example in *Forked Tongues,* focusing on "the mediator or interpreter, rather than what he is pointing to" (1). We can look next at how the writing itself inscribes the experience of the translator, refracts the role of the native collaborator, and speaks to the imagined expectations of the Anglo reader. Finally, we can consider the reading community that the text itself creates. As opposed to the "utopia of plural authorship" that Murray warns "may be only a dream of no meaning" (151–52), Lummis's translations imagine a utopian relation between the text and its Anglo readers.

While late nineteenth-century translators wrote primarily for English-speaking readers, postmodern ethnographies and ethnopoetic texts seek to communicate in both the translator's and the original speaker's languages, and thus function simultaneously as translation and criticism. Whether such bilingual communication is possible, or even desirable, is a question that white scholars alone cannot resolve. Bilingual Native American scholars are now in a position to contest and produce both translation and criticism, though according to Craig Womack they "haven't yet done enough to articulate how the oral tradition provides the principles for interpreting our national literatures—the genres; the unique approaches to character development, plot, theme, setting, and so on; the effect on the structuring of stories; the philosophies that come out of this tradition; the contexts it provides for understanding politics, religion, and society" (76). We should remember the difficulty of imagining what Geertz calls "the native's point of view," and seriously consider the possibility that now "translation" should go primarily in the opposite direction. A translation can communicate only *some* of "the understanding of the foreign text that foreign readers have"; this communication will "always be partial, both incomplete and inevitably slanted towards the domestic scene."[65] It may now be time for Anglo audiences to reverse the slant: to imagine the complex relations among translators, their texts, and potential communities of readers, and to listen closely to Native American stories like the foreigners we are.

The Ambivalent Rhetoric of the Modern Southwest

Although Lummis was merely one of the first writers to use Southwestern materials to capitalize on the collective Anglo yearning for relatively undeveloped spaces and alternative experiences of time, by the end of the nineteenth century the Southwest's Anglo discourse of longing and loss had become indelibly associated with his name. Soon Lummis's career consisted primarily of regional advocacy and self-promotion, for he failed to respond to the emerging demand for either specialized knowledge or popular reinvention that would drive the formation of the Anglo Southwest into the twentieth century. This failure became evident when Lummis played only peripheral roles in continuing Anglo efforts at Southwestern identity formation (such as exhibits at the 1915 San Diego Exposition, tours promoted by the Fred Harvey Company, and the founding of the Museum of New Mexico) and when he assumed a defensive position with his publisher in the 1920s. The waning of Lummis's authority marked the end of a period dominated by the regional amateur and the beginning of the modern era's self-conscious professional. As new literary figures and scientific experts staked their own claims to regional authority, Lummis still insisted on spreading his interests wide, opening himself to friendly ribbing and not-so-friendly attack.

The very range of his activities had always condemned Lummis to the status of the limited, and seemingly superficial, specialist, what Fitzgerald in *The Great Gatsby* called "that most limited of all specialists, the 'well-rounded man'" (4). His life had indeed become a collection of legendary anecdotes. Invited to the White House to discuss Indian policy before President Roosevelt's first message to Congress, he arrived wearing his habitual corduroy suit and sash, and left with Roosevelt's endorsement of the magazine he edited, *Land of Sunshine*. Zealous in pursuit of the preservationist cause, he proposed a novel defense of the Southwest Society of the Archeological Institute that he founded against its upstart rival in San Francisco, challenging that chapter's founder, Alfred Kroeber, to a fist-fight.[66] This all-around Westerner earned an ambivalent and anonymous 1923 tribute from Emily Coey, the daughter of one of Lummis's friends. Coey poked fun at Lummis's costume, his boasts, and his proprietary claims on Southwestern culture:

Who first beheld the Indian race?
Columbus, say you?—'Tisn't true!
I was the first to see his face—
I've had him copyrighted, too.

I'm local color—Sitting Bull—
Tracy the Bandit—Teddy's guest—
The atmosphere is full of Me.
Charles F. Lummis, who's the West.[67]

Coey apparently dressed up in corduroy herself to caricature Lummis's quick identification with the native cultures of his adopted region and dramatize his eagerness to inhabit and exploit the West. By the 1920s, Lummis's persona and his modes of representing the region were laughably out of date.

Late in his career, Lummis fought a new transregional economy that selectively appropriated Western materials for national consumption, as well as the disenchanting consequences of his own regional authority, his own waning power in the literary marketplace, and the ignorance of the very tourists he had worked so hard to attract. Though Lummis sensed the transformations of the Southwest as a cultural field, he could not adapt to them; instead he displaced his anxiety onto desperate attempts to salvage what he saw as the Southwest's imperiled traditions and what he knew to be his own imperiled career. An uncritical enthusiasm for the old Southwest, always evident in his treatment of the region's Spanish heritage, began to extend to every aspect of Southwestern culture. Both nostalgic and scientific, Lummis's preservation activities sought to recover models of cohesive culture and to document unstudied folk art.

Lummis worked especially hard to preserve the Southwest's traditional "Spanish" songs in the hope that communal singing could bring "saving grace to our hurried, angular lives" and cure "the unrest, the social dyspepsia, the de-humanizing and de-homing, the apartness that comes by multitudes."[68] He remembered fondly the feeling of community "under the infinite stars of a New Mexican sky" and around the campfire as he listened to "human, simple, friendly folk" sing and offered his "college songs and ditties" in return. He was eager to record the songs; in 1905, he thought the project must be started within three years or 50 percent of the available material would be lost. Accordingly, he defined the central project of the Southwest Society as the recording of this folk music on wax cylinders. Some songs he performed himself, boasting that he learned many of them by heart, since memorization was the only way to preserve them: "I had to sit by the hour before the crackling adobe hearth or by the ruddy campfire, singing each song over time after time in unison with my good-natured instructors, until I knew the air absolutely by heart—and not only the air, but the exact rendition of it."[69] Other songs were performed by Mexican musicians in Los Angeles. The singer Manuela García and her brother Ygnacio, a guitarist, performed for many of the recordings. Many of the singers were family friends, and Lummis seems to have gained sufficient access to Los Angeles's Hispano community to entice some of its most accomplished musicians to volunteer their services.[70] He paid composer Arthur Farwell to transcribe the songs, which were mostly *canciones* (traditional, popular lyric songs), some *romances* (traditional narrative songs in ballad form), and a few *corridos* (songs narrating contemporary political or historical events, heard mostly in Mexico and the Southwest after 1910).[71] Although Lummis and Farwell finally published *Spanish Songs of Old California* in 1923, much of the folkloric work Lummis organized remains, neither transcribed nor interpreted, on its original wax cylinders in the Southwest Museum's Braun Research Library.

The longing for an idealized and culturally unified past became a defensive move for Lummis, a means of repelling challenges to both the region's premodern cultures and his own authority as a Southwestern pioneer. George Wharton James wrote in 1923 that Lummis "took upon himself the task of being the censor of everything dealing with the Southwest. . . . Many a man who deemed himself almost above criticism found himself stripped naked because he had presumed carelessly to handle subjects that were within the domain of Mr. Lummis's interests."[72] Lummis's career proves that Anglo settlement in New Mexico and Arizona in the late nineteenth century, though initally accompanied by diverse dreams of new spatial and cultural experiences, soon produced a more conservative counterresponse. In the context of this period's internationalism and "in the midst of a collage of imploding spatialities," somehow "the fashioning of some localized aesthetic image" became a necessary foundation for a new regional identity.[73] In spite of his desire for mobility and self-fashioning through contact with Western spaces, Lummis came to cling to the security of a single conceptual place by the end of his career. That it took so long for the experience of modernity to take its toll on him proves a capacity to engage with the complexity of Southwestern culture that few of his contemporaries could match.

The correspondence between Lummis and his publisher regarding the revised edition of *Some Strange Corners of Our Country* confirms how difficult it was for a Southwestern writer like Lummis to sustain any position of authority, much less take conceptual or formal risks. The negotiations and revisions reveal the competing forces of commerce and preservation, and the contradictory rhetorics of invention and authenticity, that increasingly shaped representations of the Southwest. Lummis undertook the task of revision early in the 1920s. His health was poor and his finances even worse. Letters exchanged with his editor at the Century Company, James Abbott, display Lummis's prickly defense of his own importance and the publisher's repeated resistance to the author's grand claims. Lummis quickly distinguished his guide from "the ordinary Travel Book" written "only for amusement and for the edification of the Women's clubs and their reviewers." *His* book would provide guidance and accurate illustration for the 500,000 rail passengers and tens of thousands of automobile parties that traversed the region each year. He insisted, "There may be other books about phases of that vast territory, and even about the inexhaustible Indians; but an 'Omnibus' book, on the scenery, the ruins, the people, and the customs of the Southwest, Never."[74]

Throughout the revision process, Lummis and his editor argued about style. When Abbott objected to Lummis's "excessive use of capitals," which gave "the effect of a series of explosions," Lummis defended them, along with his "elastic vocabulary": "Where they are used, they are *meant* 'as explosives'; and for effect, which has been characteristic of my style for more than 20 years."[75] The hyperbolic style was clearly intertwined with Lummis's professional identity, for he explained to Abbott that he meant it to be his "Come-Back Book—after a lapse of over 20 years. It has to be a Ringer—to let them all know that the Old Man is on deck again and going strong."[76] To assuage his anxieties about stepping back in the ring, Lummis tried to dictate the book's promotional strategy as well. He reminded Abbott repeatedly that "people are not interested in warmed over pan-cakes or new editions";[77] that the book should be published near the holidays, when much travel to California occurs; and that since his earlier books had appealed to children, Century should expand its publicity to reach the juvenile market.

Mesa, Cañon and Pueblo was finally published in 1925, the same year as Willa Cather's *The Professor's House*. Reviewers noted the connection. The literary editor of the *Chicago Daily News* promised, "If your interest has been stirred by the glimpse of the cliff dweller city in 'The Professor's House' you will find in this book descriptions of the reality that are even more fascinating than the fiction."[78] On the whole, reviewers accepted Lummis's revision as a substantially new book and noted his dominant position in the field of Southwestern writing, even if they objected to the book's defensive edge or acknowledged that Lummis was "no great word poet" ("for thrilling esthetic interpretations of the southwest, one had better go to Mrs. Mary Austin," one advised).[79] Significantly, the review most closely aligned with a regional perspective, the description of the book in Santa Fe's *El Palacio* magazine, affirms Lummis's authority in the old style: "Dr. Lummis writes as one who has been part of the scenes and events he describes so vividly. The reader can rest assured that what he states is authentic, even though it is the very essence of romance and poetry."[80]

By the early twentieth century, the meaning of the Anglo Southwest lay in its promise to awaken visitors to new cultural and aesthetic experience, a promise often fulfilled at the expense of native places and cultures. The nineteenth-century "armchair travelers" who admired Lummis's intrepid adventures and shared his enthusiasm for Native American cultures were rapidly becoming consumers of Western myth: they read romances, planned their own trips, and watched Western films. The contradictory desires of these consumers, and the fiction that satisfied them, is the subject we will pursue in the next chapter.

2

Incomprehensible Brotherhood in Zane Grey's Borderlands

LITERARY HISTORIANS HAVE LOCATED the formula Western's popularity in its contradictory rejection and embrace of the conventions that shaped the late nineteenth-century literary novel. From the gunman's first ride alone into the desert to the final shoot-out, the Western typically narrates the masculine hero's antibourgeois education: a lone and innocent Easterner learns the wild lands and lawless ways of the frontier. As Jane Tompkins writes, the Western conjures "a world without God, without ideas, without institutions, without what is commonly recognized as culture, a world of men and things, where male adults in the prime of life find ultimate meaning in doing their best together on the job." As such, the genre "gets rid" of Christianity and "the female, domestic, 'sentimental' religion of the best-selling writers . . . whose novels spoke to the deepest and highest ideals of middle-class America."[1] But it is also, in Lee Mitchell's reading, a literary form committed not to resolving the "incompatible worlds of savagery and civilization, and especially of two competing kinds of masculinity," but to "*narrating* all those contradictions involved in what it means to be a man, in a way that makes them seem less troubling than they are."[2] The genre's mixture of utopia and ideology allows readers to engage more directly with its social fantasies and anxieties than the more highly mediated meanings of literary fiction.

The best-selling Western romances that Zane Grey published between 1910 and 1939 set the standard for this popular genre, constructing the mythic Southwest through repeated mappings of frontiers to the north and borders to the south.[3] This was a time when media, consumption, and Western migration coincided on a mass scale.[4] Indeed, the Western as Grey invented it cannot be separated from the expansion of the literary marketplace and the technology of mass culture, developments that were very much a part of Grey's professional struggles. Nor can the Western be separated from uneven geographic development in the Southwest, or from the social implications of what David Harvey calls "the intersecting command of money, time, and space."[5] Though the conventional and homosocial romance plots of Western novels may seem to reinforce the limits of transgression, and though descriptions of the landscape at times overwhelm readers with their contemporary social implications, economic and political contradictions finally prove difficult to contain.

In addition to the landscapes that define the Western as a genre, two geopolitical paradigms structure much of Grey's fiction: the late nineteenth-century frontier, already a mythic site of communal and masculine identity formation, and the U.S.–Mexico border, a site of accelerated political unrest and cultural conflict in the 1910s. My reading of the genre here as both an investigation of new geographical imaginaries and a formal solution to economic, political, and gender anxieties of the early twentieth century pursues the "problem of the popular" that Stephen Tatum has explored in relation to the New Western History. Tatum argues "that the history of popular Western texts—if studied and accepted as an evolving rather than frozen one—is everywhere invested in dramatizing struggles for cultural dominance, complex issues of morality, and contests for property and propriety."[6] Idealizing a lost frontier or a "real" West, whether as myth or out of the earnest conviction that myths obscure class and ethnic struggles, simplifies historical narratives and avoids the risk of engagement with the complexities of cultural production. The challenge for critics of popular texts lies in recognizing the roles that desire and imagination play in making and reconstructing spatial histories.[7] By working "between interior and exterior, myth and reality, fantasy and the actual, the imaginative and the real," as Tatum advises, we can begin to meet this challenge by locating ourselves within the field of popular literary production. Such involvement helps us to see how popular texts, and their critical assessments, might resist and reinforce the dominant cultural imaginary at the same time.

The problem of the popular is really a problem of critical distance. If we dispassionately analyze popular texts like Westerns as nostalgic hymns to the lost frontier, we miss one of their most important features: their persistent and affective power. As a result, we also tend to lose sight of their utopian potential, which is articulated primarily through feelings of longing rather than rational social plans. The American desert and the Western wilderness,

including the frontier, have commonly been interpreted as mythic compen-
sations for the social pressures that accompanied urban growth, increased
immigration, and Indian allotment. Without denying this reactionary function of the landscape, we should consider how the Western's geographic
imaginary can, in spite of its ideological or commodified value, also have a
utopian purpose. The spaces of utopia are more easily written into landscape
than realized, and attempts to produce them are frequently co-opted by
commodity culture. The Western narrates the imagination, disenchantment,
and re-enchantment of the American landscape, articulating the problematic
of creative destruction that characterizes many varieties of modernism.[8] As it
produces ideological *and* utopian spaces, the Western struggles to stabilize
continuing forces of change.[9] It maps modernity's temporal and spatial contradictions, showing us in the process how popular culture might, in Perry
Anderson's words, "intimate" what a consciously "utopian fiction cannot
embody."[10] The best-selling status of Grey's novels proves that his intima-
tions of utopia spoke very effectively to the desires of Eastern, middle-class
consumers.

The period in which the Western emerged as a distinct genre was also
the period of greatest *corrido* production along the border. José Limón describes the heart of the *corrido* as "an aestheticized and eroticized figure of
strong, attractive masculinity confronting other men with the phallic power
of his pistol in his hand," referring to "The Ballad of Gregorio Cortez," first
sung along the Rio Grande in 1903 and explicated by Américo Paredes.[11]
Paredes had asked why a similar epic and folkloric tradition did not develop
along the Anglo side of the border, in Anglo-Texan folk songs, for he would
have expected victors in the region "to celebrate their ascendancy with
heroic epic song." Limón concludes that the folk cultures of colonizer and
colonized function according different logics: while Mexicans produced *corridos* "as a compensatory form of resistance for a *lack* of victory in the material
realm" (106), Anglos produced folk songs (or *gringo corridos*) about romances
between cowboys and Mexican women to express "ambivalence toward [the
Anglo's] own capitalist and colonialist culture" (113). Beside the Mexican
celebration of masculine violence we can read the Anglo lament for the lost
possibility of cross-cultural romance. Following Limón's suggestive pairing
of the two types of ballad, I consider how Grey's novels themselves combine
a "theme of superiority and social domination" with "a ritualized and ambivalent rhetoric of desire and self-doubt" (103).

Whether the novels resolve, neutralize, or sustain ambivalence about the conflicts they raise determines the generic status of these Westerns as mythic, utopian, or popular.[12] Grey flirts with each of these possibilities in his early attempts at the genre before arriving at the ambivalent mixture of mythic plot, ideal landscape, and historic context that would best perpetuate the desires of his readers and enable him to reap substantial financial rewards. In this chapter I consider why three of Grey's early novels—*The Heritage of the Desert* (1910), *Riders of the Purple Sage* (1912), and *The Rainbow Trail* (1915)— are preoccupied with Mormon economic, domestic, and gendered arrangements along the Utah frontier. Even as they sustain the myth of opportunity for newcomers to the West, these novels challenge the economic and religious foundations of traditional frontier communities. A fourth novel, *Desert Gold* (1913), uses the alternative borderland space between Arizona and Sonora to represent political conflict and imagine relations between Anglo and Indian men. Through reconfigurations of these northern and southern borderlands both within and across his early narratives, Grey exposes the tensions between fantasy and development that define the twentieth-century West.

Crucibles of the Metropolis and the Desert

The popularity of Grey's novels depended on the growth of two homologous economies: the uneven expansion of capitalism that the novels imitate, and the mass cultural market in which they participate. In their details, Grey's representations of Anglo, Mormon, and Navajo economies on the Southwest's northern frontier and his depictions of Anglo, Mexican, and Yaqui economies on the Arizona-Mexico border are not meant to be accurate. The relations they tell among borderland cultures, however, speak to the increased dominance of Anglos in the region, and to the self-doubt that accompanied that dominance. In the late nineteenth century, "the extension of the market economy to the most remote corners of the American West" proved "capitalism's propensity to expand, its persistent drive toward accumulation, and its inclination to repeated technological change."[13] As this market spread farther across the border into Mexico, it destroyed local subsistence economies and replaced them with complex legal arrangements that granted primacy to private property.

Grey's Westerns rewrite this economic conflict pursued by violent means as religious or cultural difference. In Utah, the perceived fanaticism of the Mormons made frontier settlements seem incompatible with the new order; to the south, Mexico was the "country of the capitalist and the tourist," territory available for development and for pleasure.[14] Each of Grey's early texts begins to narrate the transition from a subsistence to a credit economy, and from communal organization to multicultural society. Yet, each also suspends a resolution of this transition, either by displacing narrative attention to a newly enchanted natural site, thereby collapsing the plot structure, or by staging a violent confrontation that leads toward simplistic resolution. These evasions, duplications, and violent displays are critical to the emerging genre's capacity to spatialize capitalist expansion in the West. As David Harvey explains the process, "capital builds a geographic landscape in its own image at a certain point in time only to have to destroy it later in order to accommodate its own dynamic of endless capital accumulation, strong technological change, and fierce forms of class struggle."[15] The formula Western imitates, and at times resists, this kind of capitalist production of Western spaces.

As popular fiction dependent on the expansion of mass culture, the Western occupied a field of cultural production different from that of high modernist literature. If high modernism was forged in what Raymond Williams called the "crucible of the metropolis," the popular Western was forged in what Grey called the "crucible of the desert."[16] Pierre Bourdieu argues that the opposition professional writers insisted on between creative liberty and the laws of the market, an opposition which intensified in the modernist period, was merely "a defence against the *disenchantment* produced by the progress of the division of labor."[17] Already divided from the field of high, relatively autonomous culture, the popular marketplace in the 1910s intensified that rhetorical opposition and, at the same time, required ever-clearer genre distinctions.[18] In the case of the Western, market pressure would encourage the genre to become self-referential; Westerns "are continually bordering on pastiche or parody of previous authors, against whom they measure themselves."[19] It would take the self-conscious artists of the classic Western film (John Ford), the spaghetti Western (Sergio Leone), and the postmodern Western (Jim Jarmusch) to exploit fully the ironies of the genre in nuanced forms. But by working out the critical elements and formulas, and then borrowing from his own models, Grey initiated the spatial transformations that would manage these cultural anxieties and longings.[20]

Success did not come easily for Grey. He spent his childhood in his hometown of Zanesville, Ohio, fishing, playing baseball, and pulling teeth (though the young Grey was unlicensed, his little practice supplemented his father's income). When he attended the University of Pennsylvania on a baseball scholarship, he struggled to pass his classes; despite his early literary aspirations, he seemed unsure of his technical proficiency and would always rely on his wife, Dolly, to edit his prose. Perhaps this insecurity was behind his stubborn persistence to succeed as a writer and his gloomy preoccupation with bad reviews. Biographers and critics note Grey's untiring efforts to publish his early work, beginning with *Betty Zane*, a novel recounting ancestral exploits that Dolly finally persuaded him to publish himself. A. L. Burt & Company, a publisher specializing in reprints and juvenile books, eventually took on Grey's next attempt at fiction, *Spirit of the Border* (1906); Outing Publishing Company, publishers primarily of sporting magazines, accepted *The Last Trail* (1909) but could not afford to pay. Grey kept trying to interest Harper's in his work, but his submission of *The Last of the Plainsmen* was rejected by twelve publishers and elicited editor Ripley Hitchcock's scorn: "I do not see anything in this to convince me you can write either narrative or fiction," he told Grey.[21] Although he had considerable success selling his fishing stories to *Field and Stream,* only with *The Heritage of the Desert* (1910) did Grey win commercial and literary approval: Harper and Brothers and *Popular Magazine* accepted the novel on the same day.[22]

The professional and public response to *The Heritage of the Desert* suggested a potential for mass readership that was realized by *Riders of the Purple Sage,* the novel that finally secured Grey's relationship with Harper's. From 1910 through the 1920s Grey would issue about a novel a year with Harper's, and they were soon assured that any book bearing his name would sell at least 500,000 copies. In an unprecedented feat, he produced a best-seller every year from 1917 to 1924. The rapid expansion of the periodical market between 1880 and 1920 had prepared the way for Grey's runaway success. In that period the population more than tripled, while illiteracy rates declined dramatically; urbanization made the sale and distribution of magazines easier and more efficient; free rural delivery was introduced; new, lower-priced magazines became available; and the business of advertising and promotion expanded nationally.[23] The corresponding growth in trade books was less dramatic but still significant, and together these markets created a demand for fiction which Grey satisfied.

In some respects we might consider the formula Western of the 1910s as the mass-culture successor to regional fiction of the late nineteenth century. Both provided a means of literary access to groups of writers outside of established literary culture; both required limited literary skills once the formulas were conventionalized; and both capitalized on the writer's knowledge of marginal cultures. Richard Brodhead argues that these elements characterized postbellum regionalism, and "made the experience of the socially marginalized," particularly women living outside of urban centers, "into a literary asset."[24] Though by no means as socially marginalized as the regionalists Charles Chesnutt, Sarah Orne Jewett, and Hamlin Garland, Grey was initially excluded from the New York literary scene. As he became aware of his literary marginalization, he chose to cultivate knowledge of regions still largely unknown to Eastern readers. Whereas nineteenth-century regionalism enabled writers to fit their otherwise unexceptional experiences into popular "local color" formulas, later variants on the genre required the writer to claim a foreign region and then narrate the process of gaining access to its local cultures. For Grey, as for Lummis, going west was a means of producing regional experience *and* potential readers; Grey's job also was to secure the right formula for his material to reach that audience.

The audience for the Western, however, would be significantly different from the genteel readers of nineteenth-century regionalism, which appeared in elite journals like *Atlantic Monthly, Harper's,* and *The Century.* Grey's potential readers bought dime novels and "pulp fiction" printed on inexpensive paper; already familiar with frontier adventure fiction, they simply expanded their range to include Westerns and tales of exotic adventure.[25] Grey's novels often appeared simultaneously in slick magazines, miscellaneous monthlies, and weeklies aimed at readers unable to afford glossy periodicals. *The Heritage of the Desert,* for example, was serialized in *Popular Magazine,* a bimonthly periodical of detective stories, romances, and Western adventure tales. The magazine's fiction, its price (15 cents), and its advertisements indicate an audience of lower-middle-class readers intent on self-education and social advancement.[26] *Riders of the Purple Sage* appeared in *Field and Stream,* the "official organ of the Camp-fire Club of America," which appealed to hunters, sportsmen, and wilderness advocates. At first glance, this serialization seems a surprising choice for Grey. Printing virtually no fiction, the magazine typically addressed such problems as finding the right sporting equipment: an all-round rifle, a sturdy rucksack, an effective fishing bait. Its articles recounted adventures chasing wild game like cougars, bears, and elk. But Grey had already written fishing tales of his own, and the editors probably hoped his name and the novel's exciting chase scenes would lure their readers. Other novels were serialized in magazines aimed at farmers (*Country Gentleman*) or middle-class women (*Ladies' Home Journal*). *Munsey's* variety magazine, where Grey's *The Light of the Western Stars* appeared in

1913, appealed to the broadest group of readers: it combined stories of middle-class intrigue and working women, political commentary, photographs and gossip about theater stars, sports features, and full-length serial fiction. Both the tone of the advertisements and articles and the conventional nature of the fiction in these periodicals suggest an audience anxious to master the skills required for metropolitan life, but also longing for escape from its pressures.

Beginning in 1918, films made from Grey's novels brought him an even larger audience.[27] As Christine Bold notes, the Western was a best-selling genre in every phase of mass publishing, and Grey's mastery of the formula made him one of the first American writers to earn over a million dollars.[28] Despite his extraordinary success among diverse groups of readers, Grey continued to resist his work's accountability to the marketplace. His insistence on autonomy certainly had a distinct economic value: it enabled the magazines in which his novels appeared to boast of his genius and singularity. At a time when book advertising relied more on a writer's personality and proven record than on generic categorization, the cultivation of an image of artistic independence worked to distinguish Grey's authorial identity from other Western writers and to facilitate the promotional efforts of his publishing house. Particularly with the new phenomenon of "best-sellers," introduced in practice by *Bookman* in 1895 and in name by *Publisher's Weekly* in 1911, these rewards could be quantified both within the industry and for the public by the number of books sold.

While the conflict between individual autonomy and institutional authority characterizes Grey's long publishing career, it also structures his first attempt at the Western romance and his first commercially successful novel, the Mormon romance that sets the stage for the more critically known *Riders of the Purple Sage*. Grey wrote *The Heritage of the Desert* just after exploring the inaccessible Arizona Strip and the Grand Canyon's North Rim with the buffalo hunter Charles Jesse "Buffalo" Jones and the accused cattle thief Jim Emmett. The novel partially reconstructs the author's own adventures (which, among other things, introduced him to the region's Mormon communities) and rewrites his struggle for professional independence.

The opening finds John Hare, a young Easterner with tuberculosis, regaining consciousness in "the land of the Mormons," a place he identifies by the uses of biblical reference and antiquated diction. Hare does not speak the local vernacular, and will remain a foreigner until he does; yet, a play on his name suggests that he may become heir to the legacy of the Mormon

West. August Naab, a man who combines faith in the moral righteousness of Mormon history and religious practice with benign tolerance of non-Mormons, puts Hare to work on the fertile oasis he farms and manages. Note the props that Grey gathers here, for they reappear in each of the early novels: a patriarchal village, a subsistence economy, and an improbably fertile natural landscape. Each feature occupies a distinct space on the frontier, with the zone of greatest freedom and possibility farthest from the town center. Into an island of deliberately archaic tradition, Grey introduces an outsider who will challenge its outdated foundations, propel its destruction, and prepare the way for a more liberal community. The remainder of the plot will be familiar to readers or viewers of the Western. Hare recovers his health, falls in love with Mescal (a half-Spanish, half-Navajo woman promised in marriage to one of Naab's sons), and resolves to fight: first for Naab, to avenge the death of Naab's son Dave and the property stolen by a group of rustlers, and then for himself, for the right to Mescal. Hare succeeds, but not before Naab's wrath has been awakened and "the ferocity of the desert spirit" overpowers his Mormon pacifism. In the end, Hare marries Mescal and, though he resists converting to Mormonism on the grounds that he opposes polygamy, agrees to live and work with Naab's sons.

In *The Heritage of the Desert,* Mormon history may delimit the social space of the Southwest's northern frontier, but like many writers of sensational Mormon novels, Grey distorts this history to emphasize the differences between Mormon and dominant Anglo culture. He calls particular attention to the Mormons' primitive social structure, their anti-Protestant orientation, and their authoritarianism. Snap Naab represents the Mormon belief in traditional authority and defends his property accordingly: the Mormons first "came into this desert land to worship and multiply in peace. They conquered the desert; they prospered with the years that brought settlers, cattle-men, sheep-herders, all hostile to their religion and livelihood" (2). Even when Holderness, Naab's new neighbor and competitor, offers to prove that the government owns the land, Naab insists that "this desert belongs to the Mormon" out of finder's rights: "We found the springs, dug the ditches" (26–27). The patriarch stands for the values the Mormons brought to the Great Basin and placed at the foundation of their communities, and he attempts throughout the novel to maintain order by appealing to the group's shared beliefs in tradition and work. Acting as a model craftsman and a steward of the wilderness, Naab appears as a "great and luminous figure" in the community because of the practical skills he developed to tame the wilderness. "He was a blacksmith, a mechanic, a carpenter, a cooper, a potter . . . a mason . . . a farmer, a cattle-man, a grafter of fruit-trees, a breeder of horses, a herder of sheep, a preacher, a physician" (58–59). Grey's fictional Mormon settlement of White Sage coheres through a common history of migration, a shared work ethic, nonspecialized labor, and religious and familial associations.

Outside developments, however, soon threaten White Sage's self-sufficiency. A younger Mormon warns, "We are no longer in the old days. Our young men are drifting away, and the few who return come with ideas opposed to Mormonism. Our young girls and boys are growing up influenced by the Gentiles among us. They intermarry, and that's a death-blow to our creed" (16). When Mescal refuses to become Snap Naab's Mormon wife and Snap goes into business with the cattle rustler Holderness, aiming to ruin Naab by blocking access to Seeping Spring, the threat comes true. Unlike purely political struggles, the ensuing fight to sustain the Mormon community will require absolute victory over all who enter the town of White Sage and its cultivated surroundings, for its legitimacy depends on shared notions of proper behavior and on shared attitudes toward the world.[29] Whereas on the Southwest's southern border "conflict and interdependence are deeply imbedded in the historical experience of border Mexicans, Mexican Americans, and Anglo-Americans," this northern frontier requires settlers to follow the model of corporations: to dominate the community by monopolizing natural resources.[30] Although the novel finally blunts the community's absolute demand for social conformity and obedience, it already translates economic conflict into oppositions between insiders and outsiders, believers and nonbelievers.

One source of resistance to these conflated economic, social, and religious demands is the desert itself, the novel's deliberately asocial space. Defined as a source of faith, and the element that trumps all social forces in determining character, the landscape reveals to the Eastern outsider a code of behavior and a system of belief that will overpower the existing order. But the matter of translating the overwhelming experience of landscape into an ethos always produces anxiety, both here and in later novels. Hare initially responds to the desert with terror, and his perspective fails: "He saw a red world. His eyes seemed bathed in blood. Red scaly ground, bare of vegetation, sloped down, down, far down to a vast irregular rent in the earth, which zigzagged through the plain beneath" (47). Nonetheless, Hare's physical recovery from tuberculosis is attributed to the sparse vegetation he could not even see at first (the "strong smell of black sage and juniper" mixes with the desert air to salve his lungs), and his spiritual recovery progresses through daily views of the sunset on the once limitless horizon and contact with Mescal, "the embodiment of the desert spirit" (89).

While his body toughens, his senses become more acute: "He buried his face in the fragrant juniper; he rolled on the soft brown mat of earth and hugged it close; he cooled his hot cheeks in the primrose clusters. He opened his eyes to new bright green of cedar, to sky of a richer blue, to a desert, strange, beckoning, enthralling as life itself" (89). And, though not fully erased, time is recalibrated: "He counted backward a month, two months, and marvelled at the swiftness of time. He counted time forward, he looked into the future, and all was beautiful—long days, long hunts, long rides, service to his friend, freedom on the wild steppes, blue-white dawns upon the eastern crags, red-gold sunsets over the lilac mountains of the desert" (89). The expansion of time into what seems like an organic progression is a sure repudiation of modernity's mechanical ordering and one of the Western's principal symbolic accomplishments.

In an epiphany fraught with contradictions in mood and purpose, Grey conveys the effects of the desert on his young hero and the sensations he seeks to create in his readers. Hare's awakening seems dreamlike, but it imagines a lifetime of productive and heroic work. It looks only two months back, but envisions a long and victorious future day by day: "He saw himself in triumphant health and strength, earning day by day the spirit of this wilderness, coming to fight for it, to live for it, and in far-off time, when he had won his victory, to die for it" (89). The "spirit of the wilderness," which Hare will "earn," becomes payment for his spiritual labor. Hare emerges from life in the desert as a newly formed Western hero, innocent, healthy, and resilient, speaking the true language of the West, ready to face the future and efface the past. The landscape alternately produces the romantic's awareness and the naturalist's survival skills, the disinterestedness of the artist and the economic discernment of the capitalist. As the novel's concluding chapters reveal, responsiveness to the environment and the capacity to change—qualities that also describe the successful capitalist—must be added to traditional Mormon faith if this community is to sustain its legitimacy; the "heritage of the desert" must supplement, and temper, religious heritage. With the popular success of *The Heritage of the Desert,* the formula Western and the Western hero are suddenly defined by the intervention of the Southwestern landscape.

The formation of community in Grey's Westerns, meanwhile, requires just this kind of accommodation between religious belief and capitalist practice. Though Hare does not accept Mormon law, he professes his own secular faith: he considers ranch work a calling, "an absolute end in itself." Both the trials and the conversion suggest that Hare functions as a Protestant in the land of the Mormons, a dissenter who seeks to reform the frontier's primitive economic and political order before it becomes institutionalized. As Max Weber has written, proof of worthiness was the essential prerequisite for acceptance into the Protestant sect as "voluntary association"; prospective members had to show, often repeatedly, their moral and spiritual fitness for membership. Weber wrote "The Protestant Sects and the Spirit of Capitalism" in 1906, two years after touring America and observing the persistence of religious association throughout the country. Mainline Protestants in fact sent their own missionaries "to save the West from Mormons and from Catholics," and to reform the societies they viewed as amoral; from their point of view, Mormonism did not constitute a voluntary religious and social organization.[31] When Naab accepts Hare into his family and his community, he reconciles tradition with voluntarism, and thus restores the frontier's symbolic status as an ideal American space: Protestant, democratic, classless. But the compromise is a tenuous one, a stay against the community's imminent destruction.

Although White Sage survives the crisis of belief posed by outsiders such as Hare, it faces the most severe threat from the sudden release of rage within the community. Revolt is the ready danger and consequence of monopoly. At the end of the novel we watch an unruly mob gather to administer justice to the rustlers who stole Naab's water. Naab literally quakes with rage at being denied vengeance for the deaths of seven sons, and only the improbable interventions of Hare and the bishop prevent a blind hanging of all the accused men. Grey attempts to dissipate this tension by cutting immediately to the novel's romantic resolution, the marriage of Hare and Mescal, but the irrational force unleashed in the community cannot be contained in this way. By revealing the dark side of the Mormons' seemingly mild obedience, *The Heritage of the Desert* shows the foundation of legitimacy in this community to be as much violence as belief.[32] The appearance of the mob signals that beneath the Mormons' facade, just as beneath the paternal face of late nineteenth-century corporations, lies a social order only a step away from mass revolt. The novel may seem to leave behind the East's legal system and corporate order to investigate more primitive systems of authority and economies on the frontier, but it actually reinscribes the dynamic of capital expansion within the Mormon community. The subsequent Mormon novels deepen this threat of violence and identify discrimination against women and Gentiles as crucial to the continuity of Mormon society, further aligning capitalism and authoritarianism. In Grey's novels, Mormons stand for both the traditional, religious communities at the fringes of advanced, bureaucratic societies and for repressive corporate monopolies.

As we will see, *Riders of the Purple Sage* replaces the productive communal associations of the earlier novel with coercive plots driven by hate and greed, and pits individual freedom against forced adherence to the Mormon creed. By *The Rainbow Trail,* the judgment against Mormon practice and social organization is complete: Mormon men hide their multiple wives in "sealed villages" to avoid persecution, and subdue them with the threat of unannounced night visits that read almost like raids; here, one woman's defiance signals a "deathblow to the old Mormon polygamous creed" (270). We can locate some of the fascination with these novels in their ambivalent representation of the Mormon economy. Nonetheless, the popular appeal of Mormon social and sexual arrangements bears further scrutiny. Why did the practice of polygamy alarm Gentile men? Why are women on the fringes of Mormon society the chosen heroines for Grey's newly formed heroes? Finally, what kind of domestic arrangements will Western couples make for themselves? Pursuing these questions through subsequent novels means tracking the Western's ambivalence about feminine empowerment and masculine sentiment.

Women of the Purple Sage

In *Roughing It* (1872), Mark Twain performs a comic inquiry into "the workings of polygamy," which he claimed to be a "customary" pastime for Western travelers. Though he tried to "get up the usual statistics and deductions preparatory to calling the attention of the nation at large once more to the matter," he threw this earnest intent to the desert winds when he saw how "homely" the women were. Instead, he recounts typical Gentile gossip about "how some portly old frog of an elder, or a bishop, marries a girl—likes her, takes another—likes her, marries her mother—likes her, marries her father, grandfather, great grandfather, and then comes back hungry and asks for more" (139–40). The hunger for multiple marriages becomes humorous, in other words, only if the women are undesirable to the point of being indistinguishable from men. By the time of Twain's writing, the Mormon "law" that had ruled the Utah Territory and sustained Mormon corporate enterprise was not only losing its legitimacy, and fast; it was also ruining its women in more ways than one.

Riders of the Purple Sage, "the most important single source of the modern 'formula' Western," organizes each of its romantic relations around the Mormon problem of controlling women.[33] Grey's most popular novel is set in 1871, the beginning of the decade when Americans organized the local and national crusades that threatened Mormon control in the Utah Territory in the name of protecting Mormon women. Even then, the Mormon economic and communal model would have seemed outdated; its polygamous practices, barbaric. Mormonism was "characterized by economic equality, socialization of surplus income, freedom of enterprise, and group economic self-sufficiency."[34] Under the Mormon law of consecration and stewardship, each family was granted "stewardship" of property owned by the bishop, and the church redistributed the surplus among church members. Following Joseph Smith's lead, Brigham Young took as his model order the "well-regulated family" to promote a "concern for the welfare of others in the group that transcended selfishness and promoted harmony and unity."[35]

But whereas Smith's "experiments took place during the heyday of communal experimentation in America," Brigham Young's return to Mormon communitarianism was "out of time and place—an unusual manifestation of anticapitalist economic idealism at a time when Andrew Carnegie and John D. Rockefeller were becoming national heroes."[36] Howard Lamar summarizes the fate of the Mormons: "not only to be out of touch with all the major economic and social trends between 1830 and 1890, but to have developed their own society while isolated in an extraordinary environment." In Lamar's view, Utah was a good example of territory that "always seemed to be out of step" with the others in an "evolving, continuously expanding nation," and the Mormons constituted an ideal case study for the frontier community long after the frontier had closed.[37]

Though Mormon groups had provoked hostility throughout the sect's history, beginning with the murder of Joseph Smith by a mob in Carthage, Illinois, in 1844 and fueled by the Mormon Church's alleged complicity in the 1857 Mountain Meadows Massacre, by 1870 opposition to Mormonism centered almost exclusively on a single issue: the evils of polygamy. The 1870 Newman-Pratt debate between John P. Newman, a Methodist minister from Washington, D.C., and Mormon Apostle Orson Pratt on the topic "Does the Bible Sanction Polygamy?" advanced anti-Mormon sentiment on religious grounds, and as a result many "would-be reformers seized on polygamy as the most visible symbol of Mormon peculiarity." Then the Poland Act of 1874 "extended federal juridical control over all criminal, civil, and chancery cases and placed the offices of territorial attorney general and marshal under federal direction."[38] This was also a time when Gentiles took advantage of the newly joined Union Pacific and Central Pacific railroads at Ogden, Utah, and began to settle in the Salt Lake Valley.

Recent historians of Mormon communities in Utah argue that plural marriages might not have oppressed women as fully as opponents have claimed, for Mormon women occupied new social roles and exercised considerable power under cooperative economic organization and in polygamous communities. Brigham Young specified that women should "keep books and sell goods" while the idle men "go to raising sheep, wheat, or cattle, or *go do something or other to beautify the earth*" (emphasis added).[39] Exactly what Young expected the men to do to "beautify the earth" is anyone's guess. By contrast, women ran several cooperatives in Salt Lake City, Ogden, Brigham City, and Provo that gave them "employment and a sense of independent achievement."[40] Because their husbands were often away, Mormon wives assumed responsibility for the household and divided the labor for farms and business. One study concluded "that in polygamous marriages, husbands and wives exercised approximately equal responsibilities in financial management"; in monogamous marriages, men dominated.[41] Plural marriages may also have enabled the group as a whole to adapt to the difficulties of migration. Lawrence Foster argues that they were "part of the necessary subordination of individual desires to long-term group goals that underlay Mormon success in the rapid settlement and development of the Intermountain West."[42]

Women's autonomy in Mormon society was further developed through organizations like the Relief Society; publications like the *Woman's Exponent,* a periodical newspaper that advocated women's concerns between 1872 and 1914; and the suffrage movement, which led to an act by the Mormon-controlled Utah legislature extending the right to vote to women in 1870. Unfortunately for Mormon women, these freedoms were short-lived: the *Reynolds* Supreme Court ruling in 1879 outlawed the practice of polygamy (leading to greater persecution of Mormon practices in the following decades), and the suffrage act was later retracted as part of the 1887 Edmunds-Tucker Act. Such legislation curtailed women's political freedoms in the Utah Territory as it prepared Utah for statehood, but it could not contain public fascination with both plunder and polygamy. Zane Grey learned to play on that fascination.[43]

The plots of Grey's Mormon novels explore, and finally limit, the possibility that frontier settlements could sustain both a communitarian ideal and a space of feminine empowerment. Anxious to put raw materials into the hands of capable men, the plots dismantle inherited estates to allow their heroes to search anew for undeveloped territory. More concerned with making the man than emancipating the woman, they ask women to translate nature's power while initiating masculine epiphanies. Grey's heroine in *Riders of the Purple Sage* exemplifies how his Westerns interpret nature and reallocate wealth along gendered lines to solve the problem of a postfrontier economy controlled by families with inherited land rather than by gold diggers. Jane Withersteen manages her property by supervising its productivity and employing at least a hundred people; her love for the beautified earth moderates her tough business sense. Jane's sentimental view extends from "the rich, green stretches of alfalfa, and the farms, and the grove, and the old stone house, and the beautiful, ever-faithful amber spring, and every one of a myriad of horses and colts and burros and fowls down to the smallest rabbit that nipped her vegetables" (137). In her eyes, nature is both cultivated and uncultivated land. When she walks through Cottonwoods one day, on the way to the Gentile end of town, she realizes that she owns nearly all of it, but professes that her real satisfaction lies in the love people there have for her, particularly in the love of the orphan girl, Fay. Jane's sentimentality moderates the impact of her wealth, but not enough for either the Mormon patriarchy or, I suspect, Grey's readers. At a time when Mormons struggled to maintain their economic self-sufficiency in Utah by boycotting Gentile merchants and establishing cooperatives, a single Mormon woman's private accumulation of capital would have violated both Mormon law and the patriarchal structure of the community.

Even as Grey constructs his most popular heroine as a sincerely devout Mormon troubled by "the salvation of her soul" and loyal to her belief in the bishop's direct communication with God, he uses her to assert both the difficulty of sustaining economic cooperation in a period of capitalist expansion and the tendency of inherited property to corrupt. Tatum has read the novel's characterization of the "invisible hand" as Grey's gloss on Adam Smith, a "characterization of a soulless Mormon patriarchy working in the dark to fulfill a cold, inscrutable policy reducing individuals to atoms" (177).

In this reading, *Riders of the Purple Sage* continues the earlier novel's critique of the emerging corporate order. But we should not ignore the novel's gendered redistribution of wealth, either. Jane's suitor, appropriately, is the leather-clad outlaw Lassiter, "a man with a marvelous quickness and accuracy in the use of a Colt," a man "born without fear" (21). Lassiter will demand that she leave her hard-earned ranch behind, though his own motivations are hardly revolutionary: he seeks revenge against the man who took his sister, Milly Erne, away from her marriage to a handsome Southern gentleman. As Jane becomes the proper woman at Lassiter's side, she sacrifices profitable cultivated property for Surprise Valley's natural potential. For Western heroines, good sex requires unimpeachable virtue *and* economic dependence.

For Western heroes, meanwhile, sex comes first, but money is sure to follow. As *Riders of the Purple Sage* opens, the powerful Mormon elders of Cottonwoods prepare to beat the emasculated Bern Venters in order to drive him away from his adopted town and to sever his association with Jane, for whom he works as a ranch hand. With Lassiter's sudden arrival and intervention, Venters escapes the Mormon whipping that would make him a man. Instead of revenge, he expresses a quaint concern with respect, proof that he has a long way to go before he can be a proper hero. He worries that he has lost "everything": "good-will, good name—that which would have enabled me to stand up in this village without bitterness" (18). Thinking that he is rebelling against Mormon fanaticism and exclusivity, he flees to the desert to toughen mind, body, and reputation; crosses Deception Pass, where the rustler Oldring and his men are rumored to live; and shoots Oldring's mysterious "masked rider," who turns out to be a young woman named Bess. It is Bess who will awaken his natural masculine desires and sanction his claim to the valley's supply of gold. But first, Venters must yield to the fantastic landscape.

In search of a hiding place from both Mormons and rustlers, Venters carries the wounded Bess up steps carved by cliff dwellers and discovers an enormous rock resting on a pedestal; further exploration of the narrow gorge descending behind the rock reveals, beyond an arch of stone, a valley green with trees: aspens, oaks, cottonwoods, and willows. Venters's first act is to name the place Surprise Valley and the rock Balancing Rock; only when he returns carrying Bess does he find "a glade that surpassed, in beauty and adaptability for a wild home, any place he had ever seen" (93), and proclaim the valley's "singular beauty." Unlike the Painted Desert of *The Heritage of the Desert,* nature in Surprise Valley has been tamed; it is not wilderness but a contained and naturally cultivated space ready for habitation. Venters discovers plenty of game, but no predators; evidence of the cliff dwellers, but no human enemies; nuggets of gold, but no prospectors. Here natural abundance and the absence of competition render Mormon greed and the work ethic irrelevant. Instead, we have an environment that produces physical pleasure and true love, the ideological opposites of the Mormon economy. Needless to add, Surprise Valley is every westward–moving pioneer's expectation.

In the chapter "Solitude and Storm," Bess mediates the violence of a thunderstorm in Surprise Valley to evoke an "inward storm," or an awakening of sexuality, in Venters. "The dark spruces were tipped with glimmering lights; the aspens bent low in the winds, as waves in a tempest at sea; the forest of oaks tossed wildly and shone with gleams of fire." It is not long before the glimmers and gleams yield to fireworks, though they are set off beyond the reader's gaze. The dissonant chord of rain, wind, and thunder at first makes Venters feel "deadened and drowned in a world of sound." But Bess's touch abruptly shifts his awareness from the physical storm to his own tumultuous longing, "the tingling of new chords of thought, strange music of unheard, joyous bells, sad dreams dawning to wakeful delight, dissolving doubt, re-surging hope, force, fire, and freedom, unutterable sweetness of desire." Contact with Bess, in short, enables him to transform nature's raw power into "a storm in his breast," which he suddenly realizes must be "a storm of real love" (158).

We find a similar scene in *The Rainbow Trail,* when Shefford follows Fay Larkin to the high rim of interconnected desert clefts; looks ahead to the endless stretch of red, dark blue, and purple canyons and back toward Fay; and sees that her "eyes were large, dark grey, the color of sage. They were as clear as the air which made distant things close, and yet they seemed full of shadows, like a ruffled pool under midnight stars. They disturbed him" (121). Just as he is now lured by Fay's mysterious shadows, Shefford was previously enticed by Hidden Valley's imitation of Fay's body.

> The air was hot, still, and sweetly odorous of unfamiliar flowers. Piñon and cedar-trees surrounded the little log and stone houses, and along the walls of the cañon stood sharp-pointed, dark-green spruce-trees. They were not imposing in height, but they waved like the long, undulating swell of a sea. Every foot of surface was perfectly smooth, and the long

curved lines of darker tinge that streaked the red followed the rounded line of the slope at the top. Far above, yet overhanging, were great yellow crags and peaks, and between these, still higher, showed the pine-fringed slope of Navajo Mountain with snow in the sheltered places, and glistening streams, like silver threads, running down. (79)

With striated layers of green trees and glowing earth, the valley pulses with Fay's life; the "silver threads" of the streams dangle the promise of natural riches and female responsiveness. The meaning of this landscape seems to be as explicit as sexual experience under polygamy is private. Still, we should not rush our interpretation. As Tompkins argues about Surprise Valley, here "sexuality pervades the universe," blurring the distinction between human and nonhuman worlds; along with sexuality, the landscape registers a whole range of powerful emotions like "grief, rage, frustration, vengeance, longing, and other, unnameable feelings" which produce a dazzling "kaleidoscope of desire" (170). Though the awakening of desire is finally not disruptive but socially regulatory in each novel, women and the landscape provide access to feelings deeply buried in each man. Significantly, it is the women who allow the men to recognize such unfamiliar emotions in themselves, providing the objects to which such emotion can be attached and converted into a socially symbolic romance.

"Natural" women like Bess and Fay obviously counter the "New Woman" so threatening to men of Grey's class, and their presence in the formula Western confirms the genre's re-inscription of traditional gender roles. Within Grey's imagined world, this female type also performs the role of the regional insider, translating the "heritage of the desert" to the male outsider.[44] Once this duty has been fulfilled, however, the women's own histories must be erased, their innocence restored. Venters suspects Bess of being first Oldring's mistress and then his daughter, before Lassiter reveals her true heritage and proclaims her "the innocentest of the innocent" (265). In *The Rainbow Trail,* the evil attributed to Mormon polygamy serves to accentuate the women's virtues. Both a captive and a prospective Mormon wife, Fay "was utterly innocent of any wrong having been done her" (229). It is essential, too, that she be cleared of the murder of her intended Mormon husband; the Navajo Nas Ta Bega's confession removes the "shadow" of guilt from Fay, and her public innocence assures Shefford's economic and romantic success. Now he could claim, "He had found her. He had saved her. She was free. She was innocent" (330). The Mormon novels show that no matter how strong Grey's heroines appear at first, they can exercise their power only by relinquishing their property titles and proclaiming their innocence, and can rebel against the dominant order only with a strong man's support. Alternately strong and passive, these heroines restore the "original" masculine identities of their heroes and then retreat to subordinate status.

It might seem that polygamy, which makes multiple sexual partners available, would itself have been a situation for male fantasy, but fantasy in the Western tends to be diffused through natural rather than social spaces. Perhaps the initial experience of the Western landscape is too powerful, and cannot be duplicated. Perhaps Grey's virile Western heroes expect marriage to manage their "hunger," and seek to detach themselves from Mormon men who cannot seem to curb their appetites. They might find widely available sex too threatening, preferring instead to impose the "natural" limits of a single heterosexual partner. The discovery of a single woman focuses both the land and the chaotic masculine desire it awakens. Although these explanations are informed guesses, we can note the imaginative forms that masculine desires and anxieties consistently take in formula fiction. Most significant in Grey's writing, and critical to a genre defined by landscape, is the projection of male desire onto the landscape, the saturation of the environment with sexual and emotional meaning, and the subsequent redistribution of that desire to women and men in socially sanctioned quantities. One can see in Venters, Lassiter, and Shefford not a chivalrous outlaw like Owen Wister's Virginian, the genteel Western hero out of the South who possesses superior speed at riding horses and drawing a gun, but the anxious, modern bourgeois man. Do Grey's Western heroes really rebel out of a longing for a single transformational experience, followed by the assurance of respect within a small community, marriage, and property? To judge by their plots, yes. John Cawelti defines an "essential subject" of Grey's Westerns as "the domestication of the wild hero" (235), particularly in works of the 1910s and 1920s. But consider what these heroes have gained from their rebellion: not just the form of middle-class domesticity but, even more difficult, its spiritual content.

Fantasy or Utopia?

The Western provided geographical imaginaries at least as powerful as those promoted by the tourist industry. If we read a fantastic landscape like Surprise Valley as merely an expression of nostalgia for an undeveloped West, we miss the moments of ambivalence and uncertainty that prompt a deeper imagining of the landscape's historical and social meanings. When Venters notices an enormous cavern in one of the valley's cliffs and focuses on the "little black, staring windows" of abandoned cliff dwellings, he enters into such a state of ambivalence, releasing its imaginary potential.

> Like eyes they were, and seemed to watch him. The few cliff-dwellings he had seen—all ruins—had left him with haunting memory of age and solitude and of something past. He had come, in a way, to be a cliff-dweller himself, and those silent eyes would look down upon him, as if in surprise that after thousands of years a man had invaded the valley. Venters felt sure that he was the only white man who had ever walked under the shadow of the wonderful stone bridge, down into that wonderful valley with its circle of caves and its terraced rings of silver spruce and aspens. (97)

Venters's claim to be "the only white man" to see the valley and his assertions of its wonder translate the rhetoric of the Southwestern explorer into fictional form; his earlier impulse to name the place confirms his role as conqueror. But note, too, that he feels his "invasion" is being watched by the valley's previous inhabitants, his identity merged with theirs, and his own individuality overpowered by their history. Though unpopulated, the cliff dwellings take the form of a monstrous body, with the gaps in the rock as eyes, and the landscape a living memory. The landscape and the protagonist watch each other, with the reader as witness. Surprise Valley becomes at once a historic place *and* a social body, and Grey insists that any attempt to reinvent its modern meaning must incorporate the presence of its ancient inhabitants.

Venters's previous contact with cliff dwellings left him with neither a concrete image nor an experience of contact, but a feeling: the "haunting memory of age and solitude of something past." By constructing the relation of Venters to the cliff dwellers through partly articulate sensation, the scene evokes the social harmony of the valley's ancient inhabitants as an idea incapable of realization rather than a historical truth. The intangibility of this feeling makes the subsequent alignment of vision between the protagonist and the spirit of the past all the more surprising. Suddenly Venters shifts his perspective from distant observer to native: suddenly "[h]e had come . . . to be a cliff dweller himself." The profession of brotherhood is unexpected, and difficult to comprehend. Though outsider and vanished native now share an imagined time and space, and both might share the common fate of dying and vanishing in the valley with the ominous Hanging Rock still standing, the commonality is something that is felt, not rationalized. Further exploration produces material evidence of ancient culture (dwellings on the scale of a city, black fire stains, shards of pottery, and stone pestles), causing Venters to oscillate between spells of unreality and intense scrutiny of the canyon's material history. Jameson has observed that utopian writing is characterized by the "incompatibility between action or events" common to travel narratives and "that timeless maplike extension of the nonplace itself."[45] Here, the descriptive encounter with the ancient city suspends the progression of the plot and accomplishes such geographic expansion. The encounter, like the hero's initial apprehension of the Southwestern landscape, also provides the opportunity to explore an alternative temporality. The incomprehensible feeling of cross-cultural and historical identification is both recorded *and* removed from the necessary sequence of events.

The dramatic conclusion to *Riders of the Purple Sage* puts Jane, Lassiter, and Jane's adopted child, Fay, at the entrance to Surprise Valley, poised to dislodge Hanging Rock, with the Mormon elders in hot pursuit. For a long moment Lassiter's strength and resolve falter—until Jane screams a declaration of love. Only then, with their marriage effectively professed, can Lassiter summon the effort necessary to send the rock crashing through Deception Pass, sealing the only entrance to the valley and killing the Mormon elders in one fell swoop. Bess and Venters, meanwhile, also have escaped, and intend to return to Illinois with their gold in hand. The resolution thus offers two choices: return to the commodified and disillusioning space of the East, or enter a mythic landscape. At this moment, though, the novel activates both anxiety and hope, the ideology of home and the utopian possibility of a new West—the perfect combination for a serial enterprise. Jameson explains that "the works of mass culture, even if their function lies in the legitimation of the existing order—or some worse one—cannot do their job without deflecting in the latter's service the deepest and most fundamental hopes and fantasies of the collectivity, to which they can therefore, no matter in how distorted a fashion, be found to have given voice."[46] This prolonged moment of indecision at the end of *Riders of the Purple Sage* excavates these hopes and makes them visible, even if the spatial forms they take in the novel's sequel become distorted or degenerate.

With the creation of Surprise Valley in *Riders of the Purple Sage,* Grey maps a utopian space that articulates the possibility of inhabiting the West anew, beginning with a single family. With the re-creation of the valley in a sequel, *The Rainbow Trail,* he demonstrates how the memory of a place can outlast its physical existence and continue to work as an opposing social force. Shefford sets out for the West with a dual purpose: to rescue Fay (and, in the process, fulfill Venters's promise to return to Jane and Lassiter) and to recover his own lost identity. While the first purpose drives the narrative, the second offers readers the chance to share the hero's process of discovery. We, too, have heard the legend of Surprise Valley, and the creation of Shefford suggests that the legend may do more than just haunt us. It may spur us to action, urge us to challenge social conventions, and enable us to recover our lost spirituality. The novel tells us that religious study frustrated Shefford's desire to be an artist, but with his first venture into the desert, his "instinctive but deadened love of the beautiful in nature stirred into life, and the moment of its rebirth was a melancholy and sweet one. Too late for the artist's work, but not too late for his soul!" (23). Too late for art? Not if Shefford gives himself over to the influence of the desert as Grey manages it, and we to the novel. Once molded "in the stern and fiery crucible of the desert," he returns to "this wild upland of color and cañons and lofty crags and green valleys and silent places with a spirit gained from victory over himself in the harsher and sterner desert below" (152). Then the hidden artist emerges: "He found his old self, the dreamer, the artist, the lover of beauty, the searcher for he knew not what, come to meet him on the fragrant wind" (156). Instead of producing a new self, Grey unites Shefford with the old true self that modern life has obscured.

It is striking here in the sequel how completely the old romance has faded. Once a youthful vision of femininity all dressed in white, Jane is now "barbarously clad in garments made of skins and pieces of blanket," her hair gray. The virile outlaw dressed in black leather is now "a lean, stoop-shouldered man whose long hair was perfectly white," and whose wrinkled face framed "mild, surprised eyes" (287). Grey dares to destroy Shefford's—and our—fantasy of rebellious heroes caught in a utopian valley because they have exhausted their symbolic functions as figures of opposition, both within the novels and for the readers. In place of Surprise Valley the novel leads us to a new place of enchantment that will provide "a singular and revivifying freshness" (323): Nonnezoshe, the "Rainbow Bridge" sacred to the Navajo people. This "was the one great natural phenomenon, the one grand spectacle, which Shefford had ever seen that did not at first give vague disappointment, a confounding of reality, a disenchantment of contrast with what the mind had conceived" (322). Although Shefford does not say so, Surprise Valley did disappoint him, as will all Western landscapes once they have acquired history. Like the continuous destruction and expansion of capital, the process of deterritorializing and re-enchanting Western spaces that the formula repeats enmeshes the genre in the commodity culture its heroes keep struggling to escape.

Desert Gold: Where El Norte Meets the Southwest

To conclude my survey of spatial formations in the early Western, I want to focus on which elements repeat, and which change, when Grey represents the U.S.–Mexico border. By shifting the historical and geographic context of the novel from Utah in the 1870s to the Arizona-Sonora border thirty years later in *Desert Gold* (1913), Grey directly addresses the politics of transnational development as he heightens the fantasy of territorial conquest and strengthens the relations between Anglo and Native American men. The attraction between the Anglo heroes and a Yaqui survivor, like the repulsion between American and Mexican heroes in the novel, seems to require a degree of incommunicability that allows differences to remain untranslated. Though the plot may contain surplus desire through imposing familial relations and stereotypical cultural differences, the moments when the plot pauses to contemplate the relations among the male characters delay this familiar conclusion. In the end, male desire usurps the heterosexual romance plot while it reinforces political tensions in *Desert Gold*'s revolutionary borderland.

Following Oscar Martínez, we can distinguish between a frontier and a border as follows: while a frontier is "an area that is physically distant from the core of the nation" and a zone of transition, a border is "a line that separates one nation from another or . . . one province or locality from another" with the aim to "keep people in their own space and to prevent, control, or regulate interactions among them."[47] Borderlands, then, are special cases of frontiers that involve transnational interaction, international conflict, and mutual accommodation; in this geopolitical space, cultural and national differences are continuously interrogated and re-inscribed. Historians of the U.S.–Mexico border emphasize the arbitrary nature of the national boundary drawn as part of the Treaty of Guadalupe Hidalgo and revised with the Gadsden Purchase of 1853 to include rich northern copper deposits. The border halved the Mexican nation, severing the northern territories from the old Mexican empire and drawing an artificial line across ranches, farms, and the territories of native peoples.

Lawrence Herzog lists the ecological, cultural, and historical levels on which the border made no sense. For example, the border follows a physiographic feature, the Rio Grande, for only half its length; at El Paso, the border becomes a geometric marking.[48] Whereas both sides of the Rio Grande began to be settled in the eighteenth century, Sonora had few permanent settlements along the newly drawn border even in the late nineteenth century. In William Robbins's account, "[T]he boundary itself was a chimera, a fiction in the sense that it had little relevance to the persistent transborder movement of both capital and people" (24). In fact, the four border states of the greater Southwest—New Mexico, Arizona, Chihuahua, and Sonora—continued to strengthen economic ties and were "integrated into the industrial infrastructure of world capitalism at approximately the same time" (38). A political and cultural construction rather than an ecological or economic reality, the U.S.–Mexico border has become a figure for cultural hybridity and uneven transnational relations.

After 1876, Mexican president Porfirio Díaz encouraged foreign investment and fueled an economic boom in the states of northern Mexico. Díaz systematically encouraged the flow of capital across the border through his modernization policies, granting land to corporations like the Sonoran and Central Mexican railroads; inviting foreign investment in the silver, copper, tin, oil, lead, rubber and coffee industries; and stimulating trade by extending a free trade zone, or *zona libre,* to all border cities. The same venture capitalists invested in the American Southwest and the northern states of Mexico. According to Martínez, by 1910 the northern border states had received nearly a quarter of all the American capital invested in Mexico. In Sonora, Americans invested most heavily in mining, spending nearly $28 million on the industry by 1902.[49]

An especially important area of agricultural development in the state was the area Mexicans called the Yaqui Valley. The territory of the Yaquis in southern Sonora, extending from the Sierra de Bacatete to the Gulf of California, had long been the inaccessible "arid kingdom" or the "faraway desert" to colonial Spaniards.[50] It is also the site of the longest river and largest watershed in northwest Mexico, a land made highly productive through irrigation, and the beneficiary of a predictable climate with two regular rainy seasons. Over hundreds of years, the Yaquis practiced subsistence farming in the valley, taking advantage of the river's regular overflows to grow tobacco, squash, corn, and legumes. By strategically aligning themselves with the Jesuits, the Yaquis long resisted European assimilation. However, with the construction of the Southern Pacific Railroad, the cultivated land of the Yaquis became attractive to investors, and in the 1870s and 1880s Díaz granted large land parcels there to loyal supporters for cash crops. Many of these Mexican landowners in turn sold their land to American business interests. The water from the Yaqui River was necessary to sustain such development; by damming the river and building a system of canals, the government redistributed the water managed by the Yaquis for centuries to corporations and to Mexicans and Americans who settled in the southern plains.[51] The Richardson Construction Company, which founded the Yaqui Land and Water Company in 1905, then aggressively recruited North American colonists and investors to the valley.[52]

Meanwhile, tourists came to Mexico in the late nineteenth century for the same reasons they came to the American Southwest: the exoticism of Spanish heritage, natural scenery, and local color. Major pre-Columbian ruins had not yet been excavated, and other ruins attracted only archaeologists. According to James Oles, travel literature was often sponsored by railroad interests, and accordingly "depicted Mexico as a land of traditionally dressed peasants, of volcanoes and exotic cacti, of ancient pyramids and elegant colonial palaces."[53] Alluring accounts of Mexican travel circulated in American magazines: Mary Hallock Foote published a three-part article in *Century* between November 1881 and 1882; Helen Hunt Jackson published "El Paso del Norte" in 1882 in *Atlantic Monthly;* Fredrick Remington and Charles Dudley Warner wrote for *Harper's* (1893–94 and 1887–88, respectively); Stephen Crane published sketches titled "The West and Mexico" (1894–1900). In the years Grey conceived his fiction, the major literary accounts of Mexico were Charles Flandrau's *Viva Mexico!* (1908), a travel book based on visits to his brother's coffee plantation in Veracruz, and John Kenneth Turner's *Barbarous Mexico* (1910), an exposé of Yaqui slave labor in the Yucatán.

Herzog points out the discrepancy between Mexican development and American representations of the border in this period: "[t]he dramatic economic transformation of this zone in the early twentieth century contrasts rather starkly" with Lummis's 1925 characterization of the border zone as a " 'land of sunshine, adobe, and silence' " (38). Whether or not we consider Lummis a "historian" of the border zone, it is clear that popular American impressions of the border articulated opportunities for development and expressed the desire to consume premodern Mexican culture. On the border, the uneven nature of transnational development took spatial and politically charged forms.

Evidence that Grey had read *Barbarous Mexico* can be found in the solitary history of the Yaqui character who represents Sonora's vanishing Indians. Through the character of Tom Belding in *Desert Gold*, Grey summarizes Turner's muckraking work, reminding his readers of this continuing conflict and strengthening the novel's stance against both the Porfiriato and the revolutionaries:

> The Mexican government is trying to root out the Yaquis. A year ago his tribe was taken in chains to a Mexican port on the Gulf. The fathers, mothers, children, were separated and put in ships bound for Yucatan. There they were made slaves on the great henequen plantations. They were driven, beaten, starved. Each slave had for a day's rations a hunk of sour dough, no more. Yucatan is low, marshy, damp, hot. The Yaquis were bred on the high, dry Sonoran plateau, where the air is like a knife. They dropped dead in the henequen fields, and their places were taken by more. You see, the Mexicans won't kill outright in their war of extermination of the Yaquis. They get use out of them. It's a horrible thing. (115)

By 1913, the year of the novel's publication, the Yaquis had already faced decades of persecution under Díaz, who saw them as an impediment to liberal ideals of progress and, specifically, to American investment in and development of Sonora. Following a period of strong Yaqui resistance to the Mexican government led by Cajeme (1875–85) and the resurgence of guerrilla fighting in the surrounding mountains, the Sierra de Bacatete, Díaz ordered increased military expeditions and deportation of resistant Yaquis to the henequen plantations in the Yucatán. Between 1905 and 1907, the rate of deportation increased, peaking in 1908; by 1910, most Yaquis either had been deported or had chosen "to leave their pueblos rather than cooperate with the colonization and development of the Yaqui River."[54] With his sketch of this barbarous history, Grey situates *Desert Gold* within popular anti-Porfirian discourse and locates an alternative to commercial agricultural development in the Sonoran desert.

The novel's towns of Casita and Forlorn River are newly settled border communities whose social and cultural stability is threatened by revolutionary activity, but whose future development simply awaits realization. Casita straddles the border and feels like a "foreign country" to the Midwesterner Dick Gale, who has been "idling here and dreaming there" and has come to the border to see some "stirring life" (23). One half of Casita's main street lies in Arizona, the other half in Sonora, but most of its inhabitants live on the southern side. The saloon in Gale's boardinghouse accommodates "bare-legged, sandal-footed Mexicans in white," "Mexicans mantled in black and red," "rurales, or native policemen" in blue uniforms, American cavalrymen, and cowboys alike. Grey's young Americans, Gale and his friend George Thorne, are mesmerized by Rojas, the Mexican bandit who "proclaimed himself a leader" at the revolution's outbreak and "devastated whole counties" with his rebel followers. A hero of working-class Mexicans who pursues only aristocratic women, Rojas poses multiple threats to these American men: revolutionary violence, class consciousness, and flamboyant masculinity. Wearing a lace scarf adorned with jewels, "gold rings in his ears and diamonds on his fingers," and "a tight, bright-buttoned jacket" (39), Rojas plays a dandy rebel to the American conformists. He is also a rival in love, having abducted the aristocratic beauty Mercedes Castañeda, whom Thorne now loves and aims to rescue. When Gale stages a commotion in the saloon in preparation for his fight with Rojas and then defeats his friend's rival with a few football moves, he forces the superiority of American play and muscular manhood against their Mexican counterparts, bullfighting and displays of pearl-handled guns.

Gale is the innocent American ready to conquer the decadence of Mexican culture, subdue the rebellion of its masses, and protect the border by working as a ranger for Belding. The novel pursues his physical, spiritual, and moral progress, clearly aligning us with his perspective and endorsing the guidance of the Belding family. The newcomers Ben Chase and his son, on the other hand, arrive in town as prototypical American capitalists, like the Richardson brothers in the Yaqui Valley: with ownership in a gold mine in Sonora, interests in the Southern Pacific Railroad and its local branch lines, political influence in Tucson, and legal land claims in the border town of Forlorn River, the Chases represent "those grasping and conscienceless agents of a new force in the development of the West" (282). The "hamlet" of Forlorn River, where Belding built his ranch, is an oasis previously inhabited and inexplicably abandoned by Papago (Tohono O'odham) people. Forlorn River needs only a steady water supply, an irrigation system, and a branch rail line to secure its growth. Such development was Belding's distant dream, but the Chases beat him to it. With their arrival, the town grows almost over-night: tents suddenly appear, along with a makeshift mescal house dispensing escape for Mexican laborers. As elsewhere along the border, Americans and the Mexican elite claimed the land and its resources while depending on Mexican and Indian laborers to work the ranches and the mines.

Grey's novel argues that the accelerated development of the border threatens the unwritten code of the West. "Conceited" and selfish men like Ben Chase who invoke North American law rather than the Southwestern belief in "a man's word and a gun" are not properly "Western." Belding calls Chase "a timber shark," "one of the land and water hogs that has come to root in the West" (231). Whereas Belding witnessed the passing of the Old West, of "border life in Texas in the early days" when "the law in the West depended on a quickness of wrist," the Chases are set to ruin the old ways. We have seen that the Western operates both by its code of honor and by its seeming indifference to productivity and inherited wealth, an antimaterial-ism which is "rewarded" by the discovery of natural treasure (a fertile valley, gold, smugglers' spoils). Belding insists that "[m]oney's the last thing we think of out here" (81). He raises fine horses and uses his precious spring to grow pale ajo lilies and graceful willow trees. Furthermore, Grey dissociates his unhappiness toward the end of the novel from his financial status: "He had been rich and was now poor, but change of fortune such as that could not have made him unhappy" (283).

The Western hero typically claims an ecological relation with the desert landscape, and in this novel Chase's most egregious offense to the unwritten code of the West is his destruction of Belding's water source: "No Westerner, no Indian or Mexican, no desert man could have been guilty of such a crime" (287). As we have come to expect, the beliefs of the "true" West-erners finally pay out: Gale and Belding make off with the gold strike, with water rights (the desert's most precious commodity), and with the innocence of their women. Grey's plot introduces local variations on a familiar formula, but after the first few chapters it refracts little of the geopolitical context of the border. If Grey re-imagined the Southwest's northern frontier with an acute awareness of its official close, he approached the U.S.–Mexico border without a clear sense of its future.

What remains new, and unincorporated into the plot, is the relation between men. Significantly, the novel begins with a male friendship forged in the desert. Cameron, whose quest for his lover's memory constitutes the novel's prologue and legitimizes its resolution, "was a prospector for gold, a hunter of solitude, a lover of the drear, rock-ribbed infinite" (1). He hunts for gold "in a desultory way, without eagerness" because the opportunities to reflect, "to look, to listen, to feel" (3), are more valuable to him than the price of the metal. Only when he encounters a stranger in the desert does he become aware of his solitude and begin to sense "a subtle affinity, vague and undefined, perhaps born of the divination that here was a desert wanderer like himself, perhaps born of a deeper, an unintelligible relation having roots back in the past" (3). The feeling of common purpose, and perhaps a common past, draws him closer to the strange man and prompts him to say, "I reckon we're two of a kind." There ensue mutual confessions about the women who drove them to the desert: Warren's daughter, who had fallen in love with a "wild fellow" and fled west to have her baby alone, and Cameron's lover, whose letter announcing her pregnancy arrived too late for him to "save" the child properly through marriage. When Cameron realizes that the man's daughter is his Nell, and admits as much, Warren starts to strangle him—desisting only when the younger man repeats that he *did* find Nell and marry her, though she refused to stay with him. Reaching the end of a cycle of attraction, confession, and violence calms each man, and makes sensible the "haunting presence of invisible things" in the desert. With their relation redefined as father-in-law and son-in-law, Warren and Cameron strike gold, but it will be their last act and the containment of their homosocial relation: both die after marking their claim.

The second, and most significant, friendship forged along the border is the relation between Gale and an unnamed Yaqui Indian. Seemingly conjured from the desert to fulfill—and perhaps surpass—Gale's desire for Nell, the Yaqui appears with a Papago companion at a camp of "mescal-drinking raiders" (107). Knowing "a Mexican's hate for a Yaqui," which "recalled the barbarism of these savage peons," Gale springs to the Yaqui's defense, saves his life, and transports him back to Belding's ranch. To Gale, the Yaqui stands primarily for the "tragic desolation" (112) and "all the darkness, the cruelty, the white, sun-heated blood, the ferocity, the tragedy of the desert" (182). He becomes not only Gale's teacher in the ways of the desert but also a brother and "a colossal figure of strange honor, loyalty, love" (278). With the Yaqui's guidance, Gale finally discovers the critical source of water for Forlorn River, the abandoned cache of gold, and proof of his lover's legitimate birth. "*Lluvia d'oro*"—or shower of gold—is the reason the Yaqui gives for leading him up the mountain. The phrase puzzles Dick at first. It was the

Yaqui's name for Nell, but Dick quickly learns that it also refers to the double treasure of water and gold. As the Yaqui shows him the source of Forlorn River and relinquishes any claim to ownership, Dick's imagination takes a more mercenary turn: in "flashing thoughts" he resolves to "stake out a claim here and never be cheated out of it" (318). In this final twist, the vision of the artist cannot be separated from that of the capitalist, nor from that of the family man; both types are lured—but not limited—by the border.

The relation between the Yaqui and Belding, meanwhile, works on a different level: it aligns the disempowered Anglo man with the dispossessed Native American. Belding suspects the Yaqui is "dying of a broken heart" (116) for his own mountains, and through a combination of sympathy and partial knowledge of the Yaqui language he "translate[s]" the Indian's advice regarding the route of the raiders who took Belding's prized horses "as best he could" (131). His translation is crude, as if imitating what he imagines the Yaqui's English speech would sound like: "The raiders were heading south-east toward the railroad that ran from Nogales down into Sonora. It was four days' travel, bad trail, good sure waterhole one day out; then water not sure for two days. Raiders traveling slow; bothered by too many horses, not look-ing for pursuit; were never pursued, could be headed and ambushed that night at the first waterhole, a natural trap in a valley" (131). By speaking for the Yaqui, Belding asserts their common predicament and strengthens a tie that "was no less brotherly because it could not be comprehended." Although Grey knows that this irrational tie is fantasy, he nonetheless asserts a positive fiction of brotherhood. The incomprehensible brotherhood between Beld-ing and the Yaqui remains a feeling, like Venters's imagined identification with the cliff dwellers. It exists, somehow, beyond individual and communal understanding. Because it has no material equivalent, it can be represented only through the greatest natural riches its author can imagine.

To the end, the Yaqui continues to inspire the love of both of his Anglo friends but remains "emotionless," "inscrutable," and finally incomprehensi-ble. In a reprise of Leatherstocking at the end of James Fenimore Cooper's *The Pioneers*, Grey concentrates their relation in an aesthetic moment: "The last the watchers saw of Yaqui was when he rode across a ridge and stood silhouetted against the gold of desert sky—a wild, lonely, beautiful picture" (325). Then the Yaqui vanishes, and with him any emotional obstacle to concluding the conventional romance. With the Yaqui, Grey begins to use relationships between Anglo and non-Anglo men to represent surplus desires that not only Anglo society, but even his own romance plots, cannot contain.

Readers familiar with subsequent reworkings of the Western, whether in fiction or in film, will undoubtedly recognize other ways that the genre takes up Grey's model of the West as a set of spaces containing the contradictory forces of belief, socialization, capitalist growth, and individual desire. We have seen that Grey's symbolic spaces acquire new meanings as they engage with religious challenges, social crises, economic conflicts, or sexual awakenings, even if these meanings are finally discarded or suppressed by the plot. I have argued that it is this mixture of "superfluous" meanings that accounts for both the genre's popularity and its ability to be reproduced. The features discarded by or unincorporated into the plot are precisely those which signify the desire for social transformation: the community that integrates work and spiritual belief; the woman empowered by property, economic responsibility, or practical skill; the mutual admiration and dependence between an Indian and an Anglo man. Nearly all Southwestern writers pursued one or more of these utopian ideas, often articulating them, as Grey did, through the landscape or appropriating them through native cultures.

In the chapters that follow, I turn from popular and noncanonical writers to the more familiar figures of high culture: Edward Curtis, Paul Strand, Ansel Adams, Mary Austin, Mabel Dodge Luhan, D. H. Lawrence, and Willa Cather. Though these are the names that most Anglos recognize as essential to the formation of a modernist Southwest, they comprise a small and self-selected group, one that has remained popular but has been marginalized in conventional literary histories. The high modernists have an important role to play as I begin to reconstruct this history, for their mediation between aesthetic theory and local culture transforms significant photographic and literary genres, and for the first time identifies the Southwest as a legitimate site of artistic production. But as we survey and analyze these developments, we should remember the critically unheralded accomplishments of the Anglo Southwest's first popular writers as well. By experimenting with new literary genres and articulating collective desires for reconfigured social spaces, writers like Lummis and Grey constructed the meaning of the Southwest through a combination of the imaginative and the real. Though numbers do not tell the whole story, they still talk: millions of readers have since decided that Grey's intimation of utopian longing, and his recognition that it cannot be comprehended fully, best expresses the symbolic meaning of the American West.

3

A Little History of Southwestern Photography

THE TITLE OF THIS chapter is stolen from Walter Benjamin's 1931 essay "Little History of Photography."[1] The theft is apt, for Benjamin ends the essay with a celebration of the photographer's role as voyeur of past crimes. "It is no accident that [French photographer Eugène] Atget's photographs have been likened to those of a crime scene," he observes. "But isn't every square inch of our cities a crime scene? Every passer-by a culprit? Isn't it the task of the photographer—descendant of the augurs and huruspices—to reveal guilt and to point out the guilty in his pictures?" (527). To Benjamin, the photographer records traces of the bourgeois world's empty structures and everyday acts of violence. More significant than the individual crime, then, is its exposure. Accordingly, my own short history opens the shutter on Southwestern iconography in search of fleeting images of guilt and innocence, crime and consecration, spontaneity and artifice, reflection and projection.

Let me explain my motives for this visual interlude in an otherwise textually oriented book. My photographic exhibit offers an alternate and perhaps more concise account of the transition from turn-of-the-century popular culture to the high culture of the 1920s—a transition that I document throughout the study. As exhibit, it also addresses the role of technological innovation in cultural change, an issue that literature raises only indirectly through patterns of distribution and consumption. Furthermore, photographs make visible the politics of regional representation in the kinds of "crime scenes" Benjamin imagines. By objectifying natural sites and native peoples, photography between 1870 and 1940 produced the Southwest as both a "qualitative space" for consumption and an abstract regional ideal.[2] The tensions between science and commerce, fantasy and nostalgia that structure story translations and Western romances also shaped the choices of photographic subjects, an analogy I display in the first two sections of this chapter when I juxtapose the elegant invitations to Western wilderness issued by Carleton Watkins and William Henry Jackson, the exploration of Indian identities by two members of the "Pasadena Eight," and the romance of the vanishing Indian in the work of Edward S. Curtis.

As Southwestern photography offered native places as "counter-spaces" or sites for leisured Anglo contemplation, it also introduced habits of looking at and consuming landscape. The history of this photography asks us to consider the relations among consumption, reproduction, and modern experience. It also asks us to think about how photographs have become the primary language of tourism, figures of art's mechanical reproduction, and the private as well as public means of mediating the difficulty of new places and cultures. I take up these implications of photography and regional romance in the second part of this chapter, when I shift our gaze to the canonical photographs of Ansel Adams and Paul Strand. Their images extended the male photographic tradition in the West to create the Southwest's Anglo sense of place in the twentieth century, and I argue that the modernist version of "aura," or aesthetic purity, infuses this sense of place.

Benjamin wrote his essay because photography had developed so rapidly in the preceding hundred years that "the historical or, if you like, philosophical questions suggested by the rise and fall of photography have gone unheeded" (507). He tells a "little history" of the medium's stages of development, contrasting the first "flowering" of the daguerreotype (when subjects were produced innocently and without inscription, innovation was greatest, and industrialization had yet to control photographic production) with the later emergence of a decadent pictorialism and a corrective surrealism. Against the self-indulgent aesthetics of pictorialist photography, which constructed a false "aura" around its subjects, Benjamin reads the protosurrealism of Atget as a photography that began "to disinfect the stifling atmosphere," to "suck the aura out of reality like water from a sinking ship," and to set "the scene for a salutary estrangement between man and his surroundings" (518–19).

Benjamin would return to the problem of aura in his 1936 essay "The Work of Art in the Age of Mechanical Reproduction," and to the theory of photography as a means of revising his conception of modern art; the later essay argues that repeated duplication can dispel "aura" altogether, and with it bourgeois ideology.[3] I am interested in the earlier critique because it posits an irrecoverable moment of innocence against a present that is at best disenchanting, and at worst deceptive. While his particular analysis of European photography may not hold in the Southwest, Benjamin's modernist narrative of disenchantment does. It seems to me that we still must work to expose the truth of how natural resources and native peoples have been exploited, that we unwittingly conceal that truth by limiting our view, and that we often fail to recognize the particular "aura" of modernism. Southwestern artists who were Benjamin's predecessors and contemporaries faced—and often finessed—that choice. They were, after all, modernists with very particular and time-bound regional needs.

Does Southwestern photography, too, begin with an innovative innocence, proceed through commercialized refinement leading to a false aestheticism, and then empty itself of this artiness, as in Benjamin's little history of European photography? Or, as landscape historian J. B. Jackson suggests, does the late nineteenth-century school of photography—" 'timeless' photography that flourished at a period when all of New Mexico was described by outsiders, even admiringly, in terms of a particular notion of time"—yield to a mid-twentieth-century photography of time passed, of local ruins?[4] Given the degree of repetition within the conventional categories of Southwestern images, can a place-centered photography produced for nonnative viewers work only through irony? As I display a highly selective sequence of Southwestern photographs, my history will play Benjamin's socially conscious but universalizing modernism against Jackson's more playful but regionally aware postmodernism. Rather than condemn all displays of "aura" in Southwestern images as tainted with Anglo fantasies, Jackson judges the region's modernist iconography, though constitutive of our current habits of seeing, to be guilty primarily through omission. I aim for a critical perspective on both theories, and a reconfiguration of scenes of Southwestern modernity.

Wilderness

Carleton Watkins's photographs of Yosemite, made independently in the 1860s from mammoth glass plates, and William Henry Jackson's photographs of Colorado and the Wyoming Territory, made as part of the Hayden Surveys in the 1870s, initiated the practice of contemplating Western landscapes from a comfortable and elevated distance.[5] According to John Szarkowski, images such as Watkins's "were intended for customers who believed that there was something close to religious meaning in wilderness—especially spectacularly beautiful wilderness—and spiritual value in its contemplation."[6]

These photographs were well received by Ralph Waldo Emerson; by Eastern audiences in New York, Washington, Boston, and New Haven; and by Western audiences in San Francisco, the site of Watkins's studio. By the middle of the 1870s, "viewing landscape photographs had become a national pastime."[7]

Whereas landscape paintings, like those of Albert Bierstadt and Thomas Moran, "represented the very essence of the West of the imagination—a West that embodied a sense of sublime scale, of naturalistic wonder, of geological drama, and nationalistic pride," landscape photographs seemed to present a West of magnificent wild fact.[8] Their claim to verisimilitude relied on a combination of iconic and indexical relations to reality; they both resembled and contained physical traces of the referent.[9] Watkins's images in particular embody what Joel Snyder calls "a distributed vision, one that transcends individual subjectivity and, accordingly, individual interest" (183). This vision—detached, scientific, cool in its appraisal of landscape—alternately asserted and diffused mastery over the territory, encouraged and resisted worship. In many cases, however, the power of Western landscape photographs lay in the canny combination of nature and artifice that photographers learned from painters—that is, in a selection that made the landscape intelligible.

Although any visitor to Watkins's chosen sites might confirm their spectacular effects, his technical expertise enabled him to heighten ordinary impressions of purity and spatial expanse. The 18 x 22-inch plates Watkins produced during his first visit to Yosemite in 1861 required a special, oversize cabinet; pack mules were required to carry all of his equipment, which also included a stereo camera. When Watkins worked for the California State Geological Survey in 1865–66, he aimed for a slightly different effect by working with a wide-angle lens capable of recording both broad scope and intense detail. Each project demanded that he reconsider his desired effects and re-evaluate his equipment, and he placed a steep price on the results of such efforts: thirty mammoth prints of Yosemite cost $150 in 1866.[10] This price necessarily limited his viewers to "entrepreneurs, scientists, and first-class coach passengers," an audience "disciplined in habits of seeing specific to nineteenth-century bourgeois experience."[11]

If Watkins's pioneering work in the 1860s set the standard for spectacular wilderness photography, in his subsequent work he faced a new challenge: that of returning to familiar and increasingly clichéd sites. Hambourg observes that his photographs of Yosemite from the 1870s are more "disengaged," either repetitive or excessively dramatic, as if he were aware that "a tourist park laced with easy roads and hotel accommodations" could not provide "a truly stimulating subject."[12] A number of pictures from this later period posed mountains to include their reflections in still water, implicitly testing the camera's capacity to mirror a scene against nature's. In "Mirror View of El Capitan," for instance, Watkins continues to organize space as in a landscape painting, with a fallen tree in the left foreground; a middle ground of shore, short grasses, and irregularly vertical trees; and a distant view of steep cliffs (fig. 3.1). The lake seems to question the materiality of the eminently solid mountain it reflects; not quite a negative space, it poses a challenge particular to the medium by demanding that the viewer compare the photograph and the water as natural reproductions. Watkins's artistry in arranging the scene is evident in his directional oppositions: he juxtaposes the horizontal stretch of the river and shore with the vertical reach of the trees and mountains, allowing the fallen trunk and shoreline to provide a diagonal path of access into the middle ground.

Now look more closely at the water. Though utterly still, it reflects the mountain imperfectly, blurring the sharp rock striations and creases that the camera captures so well, while diminishing the scale and shape of the distant ridge. The reflection conveys only an impression of the mountain, while the camera captures an exact copy. But with respect to the sky, we must reverse the comparison: the "actual" sky seems uniformly light and clear, though the water's reflection proves otherwise. The texture of the clouds varies, becoming more open as we look deeply into the reflection and begin to see the sky directly overhead. Even as the lake reverses the "real" orientation of the landscape, it also prevents us from looking at the photographed mountain and its watery reflection simultaneously. Watkins's camera creates the illusion of comparison while it performs and unites mechanical and natural reproduction. With this shift in focus from the pure mimesis of wilderness to its multiple reflections, Watkins marks a transition in the dominant mode of seeing the West from sublime contemplation to self-conscious reproduction.

Jackson, too, brought a new artistic quality to photographs of the Western wilderness, deliberately organizing his spaces to provide "a continuum wherein the unknown became known, the trackless waste was mapped, untamed nature was tamed and humanized."[13] According to Peter Hales, his photographs became "witnesses of men themselves witnessing," and this motif of doubled contemplation intensified as Jackson worked on U.S. Geological Surveys in the 1870s. For example, like Watkins's view of El

Figure 3.1. "Mirror View of El Capitan," by Carleton Watkins, ca. 1872. Whether as a recreational site or a photographic subject, the Western wilderness was becoming a counterspace of urban modernity. (Courtesy Cecil H. Green Library, Department of Special Collections, Stanford University Libraries)

Capitan, Jackson's "Wind River Peak [Wyoming Territory]" not only encourages us to follow the curves of nearby shores and the slopes of the middle distance toward the snow-covered peak; it also centers the mountain's reflection in the water, paradoxically creating a still image seemingly full of motion

Figure 3.2. In William Henry Jackson's "Wind River Peak [Wyoming Territory], 1878," the reflective pool, the human figure, and the implicit presence of the camera compete for the most authentic reproduction of the wilderness. (U.S. Geological Survey, 1251)

(fig. 3.2). At the same time, Jackson orients the single human figure off center and perpendicular to his view, thus introducing a second, though weaker, observational axis. As the contrast between embedded figure and implicit observer dramatizes the difference between firsthand and manufactured experience, it further suggests the potential for estrangement between viewers and their imagined Western surroundings—a condition that later photographers would both exploit and aestheticize, with not entirely "salutary" effects.

Indians

In the 1880s, Western photographers hired for commercial promotion turned their lenses on Indians, producing staged portraits and candid village scenes, documents of everyday work and monuments to the noble savage. Lee Mitchell describes the "three major elements" of this transitional time from the Civil War to the last decade of the century: "equipment was delicate yet bulky, easily broken yet hard to move; photographers were frequently on government payrolls, subject to the dictates of changing policy and bureaucratic inflexibility; and many Indian cultures were still relatively unaffected by Anglo-American society."[14] By the 1890s, dry plate technology had long dispensed with the need for a photographer's tent and George Eastman had introduced his flexible film, allowing for more candid and easily developed shots. Southwestern photography of the last two decades of the century relied on a mixture of old and new technologies, and accordingly reveals the mixture of style categories that Mitchell terms "exotica," "candid," and "Victorian" (xix).

Accessible primarily through documents of private life like postcards and albums, and through archival collections, professional and amateur Southwestern photographs in this period also reveal the politics of playing and displaying Indians. Anglo photographers like Jackson, Ben Wittick, Charles Lummis, and Adam Clark Vroman shared a broad curiosity about native places and cultures, and they met roughly similar degrees of acceptance and resistance from their subjects. More aggressive and tenacious photographers like Lummis and George Wharton James may have pushed their luck further and disregarded forceful native resistance to being photographed, while those with less at stake personally, like Vroman, may have tried harder to accommodate themselves.[15] But to describe only their dominant position in each encounter is to oversimplify the position and the cultural work of these transitional photographers. Unlike Watkins's images of wilderness, which were seen by a "first-class" audience, these portraits need to be read in the context of popular recreations, which included spectacles at expositions and fairs. The practices of juxtaposing ethnology and entertainment at the Philadelphia Exposition in 1876, the Chicago Columbian Exposition in 1893, and fairs at Atlanta in 1895, at Omaha in 1898, at Buffalo in 1901, and at St. Louis in 1904 have been well documented.[16] My two short case studies of Wittick and Vroman complement such analyses of Indian play and consumption in the late nineteenth century, while a glimpse at Edward Curtis's corporate connections will suggest an emerging alliance between high finance, high culture, and ethnographic romance.

Benjamin idealized early portrait photography for both its absence of inscription and its obstacles to dissembling. "The procedure itself caused the subject to focus his life in the moment rather than hurrying on past it," he imagined; "during the considerable period of the exposure, the subject (as it were) grew into the picture in the sharpest contrast with appearances in a snapshot" (514). This period also, in Benjamin's view, brought "incomparable groups" of people together. Though a strict photographic chronology would place this moment of unexpected contact at the time of the daguerreotype, the uneven development of photography and the asymmetrical relations between photographers and subjects in the Southwest prolonged this social function of portrait photography. And though Indian subjects surely did not "enter[] the visual space of photography with their innocence intact" (512), as Benjamin imagined the first photographic subjects to do, they did share a social space with the photographer and, increasingly, with viewers.

A prominent professional photographer in the period was Ben Wittick, a member of the "Pasadena Eight."[17] Wittick left Moline, Illinois, in 1861 to fight in the Union Army, enlisted in the Indian Service Division of the Second Minnesota Mounted Rangers, and apprenticed to a daguerreotypist in Minneapolis after the war. Though Wittick soon opened a successful studio of his own, he heeded the lure of the West in 1878 and set off with two of his sons for a job with the Atlantic and Pacific Railroad, leaving behind his wife and four other children. In return for rail fare and board, Wittick followed the track construction from New Mexico to California, taking pictures of the towns, land, and people he met along the way. He established several studios in New Mexico, first in Santa Fe, then in Albuquerque, Gallup, and Fort Wingate, and enjoyed commercial success from the start, supporting himself by selling portraits of local residents, landscape photographs, and scenes of Indian life. Finding his Indian subjects through fieldwork, Wittick shot them on studio stages set up either in one of his established galleries or in a traveling tent, and produced the portraits as mounted cabinet-sized photographs (5 1/2 x 4 inches) and stereographs.

Wittick's success between 1880 and 1900 proves how useful the combination of respect, curiosity, and timing could be. Like Lummis's photographs, his images range from documentary accounts of everyday life to staged portraits of Pueblo families, Apache scouts and chiefs, Indian schoolchildren, and traditional craftsmen. Lummis called Wittick "one of the best photographers ever in the Southwest"; had he not died of a snakebite in 1903, Wittick's intended book of travel anecdotes, sketches of sacred Indian artifacts, descriptions of ceremonials, and photographs surely would have rivaled Lummis's guides. In the early twentieth century, corporate mythmakers like the Fred Harvey Company would make Pueblo peoples into the "typical" Southwestern Indian, ignoring other groups who resisted the Anglo invasion more violently.[18] Wittick's photographs helped to create the prototype for this commercial iconography. They also began to blur the line between ethnographic document and commercial image. By securing the friendship of Hopi elders and a Snake Priest, Wittick was granted access to sacred rites and was one of the first to document the Snake Dance in 1880.[19] He photographed the ceremonial for years before tourists flocked to the annual event—and before the Hopi first imposed restrictions on camera location and finally banned photography altogether.[20] Along with the photographs of Vroman and James, Wittick's images later illustrated tourist guides issued by the Santa Fe Railway.

One of Wittick's frequently reproduced photographs shows a group assembled at Walpi, on First Mesa in northern Arizona (fig. 3.3). In the lower left corner we see a camera and the figure of a photographer (possibly Vroman or Frederick Monsen); the camera is aimed at the line of Antelope Dancers, ready to capture their performance and the arrival of the Snake Priests. More than a dramatic scene from the dance, the image shows the conditions of its performance. Composed of Anglo tourists, Hopis, and some Navajos, the mixed audience attests to the dance's growing significance outside of Hopi culture. Although the ceremonial had been performed for hundreds of years within Hopi communities, the presence of the tourists— and our indirect presence as viewers of the photograph—changes the situation. Witnesses who are outsiders to the culture make the dance a theatrical performance as well as a sacred rite to conjure the gods and produce rain; while affirming continuity with past traditions, this image also signals a break with the past, and the pressure Anglos exerted on traditional Hopi ways of life.

A series of studio portraits taken in 1885 also reveals the discontinuities and tensions between traditional Indian and middle-class Anglo cultures. The first is an informal shot of Pueblo Indians from Isleta (fig. 3.4). Hastily assembled outside of the tent that functioned as Wittick's studio, the members of the group wear everyday clothing and pose comfortably, if stiffly, for the camera. They may be a family or not; they appear as a typical subject Wittick might come across in his work and persuade to assume a conventional stance. The next set of portraits, by contrast, shows very deliberate arrangements of subject, costume, and background, and falls into what Mitchell calls the "Victorian" category. "Tzashima and Her Husband, Governor of Laguna, Laguna Pueblo" (fig. 3.5) could not be situated further from their native environment. The architecture and painted backdrop suggest a Victorian mansion complete with turrets, stone walls, and landscaped grounds; the tall, impressionistic trees evoke a humid climate that is the

Figure 3.3. "At the Snake Dance, Moqui Pueblo. The Beginning of the Dance, 1897," by Ben Wittick. As one of the first photographers to document the mixture of Anglo and native spectators at the Hopi Snake Dance, Ben Wittick had begun to transform the dance from a sacred rite to a theatrical performance by the end of the nineteenth century. (Courtesy Museum of New Mexico; neg. no. 44775)

opposite of the New Mexican desert. The props in the foreground and the figures appear as part of a world entirely different from the surrounding scene.

Benjamin recalls with shame and disdain the props that cluttered the bourgeois portraits of his childhood and found their way into albums "most at home in the chilliest spots, on occasional tables or little stands in the drawing room" (515). To him, the accessories, the pillars and curtains, "the pedestals and balustrades and little oval tables" were all left over from an era when subjects needed support to stay still through long exposure times. Stripped of function, such props now appeared as empty symbols of the sham of bourgeois life. But the incongruous settings that Wittick used over and over hardly bolster a "bourgeois" Indian life. They might indicate a deliberate effort to create an image of the peaceful, nearly assimilated Indian, but such an interpretation minimizes their strangeness. The juxtaposition of Pueblo Indians and Victorian architecture estranges both subject and setting, producing a

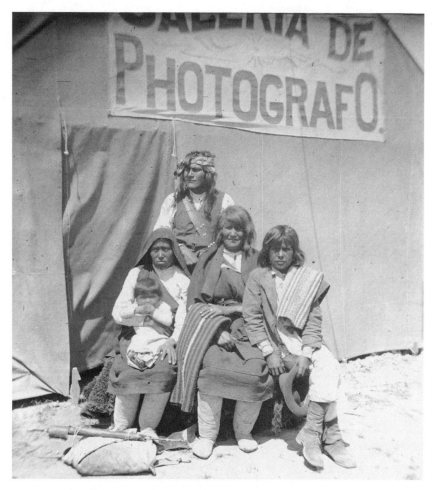

Figure 3.4. Ben Wittick's photograph of an unidentified group from Isleta Pueblo in front of the photographer's portable tent, ca. 1885. Under a father's watchful gaze and with a mother at its center, this group embodies Anglo ambitions for Pueblo domesticity. (Courtesy Museum of New Mexico; neg. no. 16157)

poetics of shock through cultural contradiction rather than surrealism. The political unconscious of these images is the failure of assimilation.

As we look at "Apache Bucks" and "Slim, Maker of Silver," however, we see portraits that costume Indian subjects as representatives of vanishing cultures. According to Patricia Broder, "Wittick's customers believed in the reality of the stereotype Indian" (23). Indeed, the "Apache Bucks" stand proud and well armed (fig. 3.6). The figure seated on the right has a blanket draped over his Western shirt, and the other two men wear fully fringed

Figure 3.5. "Tzashima and Her Husband, Governor of Laguna, Laguna Pueblo, ca. 1885," by Ben Wittick. The juxtaposition of Victorian backdrop and Indian subject estranges both setting and people, producing a poetics of cross-cultural shock. (Courtesy Museum of New Mexico; neg. no. 15984)

shirts; with grass and rocks scattered at their feet and scrubby trees rising directly behind each seated figure, the group appears to be calmly pausing from a day's work. Wittick had photographed the delegation of Mescalero Apaches to the Santa Fe Tertio-Millennial Celebration in 1883, and then proceeded to document the American campaign against the Chiricahua in 1885 and 1886, producing portraits of both scouts and chiefs. "Apache Bucks" dates from this period, when General George Crook's scouts sought to capture the last resistant Apaches; it displays forced complicity with this late episode of Anglo conquest in the Southwest.

By contrast, "Slim, Maker of Silver" provides a glimpse of the productive

Figure 3.6. "Apache Bucks, ca. 1885," by Ben Wittick. Posing as themselves, these young scouts project calm in the midst of their pursuit of resistant Apaches. (Courtesy Museum of New Mexico; neg. no. 16329)

Indian craftsman through a round aperture (fig. 3.7). Looking straight ahead and wearing silver earrings, two necklaces, and decorated leggings, the Navajo man extends a belt decorated with hammered silver disks for viewing. Beside him lie a layered tableau (a woven blanket, a leather pouch, and a careful arrangement of the tools of his trade) and a hanging display of his handiwork. This portrait, like Lummis's photograph of a silversmith named Juan Luhan (fig. 3.8) and Vroman's more candid portrait of a Navajo artisan (fig. 3.9), gives no indication that Indians had mastered silversmithing only in

Figure 3.7. "Peslakai Atsidi, or Slim, Maker of Silver, ca. 1885," by Ben Wittick. Especially in comparison with the slightly later, more candid shots of Lummis and Vroman, Wittick's photograph challenges the notion of an "innocent" period of Southwestern portrait photography. His subjects all participate, willingly or not, in the projection of traditional Indian identities. (Courtesy Museum of New Mexico; neg. no. 16333.)

the 1850s and 1860s, when the metal first became available. Silver has "no place and no ritual association" in the Navajo universe, though turquoise plays a significant cultural role for both Pueblos and Navajos, being one of four primary substances of the world for the Pueblos and one of four corners of the universe for the Navajo.[21] Photographs of Pueblo and Navajo Indians frequently show the subjects adorned with jewelry Anglo viewers only believed to be "traditional."

While Wittick took advantage of the railroad's need for publicity photo-

Figure 3.8. "The Silvermith, Pueblo of Acoma, N.M., Juan Luhan, 1891," by Charles Lummis. A typical image of an Indian craftsman in a moment of compulsory repose. (Courtesy Center for Southwest Research, General Library, University of New Mexico; neg. no. 990-009-0024)

graphs and the public appetite for Southwest exotica, other Southwestern photographers of the 1880s and 1890s, such as Lummis and Vroman, gained expertise and subsidized their work through alternate means. Leaving Illinois in search of a better climate for his tubercular wife, Vroman moved to Pasadena in 1893; after his wife's death the next year, he established a profitable bookstore there that supplied the libraries of wealthy Easterners newly arrived in southern California and sold photographic equipment as an Eastman Kodak dealer. Vroman often would buy sets of classics in New York, ship them to England to be bound, and sell the expensive-looking volumes at

Figure 3.9. "Turquoise Drilling, 1899," by Adam Clark Vroman. (Courtesy Seaver Center for Western History Research, Los Angeles County Museum of Natural History)

a good profit; he also collected books himself, specializing in anthropology and the Southwest, and joined many archaeological and anthropological expeditions to New Mexico and Arizona as the unofficial photographer.[22]

Especially fascinated, like Wittick, by the Hopi Snake Dance during his first visit in 1895, Vroman observed the ceremony eight times over ten years. His photographs have long been seen by historians as both continuing the field photography of Jackson, Timothy O'Sullivan, and John Hillers and looking ahead to a twentieth-century photography that accorded greater respect to native subjects.[23] Although Vroman sold prints to the Detroit Photographic Company (to be hand-colored and used for tourist brochures and postcards), lent his Indian images to a deck of playing cards (apparently hoping to "win sympathy for Indian rights among white socialites"),[24] and gave lantern slide lectures, he never achieved national recognition as a photographer. His glass negatives were dispersed at his death in 1916 and ignored long afterward.

Wittick, Lummis, and Vroman shared an unselective view of the Southwest; all three took as many photographs as they could, leaving the tasks of selection and promotion to others. Rather than consider their subjects as innocent, we might consider their entire body of work as documents of their own *relatively* innocent curiosity, and the few photographs that reached a wide audience as representative of an emerging Anglo taste for "authentic"—and objectified—Indians. The most comprehensive collection of unselected Southwestern prints remains the set of sixteen albums Vroman compiled himself, now at the Pasadena Public Library. Each album re-creates the experience of approaching, inhabiting, and leaving a specific place in the Southwest. The record of Zuni, for instance, first focuses on cloud formations, then reveals the architecture of the pueblo (including notes on Cushing's house), and only gradually claims a position inside the pueblo. Many people seem to be just pausing from their work, rather than forced into a fixed pose: a man inside the mission church is blurry with motion, possibly prayer; another drills turquoise beads for jewelry, leaving his tools scattered; women paint pottery, grind corn at the metate, weave, or carry jugs of water.

In his study of Zuni, Vroman identifies the mountain in the background, included at the end of the series, by its native name, Ta-a-yallona Mountain. The same album presents similar approaches to Laguna, while views of the Enchanted Mesa and Ácoma include photographs of the investigating party and its bulky equipment along with the scenery. Evidence that Vroman did not seek to produce falsely "authentic" Indians can also be found in images of Navajos on horseback with umbrellas, a Hopi woman in a store stocked with cans and fabric at Walpi, a Taos man wearing a ribbon proclaiming him "Grand Orator, Illinois," domestic interiors with tin-framed devotional pictures, and a boy standing near his tripod at Jemez. Because they were not selected by Detroit for promotional purposes, few people saw them; Vroman is known instead for pictures that seem highly conventional: straight portraits, images of ceremonial dances, and olla maidens.

Vanishing Indians

By the beginning of the twentieth century, the range of subjects of Southwestern photography became more limited as regional mythmaking came under the control of the railroad, the tourist industry, and the Anglo elite. The purpose of photography also began to change. While some documentary images became charged with moral intent, native peoples and architecture became sources for high art, first pictorialist and then modernist. Social reformers and aesthetic photographers still required financial backing, but they sought greater autonomy. Frederick Monsen, for example, originally worked on government surveys, then struck out on his own, and finally produced his only book, *With a Kodak in the Land of the Navajo* (1909), under the patronage of George Eastman. Working later than Wittick, Lummis, or Vroman, Monsen took full advantage of technological developments which he thought made the relationship between photographer and subject more intimate. The hand camera and cartridge film, he explained, enabled the photographer "to snapshot any number of *charming, unconscious* groups that show just what the Indian is like in daily life at home" (emphasis added).[25] Monsen came to define his mission as recording and defending Indian life; like Jacob Riis, who used photographs of New York City tenements to agitate bourgeois complacency, Monsen aimed to move a national audience—in this case, through illustrated lectures and a series of four articles published in Gustav Stickley's magazine *The Craftsman* in 1907.

Photographers with artistic ambitions also began to attract patrons and to publish large volumes privately. Edward Curtis sold subscriptions and solicited support from J. Pierpont Morgan and other businessmen to complete the twenty-volume *The North American Indian; Being a Series of Volumes Picturing and Describing the Indians of the United States, and Alaska* (1907–30), which eventually included over 2,000 photographs.[26] It is staggering to consider not only the scale of this project, but the fact that it constitutes only a fraction of the 40,000 photographs Curtis made of native peoples during his career. Scholarly criticism of exactly how Curtis stripped his images of modern details and posed his subjects to re-create a Native American past has been extensive.[27] But as Judith Fryer Davidov points out, his pictures "are not so different from the vast quantities of images made by missionaries, doctors, tourists, journalists, anthropologists, and geologists in the early twentieth century" (122). Curtis's subjects were popular, though his primary audience was elite.[28] He did allow some middle-class viewers possession of his romantic natives by printing individual platinum prints and "orotones" that "conveyed a moody iridescence" suitable for domestic display. Set in decorative frames, these "proved popular as upscale wedding presents."[29]

The Pueblo portraits shot in the early 1900s prove that Curtis sought stereotyped poses at a time when fast, portable cameras began to permit candid photographs; by returning to older technology, he imitated the innocence of an earlier age. These images suggest how Curtis produced a collection of everyday exotica in the Pueblos that, according to Lee Mitchell, marks "the consummation of the period's visual fascination with the Native American" (xxiii). He poses a Taos girl in a three-quarters profile, and arranges the light to rest on the girl's head shawl, sculpt her face, shine on her braids, and play with the sheen of the fabric and fur of her dress (fig. 3.10). She looks fixedly into the distance, careful not to disturb the pose. Other photographs of Pueblo women in their villages pay as much attention to the frame and pictorial accessories as posed studio shots. Many of Curtis's images heighten the visual and ideological contrasts between the graceful, neatly dressed female figures and rough Pueblo architecture, finely crafted artifacts and utilitarian tools. The few subjects in motion are moving out of their own native places, like the riders descending the trail at Ácoma and the famous vanishing Indians of "Cañon de Chelly—Navajo" (fig. 3.11). Curtis's project spread a pictorialist aura, or the mood of "timelessness" that J. B. Jackson observed in late nineteenth-century representations of the Upper Rio Grande Valley's Hispanic villages, to the entire Native American West. The result was a gap between aesthetic time and historical progression, and this gap has kept photographers, viewers, and tourists constantly in motion between accessible images and an inaccessible local knowledge.

A history of Southwestern portraiture at the turn of the twentieth century thus reveals not the production of a single type of image but an emerging pattern of iconographic consumption. Encouraged by commercial interests in the region and seduced by techniques of more experienced and deliberately artistic photographers, Anglo viewers began to develop a taste for certain kinds of Indians: craftsmen, decorative women, families. Because many Native Americans became wary of intruders who had betrayed their confidence, photographers like Monsen and Curtis often had to feign the feeling of intimacy that had existed at least to some extent between earlier photographers like Wittick, Vroman, anad Lummis and their subjects. And because all Native Americans were being forced to assimilate by curtailing their religious rituals, exercising ownership over small plots of land, and sending their children to government schools, portraits of ceremonial events and traditional domestic life would increasingly require costumes and props.

Curtis's work may represent the "consummation" of nineteenth-century Anglo practices of viewing Indians, but it also marks a shift both in the working conditions of Southwestern photographers and in the relation between regional subjects and Anglo viewers. If the first generation of photographers keenly understood the difference between portraits staged in the portrait studio and candid shots snapped in the field, their aesthetically

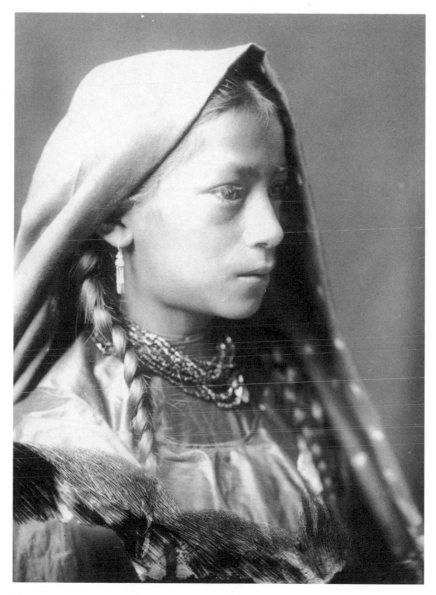

Figure 3.10. "A Taos Maid," by Edward S. Curtis. A fantasy of Indian femininity and innocence, this meticulously posed portrait might have been framed for a wedding present. (Courtesy Museum of New Mexico; neg. no. 144507)

minded successors approached the entire region as an open studio that might need rearrangement to create the proper authentic effect. Mitchell's categories of "exotic," "candid," and "Victorian" photographs became stylistic choices, each equally available. We will soon see, however, that modernist

Figure 3.11. "Cañon de Chelly—Navajo, 1904," by Edward S. Curtis. By the turn of the twentieth century, photographers and promoters began to limit images of the Southwest to a few sites that best conjured a regional aura. Canyon de Chelly was one of these sites, chosen here as a backdrop for a last glimpse of the vanishing Indian. (Courtesy Yale Collection of Western Americana, Beinecke Rare Book and Manuscript Library)

photographers who came to the Southwest rejected such artificial choices. Instead of authentic Indian subjects, they pursued the apparent purity of the natural landscape and its architectural forms.

Canyons and Sky

Ansel Adams opened his shutter on "White House Ruin," part of Canyon de Chelly, in the early 1940s (fig. 3.12). When he did so, he claimed he was not aware that he had positioned himself "in almost the same spot on the canyon floor, about the same month and day, and at nearly the same time of day that [Timothy] O'Sullivan must have made his exposure, almost exactly sixty-nine years earlier" (fig. 3.13)—even if a letter to Beaumont and Nancy Newhall suggests otherwise.[30] He was not thinking, he protested, of an album of O'Sullivan prints that he used to own, nor of Curtis's "Cañon de Chelly—Navaho, 1904." Even when he compared the prints, he continued to insist on his own originality of style: against the "luminosity" of O'Sullivan's print, a quality enhanced by the blue-sensitive emulsions of the time,

Figure 3.12. "White House Ruin, Canyon de Chelly National Monument, Arizona, 1942," by Ansel Adams. (Courtesy Ansel Adams Publishing Rights Trust; Collection, Center for Creative Photography, University of Arizona; Corbis ©)

Adams pronounced his own photograph to be "vigorous" and more authentic in its representation of "the brilliancy and clarity of the scene."[31] Why would he conceal the influence of O'Sullivan's mixture of geological precision and abstraction, and then recast his relation to his predecessor in terms of

Figure 3.13. "Ancient Ruins in the Cañon de Chelle, N.M., 1873," by Timothy O'Sullivan. (Courtesy Yale Collection of Western Americana, Beinecke Rare Book and Manuscript Library)

the photograph's mood? The answer, I suggest, combines two interwined modernist ideals: artistic autonomy and unmediated perception.

Ideally, in Benjamin's view, reproduction accomplishes "[t]he peeling away of the object's shell, the destruction of the aura which makes possible the perception of things as they are." Canyon de Chelly is just one example of a Southwestern site that has been photographically reproduced in two ways: by different (and mostly male) photographers, each seeking to express his own pure vision of remarkably few subjects, and through mass printing, whether on postcards, posters, or book pages. Whether such reproduction in fact destroyed the "aura" of the emptied landscape is another matter. Although the Western wilderness mesmerized developers and viewers in the 1860s and 1870s, rituals like the Hopi Snake Dance lured photographers and tourists through the turn of the century. The noble vanishing Indian attracted artists with pretensions to high culture in the early twentieth century, and artificially purified landscapes became increasingly powerful as sites for escape, pseudo-spiritual contemplation, and ritual return. Imbued with an aura of absolute clarity, photographs of the Southwest's characteristic features provided souvenirs of the kind of epiphany that artists had led tourists to expect in the region, or substitutes for firsthand experience. The reproduction of the landscape then brought the feeling of transformation to mass audiences, both demystifying this feeling and consecrating it anew. Benjamin's hope that mechanical reproduction might destroy the false sentiments of decorative or bourgeois art proved vain in the Anglo Southwest; it underestimated the desire of Anglo viewers to respond to a particular photographic style and to project themselves into an idealized landscape, regardless of the quality of the image.

In this part of my history, I want to consider what this pattern of production and consumption says about the desire "to possess the object in close-up in the form of a picture, or rather a copy" (Benjamin, 519) that modernity produces, and the value that modernists, including Benjamin, placed on an aesthetics of authenticity. Alfred Stieglitz, Strand, and Adams were artists in a way that their predecessors in the Southwest could not claim. They exhibited their work in art journals, galleries, and museums. As Davidov observes, the "*line* of male influence—from Stieglitz and Strand to Adams and Weston, and from Weston to his disciples" achieved and maintained its power largely through masculine claims to "quality" and "purity" (27–29). Both lines of influence, of people and of places, have much to tell us about the way scenes acquire aura through their style of representation and their reproduction.

Whether reproduction enhances or destroys a scene's "aura" is a question Benjamin leaves unanswered in "Little History of Photography." He uses nonurban spaces and leisured moments to explain how a certain kind of seeing produces "aura," or a false sense of distance from the scene at hand that creates an opportunity for projection. He begins with a definition of the term as "[a] strange weave of space and time: the unique appearance or semblance of distance, no matter how close it may be." But as he begins to elaborate on how "aura" works, he imagines "tracing a range of mountains on the horizon, or a branch that throws its shadow on the observer" at rest on a summer's noon. Such aimless looking at mountains or trees, "until the moment or the hour become[s] part of their appearance," defines "what it means to breathe the aura of those mountains, that branch" (518–19). Benjamin may conjure such a moment of indulgence for his readers so as to show how atmosphere can become distorted and infused with feeling regardless of the particularities of place. Like "the exotic, romantically sonorous names" of European cities, the mood produced through association depends more on the *idea* of mountains as a grand site than a range's specific contours or its cultural history.

Lummis's photograph of two women resting during their climb to Ácoma pueblo depicts just such conditions for creating the "aura" of the Southwestern landscape (fig. 3.14). Whereas Vroman emphasized the purposeful vigor of a central male figure when he recorded a similar pause in his party's ascent (fig. 3.15), Lummis organizes this image around leisured female figures. With their straw hats cast aside and bodies stretched against the sloping rock, the women are positioned for the viewer's contemplation as they idly contemplate the horizon. One dozes while the other gazes at the sky; both are oblivious to the Pueblo woman and man nearby, who look at the photographer rather than the landscape as they pause from their labor of transporting goods up the steep trail. Representing a triangulated relation among the photographer, Anglo visitors, and Pueblo natives, this image reveals how the experience of aura is created: through possessing sufficient leisure to lose track of time, desiring to see selectively, and thus allowing one's perspective to be manipulated. Other modernist descriptions of the Southwest's aura confirm this conjunction of conditions. When Georgia O'Keeffe taught school in Texas, she wrote often to Strand of the long sunset on the plains. One night in June she and her sister "lay down with our feet toward the north—watching the sunset for a little while the stars came out— big quiet starlight glow lasting a long time in the west."[32] Lummis's photograph and O'Keeffe's recollection suggest that the "aura" of the Southwest will be reproduced through the modernist period, extending the Anglo preference for the exotic and romanticized construction of native cultures

Figure 3.14. " 'The Morgue' Trail, Ácoma Pueblo," by Charles Lummis. Are these figures lost in a "strange weave of space and time," Benjamin's definition of the false experience of aura? (Courtesy Museum of New Mexico; neg. no. 1956)

Figure 3.15. One of many images of the Camino del Padre at Ácoma Pueblo produced by Anglo photographers, this version by Adam Clark Vroman isolates the contrast between natural rock and constructed path as it documents an organized Anglo ascent. (Courtesy Seaver Center for Western History Research, Los Angeles County Museum of Natural History)

and places that we saw in the commercially distributed Indian portraits of Wittick, Vroman, and Lummis and in the aestheticized style of Curtis's entire project.

In early twentieth-century New York, Stieglitz played the role of an American Atget and promoted the formation of a modernist community. He displayed avant-garde art at his "291" gallery and advocated "straight" photography's transformative potential in the pages of *Camera Work,* but the photographic practice and theory he promoted lacked the unflinching estrangement Benjamin applauded. Indeed, the dramatic and revolutionary claims Stieglitz's circle made for themselves would be difficult for any group of artists to realize fully. Strand explained "291" as "an experimental laboratory" in which the material under scrutiny was "the inner lives of human beings of all kinds and degrees."[33] He urged students at the Clarence White School of Photography to "look at the things around you, the immediate world around you. If you are alive, it will mean something to you, and if you care enough about photography, and if you know how to use it, you will want to photograph that meaningness." But, he warned, "[i]f you let other people's vision get between the world and your own, you will achieve that extremely common and worthless thing, a pictorial photography."[34]

Stieglitz strenuously opposed the decorative effects of pictorialism with his own intuitive visions. While he conceived all of his photographs as "equivalents of my basic philosophy of life," the photographic series of the sky titled *Equivalents* culminated his pursuit of a nonliteral visual language. His contemporary Herbert Seligman explained that Stieglitz's photography achieved a "translation of experience" that "should have ended for all time the silly and unthinking talk to the effect that the photographer was limited to a literal transcript of what was before him."[35] Meanwhile, the mixture of individual feeling and "scientific" principles took social form as an aesthetic ritual in the space of Stieglitz's gallery. "[S]uch was the purity of those little grey rooms that they finally came to be holy ground," Strand claimed.[36] Straight photography, in its "purity" of expression, inspired a new religion suited to the cultural economy of high modernism.

Strand began his career as Stieglitz's protégé, articulating the theory of "291" in such essays as "Photography" (1917), "Photography and the New God" (1922), and "The Art Motive in Photography" (1923). More important, he put the theory into practice in photographs that cultivate the abstract beauty of both urban scenes and machine-made objects. Early photographs such as "New York, 1910s" and "Telegraph Poles, Texas" (1915) illustrate the Stieglitz aesthetic well. In the first image, his view from the city street juxtaposes the array of geometric shapes that constitute building facades with delicate wisps of the sky, playing the looming shadows cast by the tallest buildings against sunlight spread from afar. By locating the bottom of the image above street level, Strand prevents the viewer from seeing the street, much less entering the scene; the windows are merely shapes that provide no access to the lives behind them. Despite its urban subject, there is a definite mood in this photograph: awe for the city's architectural grandeur.

As he traveled west, and as he distanced himself from Stieglitz's own efforts at natural photography, Strand began to notice how ordinary dwellings punctuated the plains.[37] In 1916 he wrote of Texas, "The country is perfectly flat and mostly used for cotton. But the way this monotonous plain is broken by shacks and little white houses is quite fascinating. Things become interesting as soon as the human element enters it."[38] The telephone poles in Strand's 1915 photograph likewise break up an ordinary curve in the road and a monotonous expanse of sky. Though they indicate the extension of modern convenience into rural territory, they lean precariously, seemingly no more secure than the farms they serve. Strand shows us the textures of open space: the long, variegated sky, the irregular surface of the poles, the wood grain of the barn. Whether depicting a still life of pears and bowls, the juxtaposition of a car's fender, headlight, and wheel spokes, or the gaping shadows that hover over pedestrians walking on Wall Street, Strand's early photographs emphasize the sensuous play of shades of shadow, of shape and texture, of man-made and organic objects as they alternately reveal and conceal their subjects' local histories. After seeing his work, O'Keeffe found herself "making Strand photography in my head"—that is, "looking at things and seeing them as though [he] might photograph them."[39] And when Adams saw Strand's negatives for the first time, he re-evaluated his own work. "I was turned from a quasi-pictorial approach to a far more precise and austere vision," he claimed.[40]

When he started to work in the Southwest in the mid-1920s, however, Strand wavered from his earlier austerity and moved toward the mysticism that the region seemed to encourage in Anglo and European modernists. It is true that the Indians, by now a clichéd romantic subject, did not interest him. He admitted in a letter to Stieglitz that "the Indians are not very much a part" of his experience of Taos; "I know I cant do anything for them, nor can I live with them and possibly in time get to know something about them—to penetrate the barrier that Lawrence so quickly sensed."[41] He also refused

John Collier's offer to assist in making movies on Indian reservations "to be used in a new type of Indian education."[42] While he claimed to "know the country" of the Southwest and to "have penetrated to some extent its spirit," he confessed that he knew the Indian only as an abstraction, "although I feel deeply his rituals and have good friends among them. But I have not had the opportunity to photograph him as I would want to do it."[43]

Still, like so many Anglo travelers, Strand responded to a pure and dreamlike quality in the landscape, and wondered that it had inspired so much "trashy, utterly commonplace picture-making."[44] Writing to Stieglitz from the Rocky Mountains, he described the mountains as "untouched— pure and wonderful—great," a relief after the "deadness, cheapness, standardized mediocrity, in towns and towns trying to be cities."[45] He perceived the high desert of northern New Mexico, too, as "a pure undefiled thing." Stieglitz must have grown weary of such rhapsodies about New Mexico, which he received from Adams as well as from O'Keeffe and Strand. "It is all very beautiful and magical here—a quality which cannot be described," Adams wrote from Ghost Ranch in Abiquiu in 1937. "You have to live it and breathe it, let the sun bake it into you. The skies and land are so enormous, and the detail so precise and exquisite that wherever you are, you are isolated in a glowing world between the macro and the micro, where everything is sidewise under you and over you, and the clocks stopped long ago."[46] The persistent storm clouds over Taos mesmerized Strand, creating a spell that for a time disrupted his work ethic: "The days slip by within this magical repetition of sun and storm and cold starlit nights—all too fast—So much so that if one had not made a few photographs—, paintings standing on the mantel— they might well be a kind of dreamlike mirage."[47]

Strand, Adams, and O'Keeffe would repeatedly conjure this ineffable atmosphere, a vast New Mexican sky stirred by clouds and barely anchored by the land. In pictures like Strand's "Near Abiquiu, New Mexico, 1930" (fig. 3.16) and Adams's "Thunderstorm, Ghost Ranch, Chama Valley, ca. 1937" (fig. 3.17), there is no foreground. One must jump right in or expect to be knocked sideways and engulfed by the life of the sky. The photographs are not filtered or retouched to produce a pictorialist impression of aura because both men were too committed to "straight" and "pure" photography to consider such manipulation. But the clarity of the images constitutes a new kind of aura; they create the impression of distance through a combination of transparency and human absence. As closely as we may try to approach these natural Southwestern scenes through reproduction, the air in

Figure 3.16. "Near Abiquiu, New Mexico, 1930," by Paul Strand. Pared down to its natural elements, high desert and sky, this landscape evokes a modernist aura through transparency and absence. (© 1981, Aperture Foundation Inc., Paul Strand Archive; Collection, Center for Creative Photography, University of Arizona)

them still seems to circulate and the horizon still remains a distant dream. "Modernism constitutes, above all, the feeling that the aesthetic can only be realized and embodied where it is something more than the merely aesthetic," Jameson argues. In these photographs, the landscape is more than the mere arrangement of elements; it contains a "pure undefiled" atmosphere, "a quality which cannot be described," a feeling of "magical repetition." It follows that even Benjamin, modernism's most eloquent and challenging philosopher, might be able to "describe everything about the work of art and its functions and effects," and still resist naming "what transcends all those things and constitutes the work as modernist in the first place."[48] As we historicize modernist aesthetics, however, we are left with the disenchanted possibility that photography has lost its power to produce salutary estrangement. The final images of this chapter pursue this consequence by reconsidering how Jackson's conception of a "sense of place" might still be mobilized to make visible the Southwest's vernacular landscapes.

Figure 3.17. "Thunderstorm, Chama Valley, New Mexico, ca. 1937," by Ansel Adams. (Courtesy Ansel Adams Publishing Rights Trust; Collection, Center for Creative Photography, University of Arizona)

Senses of Place: Local, Virtual, or Mobile?

"In my beginning is my end. In succession / Houses rise and fall, crumble, are extended, / Are removed, destroyed, restored, or in their place / Is an open field, or a factory, or a by-pass," T. S. Eliot wrote in his late meditation on literary modernism, *Four Quartets* (1943).[49] So could we end this part of our little history of photographic modernism with an imagined return to the beginning. Instead of the view of Canyon de Chelly, or the trail to Ácoma, we could look at the frequently reproduced Pueblo church at Ranchos de Taos and pay homage to its organic shapes. Does the church serve primarily as a place of worship? Is it a work of vernacular art re-created by each generation of local inhabitants? Or does it become high art as it is photographed and painted? Benjamin argues in a version of his essay that "[o]nce an object is looked at by us as a work of art, it absolutely ceases its objective function."[50] The buildings around the church may well have risen or crumbled, been destroyed or restored in the interval, but we have no way of knowing. Once liberated from its context, the church surely becomes an art object for Anglo spectators.

We could look at any number of Pueblo ceremonials, costumes included, to see other examples of how Anglo representations transform native practices into aesthetic and commercial objects. Or we could contemplate handmade Hispanic artifacts, like crosses, santos, and *bultos*. From Curtis's staged Navajo exit from Canyon de Chelly to Adams's return to the Canyon's pure form, the narrative of early twentieth-century Southwestern photography starts with vanishing natives and ends with vanished ones; in place of people we find abandoned buildings and artifacts. An image like Strand's "Ghost Town, Red River, New Mexico, 1930" (fig. 3.18) would reveal an artful geometry of ruins that in Jackson's terms is "less a reflection of reality than a way of expressing a nostalgic version of history: a desperate, last-minute recording of old and once cherished values, the New Mexico chapter in that once popular chronicling of 'vanishing America,' the old America of small farms and villages and small hillside fields" (23). With all the people gone, the emptiness of the modernist Southwest may have a corrective significance: it reveals social relations to exist only among Anglo photographers and viewers, and provides evidence of the familiar Western crime of a place sold as an idea. As Larry McMurtry puts it, "It's a sad, but, to my mind, inescapable fact that most of the traditions which we associate with the American West were invented by pulp writers, poster artists, impresarios, and advertising men; excepting, mainly, those that were imported from Mexico."[51] The still landscape, full of the aura of Western space, is yet another "invented" tradition.

Jackson suspects that the common understanding of what creates a sense of place derives from just such composed landscapes: from "our own response to features which are *already* there—either a beautiful natural setting or well-designed architecture." Now, at the beinning of the twenty-first century, Anglo habits of creating a sense of Southwestern places have become firmly established through repetitive viewing of scenes already known to be there. The dominant Anglo iconography of the Southwest will probably continue to resist any challenge to the familiar categories of desert wilderness, Indians, and vanishing Indians. Against this manufactured understanding of place, however, Jackson proposes his own theory "that a sense of place is something that we ourselves create in the course of time. It is the result of habit or custom" (*Sense of Place*, 151). He returns to the origins of the expression "sense of place," explaining it as "an awkward and ambiguous

Figure 3.18. "Ghost Town, Red River, New Mexico, 1930," by Paul Strand. (© 1971, Aperture Foundation Inc., Paul Strand Archive)

translation of the Latin term *genius loci,*" meaning in classical times "not so much the place itself as the guardian divinity of that place" (157). Though we have replaced the belief in divinity with "a certain indefinable sense of well-being," Jackson concludes that the phrase can still retain the "original notion of ritual, of repeated celebration or reverence" (158). Southwestern tourism, meanwhile, continues to enact a ritual of imagined spiritual return to territory Anglos would like to claim as their last, best place.

Does it follow that all Anglo images necessarily perpetuate a modernist aura of purity? Might the familiar categories of Southwestern photographs accomplish something other than the promotion of an outdated and commercially useful aura around the region? Perhaps the very repetition of familiar scenes could allow viewers to engage in repeated celebrations, and to create their own imagined senses of place. Admittedly, it would be a different sense of place than Jackson's, for his emerges through rituals of contact with the everyday, physical world. But are not images, too, "embedded in the everyday world around us and easily accessible" (158)? Arguing for the joint effects of media and migration on the imagination, Arjun Appadurai claims that they are.[52] Though he focuses on electronic media, the ubiquity of printed images prepared the way for his understanding of how we construct subjectivity through a composite of real and virtual experience. The problem with trying to produce an independent sense of place through reproduced images, however, is that exact repetition tends to reinforce existing relations rather than allow us to imagine new ones. For this reason, the challenge of resisting such dominant visions and reconfiguring regional iconography must be met by the viewer; neither the art world nor the highbrow tourist industry has an interest in rising to it.

Alex Harris's photographic work in northern New Mexico envisions one alternative to a mechanically produced sense of place that we might take as a model of how landscape, local tradition, and vernacular art interact in the Southwest. Between his collaboration with Robert Coles on *The Old Ones of New Mexico* (1973) and his own collection of photographs in *Red White Blue and God Bless You: A Portrait of Northern New Mexico* (1992), Harris spent nearly twenty years in the mountain villages of Taos County: Peñasco, Truchas, El Valle, Río Lucío, Vallecito, Córdova. His patience for learning about a new country was rewarded with a welcome that made him "feel so at ease in new rooms, so immersed in another life, that the adopted country beg[an] to look and feel like home, while the country of [his] birth seem[ed] foreign or strange."[53] Gradually, by photographing the people he came to know, the domestic spaces they created, and the cars they decorated, he came to understand his "sustained attraction to this small, uncommon island of Hispanic northern New Mexico" (30). Harris's more recent project takes its title from a rough inscription in Amadeo Sandoval's kitchen—"I Love My God. I love the Red White Blue and You. Red White Blue and God Bless You"—a declaration of Amadeo's respect for his house; the welcome he extends to family, friends, and strangers; and the mixture of religion and

Figure 3.19. "Sombrillo, New Mexico, Looking South from Ben Vigil's 1952 Chevrolet, August 1986," original color photograph by Alex Harris. Though the driver is absent, he lends the viewer his mode of expression and his habitual point of view. (Reprinted courtesy of Alex Harris)

everyday life in northern New Mexico. Amadeo has painted crosses on his cabinets and stars and stripes on his walls, unevenly but with evident joy; he has nailed printed devotional cards between blue stars and honored them with frames gilded with dabs of paint. We see a similar, if more restrained, aesthetic at work in Harris's images of bedrooms; there, religious pictures and family photographs decorate walls painted a single, exuberant color.

But it is the photographs Harris took from the back seats of cars that are the most spectacular, and the most revealing of the imagined relation between driver, decorated vehicle, and landscape. Harris positioned his cars carefully to "show what it was like for these men to be—and to see—in their cars" (42). Two of them will illustrate how still images can produce the effect of motion through natural and inhabited landscapes. "Ben Vigil's 1952 Chevrolet . . . " (fig. 3.19) gleams quietly everywhere, from its polished red dashboard to its chrome trim and gold plush seat. The car is parked for a view of high desert, sky, and mesa in Sombrillo, New Mexico, and its windshield acts like a wide screen for the drama of clouds outside. Though the driver is absent, he lends us his habitual vision. The photograph "Leví Lovato's 1972 Chevrolet Monte Carlo . . . " (fig. 3.20) also articulates a harmonious rela-

Figure 3.20. "Las Trampas, New Mexico, Looking East from Leví Lovato's 1972 Chevrolet Monte Carlo, July 1987," original color photograph by Alex Harris. Working against both the modernist poetics of estrangement and a commercially reproduced sense of place, this photograph constructs an inhabited locality for the viewer. (Reprinted courtesy of Alex Harris)

tion between owner, automobile, and desert. Through the windshield we see Las Trampas's adobe church and a few wooden houses. The perspective Harris has chosen emphasizes the continuity between rectangular shapes within the car (the horizontal stretch of the front seat, the black space in front of the seat, dashboard and glove compartment, windshield, rearview mirror, and slice of ceiling); the middle ground's stretch of dirt, grasses, fences, and walls; and the distant buildings. Though the materials of the car are synthetic and machine-stamped, while the materials of the town are primarily mud and wood, the design of the photograph argues for continuity between automotive design and built environment. The car takes on the role usually played by human figures in a landscape: it directs our perspective and articulates the relation between individuals and their surroundings.

Harris's friends in New Mexico recognized whom he resembled: a local photographer from the 1940s named Eugenio Sena, whose few surviving photographs in local houses display the ease and intimacy of a lifetime among friends and neighbors. Perhaps Harris was imitating the *idea* of Sena—Sena's local and rooted familiarity—even if he had not previously known the man. Harris's work produces an inhabited locality for the viewer, a space that is neither abstract nor mechanically reproduced, neither his or the viewer's own nor deliberately exotic. If "a landscape, like a language, is a field of perpetual conflict and compromise between what is established by authority and what the vernacular insists on preferring," as Jackson claims, Harris's artistry lies in his ability to make local preferences not only visible, but dominant.[54] Rather than deny the cumulative power of the natural landscape, Harris celebrates it by showing us how the high desert has shaped local lives and everyday art.

Benjamin's modernist belief in the shock of the real as the means to a truer social vision may not hold in our era, for single moments of recognition have a way of being assimilated into familiarity. The poetics of estrangement may also be an urban European ideal rather than a means of defamiliarizing American spaces; as any American will tell you, the surest means of seeing the strange mixture of emptiness and improvisation in middle-class life is to hit the road and pass along the "strip" between the highway and the town, cruise through neighborhoods where the cars in the yard outnumber the residents in a house, and survey the arrangements of mobile homes. In a drive through New Mexico, you are more likely to encounter any of these landscapes than an abandoned ghost town. Whether you will return to these unrecorded spaces and incorporate them into your sense of place depends on whether you share Jackson's enthusiasm for the automobile and his ability to sustain the contradictions of the modern Southwest; whether you can take the time to know the rhythms and preferences of a single community; and whether you can resist the artificial but familiar feeling of Southwestern emptiness. "Which do we value more, a sense of place or a sense of freedom?" Jackson asks.[55] If we move through its vernacular landscapes as well as return to its hallowed sites, and if we settle in for a while before we move on, the Southwest might still provide both.

4

Unconsummated Intimacies in
Mary Austin's Southwest

IN HIS BIOGRAPHY of Mary Austin, T. M. Pearce tells a story that passed among the Pueblo Indians of New Mexico:

> A fine Indian in one of the Rio Grande pueblos was being questioned by a tourist who had been reading several of the many books descriptive and interpretive of Southwest Indians. The visitor had found points of disagreement in them and kept asking the Indian to tell what was true and what false. The Indian made two or three answers on points to which he could contribute something, and chose to. Finally, annoyed by some question which was either beyond him or embarrassing to him as prying into tribal information, he said to the examiner, with brief irony, "Why don't you ask Mary Austin? She knows everything about Indians."[1]

This story, even as heard by a white man, reveals three things: the desire of Anglo-Americans to investigate Native American cultures in the 1920s, the resistance of native informants to Anglo translation, and the search for a clarifying regional authority. The availability of "descriptive" and "interpretive" books, the visitor's eagerness to conduct research prior to his or her visit, and the visitor's relentless questioning all indicate the popularity of Indians as a subject of study and as a means of entertainment. Native resistance confirms the continuing status of the Southwest in the modernist period as what Eric Cheyfitz calls a "frontier of translation," a place where the dominant culture rewrites racial and class conflicts into linguistic difference. Yet the difficulty of cultural translation and regional authenticity also emerges everywhere in this story, from the Anglo-American author's apparent need to vouch for his subject's character ("a fine Indian") and simultaneous wish to distinguish truth from falsehood through the subject's half-bewildered, half-knowing response to the visitor's questions. Did the Indian deflect the answer to the final question because of its inappropriate content, or mock the visitor's fantasy that a single white person could translate all Indian cultures? The fact that the story was so often repeated by Pueblo Indians suggests both bewilderment about and insight into Anglo preoccupations.

As we have seen, the popular Westerns of the 1910s and 1920s articulated social anxieties about Western development and established a narrative structure that could sustain the utopian potential of illusory spaces; modernist Southwestern writing of the period refracted the same tensions of uneven development, though with greater attention to language and aesthetics. As Jameson explains, mass culture and modernism process the same content in different ways, but "where modernism tends to handle this material by producing compensatory structures of various kinds, mass culture represses them by the narrative construction of imaginary resolutions and by the projection of an optical illusion of social harmony."[2] We need to read modernist texts beside mass cultural texts to understand "the dialectical opposition and profound structural interrelatedness" of the two categories of literary production, and to reconstruct the "hopes and blind spots" of the period.

The second generation of writers and photographers who settled in New Mexico in the 1910s and 1920s addressed the problems of development by negotiating—and often blurring—scientific and mystical understandings of Indian cultures. These artists produced increasingly free translations to compensate readers dulled by the routines of modern work and unsatisfied with the excessive refinements of high culture. Such translations emphasized the difference between the translator's experience and the reader's understanding, and shifted the responsibility of overcoming this difference to the reader. They functioned as models of authenticity, carrying all the moral intensity associated with the term; as Trilling explains, "The authentic work of art instructs us in our inauthenticity and adjures us to overcome it" (100). At the same time, the competition for authority that single figures like Lummis and Grey managed by defining their work in terms of region or generic formula reappeared as competition between writers for the authentic representation of local cultures. Modernists in the Southwest simultaneously asserted the truth of their own experience and devised new rationales for translation, professing sincerity and inventing authenticity at the same time. Austin especially manipulated her own relation to the Southwest, claiming true allegiance to the Mojave Desert in *The Land of Little Rain* (1903) and flaunting the autonomy of her controversial method of translation in *The American Rhythm* (1923).

In this chapter I approach Austin's career as a case study in the modernist convergence of ecological, ethnographic, and literary representations of the Southwest. I focus on her selection and appropriation of natural and native materials, a creative process common to her nonfiction sketches and her poetic "re-expressions," to interrogate each genre's strategic deployment of a regionalist ethics. Her nonfiction sketches depict the desert as a space where nature determines individual character and social organization, while her song translations test the forms and limits of cross-cultural knowledge. Because Austin's writing persistently figures the Anglo body as the site where regional knowledge is produced, it heightens the tension between perception and representation and raises issues that are critical to our interpretation of this period in Southwestern literary history. What kind of knowledge must an outsider have in order to be true to a place and its native peoples? Are sincere intentions sufficient defense against charges of cultural appropriation? How thoroughly must traditional materials be transformed before they constitute an entirely different kind of art? By stubbornly raising these questions, Austin's work articulates the region's high modernist problematic even as she promotes an emerging Southwestern authenticity.

The Land of Little Rain

Austin wrote the sketches of the California desert and its inhabitants that make up *The Land of Little Rain* early in her long and varied career as a naturalist, poet, novelist, translator, literary critic, and social activist. She had been raised in a middle-class family in Carlinville, Illinois, a small town with Methodist roots; educated at Blackburn College; and, like many Midwesterners, had set out with her mother and brother in the mid-1880s to seek better fortune in the West. By the time her family settled on their homestead in the Tejon Valley south of Bakersfield, California, Mary was eager to turn her attention to a subject that would engage both her scientific and her literary interests: the natural life and human communities of the Mojave Desert. As she wrote to Lummis's second wife, Eve Douglas, the "perpetual wonder of the hills, the trout fishing, the new plants discovered, new cañons explored" was one of the "real happy things" that "can hardly be put on paper."[3]

Her first story, the sentimental "The Mother of Felipe," was published in

1892 in *Overland Monthly,* the San Francisco periodical dubbed "the *Atlantic Monthly* of the West." Edited by Ina Coolbrith, the magazine was known for its local-color poetry, its descriptions of the California landscape, and its contributions by Bret Harte, the author whose stories such as "The Outcasts of Poker Flat" (1869) and "The Luck of Roaring Camp" (1868) had defined the California frontier for the previous generation. Soon afterward Austin began to receive encouragement—and criticism—from Lummis. From the time they first met in 1899, Lummis took Austin's talents seriously and provided a model for the kind of writer she aspired to become. He was prolific, sure of his own knowledge, active in preserving local cultures, and possessed of a personality strong enough to attract artists and writers to his Los Angeles house, El Alisal. Austin met Lummis when she moved to Los Angeles to teach; she was just beginning to consider writing her profession and was anxious about the domestic duties that compromised her work, so Lummis's support was critical at this time. He asked Austin to work with him on *Out West,* and eventually published a variety of Austin's work: seven poems, four stories, a serialized novelette, and one essay. He also encouraged her to send poems to the children's magazine *St. Nicholas,* where they were handsomely illustrated, and stories to the *Atlantic Monthly* (which published Austin's "The Shepherd of the Sierras" in July 1900).[4]

T. M. Pearce describes the relationship between the two Southwestern writers as one of "friendly adversaries." Lummis upbraided Austin for her "ignorance" of Spanish derivations that Eastern readers would assume to be accurate. Lummis wrote, "If you want to take a historic period, or a geographic setting, to make fame or money, for you—or even, let us say, in the very extreme of liberality, to fulfill your mission toward rounding out literature—you are entitled to give them a fair bargain. It is your business to treat them with the respect that you would like to have for your own work. If you ignorantly and carelessly mutilate them, then by all justice your work ought to be laughed at. Fair exchange is no robbery; but to feather your nest with stolen plumage is worse than robbery."[5] Lummis further insisted that it was an "iniquity" to "misrepresent" regional details or language, and that Austin was enough of an insider to "have a right to be" correct. He implied that the Eastern literary establishment would reward her with a literary reputation and generous payments only as long as she adhered to the implicit regionalist contract.[6] Effectively asserting his own Southwestern authority, Lummis's letter articulates the new rules of the region's literary marketplace: one succeeds by specializing, whether by genre or by place, and by using local details accurately. To mix truth and invention is to violate the terms seemingly dictated by the place and to sacrifice literary status.

Austin in fact had already taken up Lummis's challenge to conduct a "fair exchange" with the geographic setting of the Mojave Desert, setting her own terms for fairness in *The Land of Little Rain*. Toward the end of her career Austin herself echoed Lummis's distinction "between a genuine regionalism and false presentiments of it." In an essay titled "Regionalism in American Fiction," she juxtaposes "genuine" examples of regional fiction (Jewett's *The Country of the Pointed Firs*, Wharton's *The House of Mirth,* and Cather's *My Ántonia*) with "false" ones (the stories of George W. Cable, Stowe's *Uncle Tom's Cabin,* and Cather's *Death Comes for the Archbishop*).[7] Applying a regional ethic to fiction means not just respecting one's material, she argues, but also incorporating the long-lived experience of place into literary form. "The regionally interpretative book must not only be about the country, but must be of it, flower of its stalk and root" (139), and the country must become either "another character" or "the instigator of plot" (132). In the modernist period, regionalist theories and literary texts continue to emphasize firsthand experience and fidelity to place, but combine this ethic with linguistic and formal experimentation. In sketches collected in *The Land of Little Rain,* Austin developed both aspects of modern regionalism.

As Lummis predicted, Austin first achieved significant success in the literary magazines produced for Eastern readers. Bliss Perry, editor of the *Atlantic Monthly,* accepted six of the sketches that would form *Land of Little Rain,* proclaiming that "it is not often that prose sketches of outdoor life have given us such unalloyed pleasure."[8] Between 1900 and 1910 Austin published much of the material in her books *The Land of Little Rain* (1903), *The Basket Woman* (1904), *Isidro* (1905), *The Flock* (1906), and *Lost Borders* (1909) in periodicals such as *Out West, Sunset, Harper's, Munsey's,* and *Century.*[9] One of the reasons for the sketches' success was that they juxtaposed an intimate appreciation of nature with social details of the desert communities, and embedded factual observation with new narrative invention. Written out of the tradition of nineteenth-century regional realism, they borrowed the flexibility of the short story, which Perry described as the literary form best suited to the portrayal of "new corners of the world" and most satisfying to the contemporary sensibility. Referring to the work of Mary Wilkins Freeman, Bret Harte, and Stephen Crane, Perry explained how "the modern feeling for landscape, the modern curiosity about social conditions, the modern aesthetic sense for the characteristic rather than the beautiful as such, all play into the short story-writer's hands."[10]

Austin's "Jimville: A Bret Harte Town," published in the same issue as Perry's article and later included in *The Land of Little Rain,* serves just such a modern mixture. On the one hand is the forbidding, immutable desert and the legendary mining territory: the "white, hot land," lava flats, canyons, craters, and scrub-filled valleys one passes on the way to a town erected haphazardly between the mines and a ravine called Squaw Gulch, named after the men who discovered the local deposits of gold and organized around its four saloons. On the other is the transitory cast of characters "who had walked out of Mr. Harte's demesne to Jimville" (76): Mr. Fanshawe, "the gentlemanly faro dealer," who used his air of respectability to turn quick tricks; Side-Winder Smith, who divided his saloon to accommodate the church fair and traveling ministers; and men like Alkali Bill, Pike Wilson, and Mono Jim, who had had, at some point, the distinct good fortune of owning a mine and who passed their time by incessantly recounting their adventures.

The story warns that making meaning from Jimville's mixture of harsh natural environment and fugitive human settlement is not easy. On the way you will see discarded stagecoaches that failed to weather the trip, and your own driver may stop "to rummage for wire to mend a failing bolt" (71); once there, you must wait until the town's idiom and society become familiar before you can reproduce its language and tell its story. Whereas "Bret Harte would have given you a tale," Austin's speaker boasts to the reader, "you see in me a mere recorder, for I know what is best for you" (73). Of the miners' talk she warns, "Do not suppose I am going to repeat it all; you who want these things written up from the point of view of people who do not do them every day would get no savor in their speech" (76). By situating her own sketch in territory previously claimed by one of the most popular storytellers of the frontier, Austin takes apart the tall, romantic tales of the West told by outsiders to expose the truths of Western communities as told and embroidered by locals. And by simultaneously claiming to be a "recorder" and flaunting the information withheld from the reader, Austin clears the land for her own mediated transcription of local voices.

A glimpse at some of the issues of the *Atlantic Monthly* in which Austin's work appeared confirms the contemporary appeal of her subject. Several articles in the *Atlantic Monthly* explored both the necessary human adaptations to an extreme environment and the desert's surprising variety of natural life.[11] Articles by Frederick Jackson Turner and David Starr Jordan promoted the idea of the West, and California especially, as America's most characteristic region.[12] The July 1903 issue was devoted entirely to "the literary development of the Pacific Coast." Herbert Bashford introduced it with an analysis of two periods of literary growth in California, the first occurring during the gold rush, "when Bret Harte began his contributions to the world's enduring fiction" and Joaquin Miller wrote his poems, and the second beginning with the completion of the transcontinental railroad that brought commerce, agriculture, and culture to Western regions. Bashford divided the area bordering California into Northwest and Southwest; among the writers he thought evoked the feeling of the desert were Sharlot Hall, Austin, and Lummis. Then he predicted, "This veritable wonderland, with its prehistoric ruins and solitary mesas, will without doubt figure more prominently in the nation's literature henceforth."[13]

In the previous year, *Poetry* magazine editor Harriet Monroe had made an impassioned discovery of Arizona as "the inspiration of the future." Though she had traveled to see the works of Giorgione and Donatello in Florence and to attend the Queen of England's jubilee, Monroe claimed that "face to face with the bare desert, I felt ashamed of my long preoccupation with all these." Still, she wrote, "I cannot repent of seeing Italy before Arizona, for only thus may I be sure that Arizona is more inspiring than Italy, that for us of the new world and the new century it has the richer and profounder and more mysterious message of beauty."[14] Thus Austin's sketches appeared just as American writers and critics canvassed their native territory for new sources of literary material.

Surrounding Austin's work were investigations of other local landscapes (the Alleghenies, the northern Rockies, the Sierra, and Florida farmland) that enabled readers to indulge in the genteel recreations of bird-watching and mountaineering. The naturalist John Muir published many pieces to promote the Western wilderness at this time, starting with two articles he agreed to write in 1889 for Robert Underwood Johnson, the editor of *Century* magazine, in exchange for Johnson's support in lobbying for wilderness preservation.[15] With the founding of the Sierra Club in 1892 and his appointment as its president, Muir continued to write about the California forests and mountains, lead tour groups through Yosemite, and attract a large audience for his cause. *The Mountains of California* (1894) sold 10,000 copies; *Our National Parks* (1901) collected all of the articles that appeared in the

Atlantic in the 1890s and ran through twelve printings in six years. Muir observed that "thousands of tired, nerve-shaken, over-civilized people are beginning to find that going to the mountains is going home; that wilderness is a necessity; and that mountain parks and reservations are useful not only as fountains of timber and irrigating rivers, but as fountains of life."[16]

For affluent Anglo readers worried about feminized or hybridized culture, going back to nature while on vacation, or vicariously through reading, provided "the hope to recover the lost manly virtues—courage, self-reliance, physical strength and dexterity."[17] *The Land of Little Rain* similarly advocated escape from a frivolous, dehumanized urban culture (featuring foods like mulligatawny soup and tinned lobster), but balanced Muir's masculine emphasis on individualism with a concern for communal organization.[18] Read in the contexts of high literate culture and the emerging conservation movement, Austin's sketches represent the Mojave in a way that engages a cluster of antimodern concerns: the mental exhaustion and spiritual sterility of city life, the breakdown of community, and the impending loss of folk culture.

The title essay of *The Land of Little Rain* exemplifies how Austin manipulated literary and popular expectations of the Southwest in order to promote an ecological relation to the environment and claim a new position for the regional writer in the modernist period. The essay was published first in the *Atlantic Monthly* in January 1903, next to Frederick Jackson Turner's "Contributions of the West to American Democracy," an essay that reiterates Turner's grand interpretation of the West as the source of opportunity and the instrument of individual freedom. Austin's sketch proposes that we approach the legendary freedom of the West quite differently. She advises her readers to submit to its unfamiliarity, to relinquish individuality, and to dispose of social expectations. The sketch also advocates a new kind of regional sincerity. Lionel Trilling defines sincerity as the "convergence between avowal and feeling" and the "avoidance of being false to any man through being true to one's own self."[19] For Austin, avowal and feeling are indeed inseparable, and being "true" means being true to the place she represents. For example, while most Anglos would emphasize the desert's absence of human life, Austin chooses to call it "the land of little rain," a literal translation of its Mojave name. Rather than a beautiful landscape, she presents a modern sublime: grotesque hills "squeezed up out of chaos, chrome and vermillion painted" and menacing "black, unweathered lava flows" (3). The sketch shows how the region disorients the initiate physically, aesthetically, and linguistically. It further unsettles the notion of seasonal progression by announcing that the desert progresses through only three seasons: one hot and still, the next chill and quiescent, the third hot and seductive.

Having dispensed with the task of asserting what life in the desert is *not* (a confirmation of familiar scenes and rhythms, an opportunity to assert individual mastery over the environment), "The Land of Little Rain" proceeds to explore the interdependence of climate, vegetation, and animal life. Austin asserts throughout that "the true desert breeds its own kind, each in its particular habitat" (6); here she illustrates the maxim with descriptions of the smelly creosote shrub in Death Valley, the "tormented" tree yucca of the high mesas, the painted lizards among the rocks. In "Shoshone Land" she shows how place produces character and organizes community, observing that "the solitariness of the life" in this land "breeds in the men, as in the plants, a certain well-roundedness and sufficiency to its own ends" (60), and that "the Shoshones live like their trees, with great spaces between" (59). The discursive path of each essay leads the reader through patterns of desert life indecipherable to one who has not followed Austin's dictate to "summer and winter with the land and wait its occasions" (xvi). With what Lawrence Buell calls an "aesthetics of relinquishment," Austin deliberately suspends her own Anglo perspective and constructs a diffuse narrative persona to advance an ethical, ecocentric concept of region notably absent in Lummis's work. She shows that every part of nature has its local use, from the adhesive gum of the creosote bush to the nourishing kernels of resin-dripping pine cones. Although she rarely interprets the landscape in religious terms, as does Muir, who calls the Sierra range a "divine hieroglyphics written with sunbeams" and a "divine manuscript"—and who "tremble[s] with excitement in the dawn of these glorious mountain sublimities"[20]—she shares Muir's belief in learning from the natural world.

Also out of her willingness to yield to the real, intricate demands of the environment comes the possibility of fiction and romance, for even as Austin advocates a conception of region as an ecosystem independent of human activity, she explores how desert places inspire dreams, legends, and specifically feminine desire. She succumbs to the pleasure of seeing the Shoshone Land "through the eyes of Winnenap' in the rosy mist of remembrance" and "in the light that never was" (57). Toward the end of "The Land of Little Rain" she alludes to the legendary waters of Hassaympa, whose consumption prevents the drinker from seeing "fact as naked fact" (13). She writes, "It was not people who went into the desert merely to write it up" who invented these waters, but people who lived there and suffered its hardships. Speculating that she "must have drunk of it" sometime in her fourteen years there, she implies that sustained interaction with the desert constitutes a kind of unconscious collaboration. Austin faults Harte on exactly this point: once he found "his particular local color fading from the West, he did what he considered the only safe thing, and carried his young impression away to be worked out untroubled by any newer fact" (69). What he should have done was to stay long enough to find his way to the sources of "more tales, and better ones," such as those Austin discovered herself in Jimville.

"The Little Town of the Grape Vines," the final sketch in the collection, provides plenty of the old-time romance Harte had to fabricate; Austin claims it is one of the few places in the West "where the quails cry 'cuidado' [careful]; where all the speech is soft, all the manners gentle; where all the dishes have chile in them . . . [where] they keep up all the good customs brought out of Old Mexico or bred in a lotus-eating land" (163–64). There you can hear the grinding sounds of the metate and the jubilant celebration of the anniversary of the Mexican republic. But in order to take part in the region's local romance, you must know where to look for it; "Where it lies, how to come at it, you will not get from me," Austin warns. Echoing Sarah Orne Jewett's narrator in "The White Heron," she withholds access to the precious site and says, "rather would I show you the heron's nest in the tulares" (163).

Like the stories of the natural world, the tales of the desert's human inhabitants require access to the imaginative life of the region, but they also register ambivalence about writing that life. Once transcribed, a story no longer belongs solely to the listener, much less the teller. Often Austin uses the struggle for control of a story to reveal the conflict between the informant's natural possession of his or her own story and the translator's forced claim. "Woman at the Eighteen-Mile," a story published in Lost Borders, begins with a declaration of the writer's bald ambition: "I had long wished to write a story of Death Valley that should be its final word." Seeking to rid herself of the "obsession" by producing Death Valley's definitive text, Austin begins to pick up details of one man's mysterious death, first from a nameless teamster, a "big, slow man" with a "big, blunt voice," and second from passengers whose conversation she overhears in between waking and sleeping while traveling in a stage from Red Rock to Coyote Hole. Efforts to obtain more information fail to yield a full story; a bartender, a Mexican man, and a dinner companion provide only fragments and rumors. Meanwhile, "all this time the story glimmered like a summer island in a mist, through every man's talk about it, grew and allured, caressing the soul" (*Lost Borders,* 204). The feeling of the story, including its desolate scenery and its romantic protagonists, precedes the narrative, which begins when Austin learns that a woman with "the desert mark upon her" was involved in the death, a woman with the rare ability "to keep a soul alive and glowing in the wilderness" (205).

Yet, even before addressing the subject of the woman's character and the plot of the tale, Austin begins to mock her own claims to the story and pronounces this woman its true author. The woman kept her soul alive "against the heart of my story. Mine! I called it so by that time; but hers was the right, though she had no more pertinence to the plot than most women have to desert affairs" (205). Although Austin passes lightly over her informant's resistance to talking (merely alluding to her threat to publish a distorted version of the story that forced the woman "to talk to save it"), it is exactly this resistance that tightens the loose threads and digressive structure of Austin's own narrative. The final story of Death Valley turns out to be not an account of a man named Whitmark meeting his death as the result of his own crimes, but an homage to the qualities shaped by that threatening, desolate land: loyalty and hidden passion. These qualities prevent the truth of the Whitmark affair from being revealed. Without relinquishing either the narrative drive of her pursuit or her sensible satisfaction at discovering the truth, Austin reasserts her "promise of inviolateness" to the woman at the Eighteen-Mile. While she admits that she usually persuades her subjects to break the promise, in this case she respects it (that is, as long as her subject is alive). The result is not the "final word" of Death Valley but a reading of her informant's mixture of local knowledge and defensiveness, a representation of the ambivalent relation between insiders and outsiders.

Many speakers display either distrust or indifference to the requests of outsiders, an attitude that Austin incorporates into her own narrative and turns against her reader. The "Pocket Hunter," though a "perfect gossip of the woods" always eager to talk about the search for ore, must be pressed to discuss the natural rhythms that orchestrate his life. Seyavi the basket maker, too, fails to comprehend "the keen hunger I had for bits of lore and the 'fool talk' of her people" (*Land of Little Rain,* 108). This everyday talk, which takes place on fall and winter afternoons, constitutes "the essential performances of life" for Indian women.[21] As with the Whitmark affair, Austin describes this talk but does not repeat it. It may be that her own desire to possess it is so fierce she cannot let it go, for in *Lost Borders* she describes her heart as "a pit, bottomless and insatiable for the husks of other people's experiences" (174). Or, like many modernists, she may not trust her reader to supply the proper context: at one point she accuses, "You, between the church and police . . . what do you know of the great, silent spaces across which the voice of law and opinion reaches small as the rustle of blown sand?" (166–67). Self-conscious about her voracious need for "other people's experiences," Austin nonetheless withholds part of those experiences in her writing to protect the place she discovered from those who might violate it. Whereas canonical modernist texts tend to demand the literary expertise of the reader, regional-ist texts such as *The Land of Little Rain* demand a willingness to respond to the natural environment and listen to local stories. Both kinds of texts, however, reveal hostility toward the casual consumer, reserving their secrets for true believers. In its resistance to easy reading, Austin's collection imitates the inscrutable land it represents *and* engages in a poetics of difficulty, thus com-bining regional ethics with modernist aesthetics.

Translating the Spirit of Place: Modernists in New Mexico

The publication of *The Land of Little Rain* brought Austin sufficient income to build a house in Carmel, California, in 1905, complete with an outdoor study in the form of a wickiup. She and Jack London were among the first writers to settle there; George Sterling and Robinson Jeffers would soon follow. Yet it was almost twenty years later, in Santa Fe, that Austin finally found a place that fulfilled her regional ideal, challenged her social con-science, and provided a productive domestic environment. After traveling to Europe, where she met H. G. Wells, Joseph Conrad, George Bernard Shaw, and W. B. Yeats, and working in New York City for many years, Austin visited Mabel Dodge at Taos in 1917 and began an investigation of the region's Spanish populations and cultural institutions for the Carnegie Foun-dation. The following summer she went on a sketching trip through the Rio Grande Valley and southern Arizona with the Santa Fe artist Gerald Cassidy and his wife, gathering the impressions that would become *The Land of Journey's Ending*. In 1924 she built Casa Querida, the house she lived in for the rest of her life, on Santa Fe's Camino del Monte Sol.

The translations and critical essays on Native American culture and art that Austin wrote in New Mexico continued to advocate the role of the environment in shaping individual subjectivity and American literature and culture. She believed that "things lived"; the experiences of the land and racial contact, rather than things "observed and studied," would produce both an authentic regionalism and a national art. She turned to Indian art for a model of "an authentic culture, a culture of 'wantlessness.' "[22] David Harvey observes that modernity has "no respect even for its own past"; instead, it seeks imaginary histories to recover, respect, and even to revere.[23] American modernists often appropriated Indian artifacts, rituals, and poetry as materials for building their own usable pasts, and Austin epitomized this practice. Her appropriations and promotions of Indian songs took place within the overlapping contexts of a localizing modernist aesthetics and the ethnographic study of native cultures. "In a time and place deeply unsettled by the experience of modernization, it is unsurprising that the figure of the Indian would once again serve a dual purpose: on the one hand, mediating Americans' changed experience of empire . . . and on the other hand, reminding Americans of some other, preindustrial moment that they could attempt to appropriate as an alternative to their own."[24] By promising the immediacy of sensory experience, insisting on the fragmentary nature of any single interpretation, and celebrating art's indigenous origins, Austin's work in New Mexico shows how primitivist ideology combined with a popular understanding of ethnographic methods to produce an "American" poetry and a modernist Southwest.

When she chose New Mexico as the source of a genuine American culture, Austin joined many artists trained in European aesthetics and primitivism who similarly "rejected the possibility that the urban landscape could provide the conditions and the means necessary to their personal, aesthetic and social visions."[25] In the 1920s and 1930s, the writers D. H. and Frieda Lawrence, Alice Corbin Henderson, Witter Bynner, and Willa Cather; the painters William Penhallow Henderson, John Marin, Andrew Dasburg, Marsden Hartley, Georgia O'Keeffe, and Edward Hopper; and the photographers Ansel Adams, Paul Strand, and Laura Gilpin all at least passed through New Mexico, and a number of them chose to live there. Drawn to the Navajo and Pueblo groups living near Santa Fe and Taos and to the mystical Catholicism of the region's Hispanic residents, Euro-American artists depicted their experience of the Southwestern desert and its native peoples through local scenes and abstracted images. These artists produced the most visible, romantic strand of Southwestern regionalism and made Taos and Santa Fe into prominent artists' colonies.[26]

In many ways Mabel Dodge Luhan illustrates most dramatically the region's lure for modernists seeking transcendence, "primitive" culture, and the opportunity to reinvent the self.[27] After holding a salon between 1905 and 1912 in her Florentine villa frequented by European and American artists, and another between 1912 and 1916 in her apartment at 23 Fifth Avenue in New York City (with rooms decorated all in white, from hand-woven linen curtains to the bearskin rug in front of the marble fireplace), Mabel Dodge longed for spiritual wholeness. While in Florence she pre-sented herself as a "Renaissance Woman" who easily assumed various identi-ties. She then adapted her persona to the demands of radical New York. In addition to running the salon, Dodge worked on publicity for the 1913 Armory show, supported the Women's Peace Party, contributed to *Camera Work* and *The Masses,* and wrote a syndicated advice column for lower- and middle-class women that popularized many of Freud's ideas.[28] But rather than providing fulfillment, these activities seemed to lead her in conflicting directions, and she went to Taos in 1916 to gather the pieces of her life.

The trip marked a fundamental fracture. "My life broke in two right then, and I entered into the second half, a new world more strange and terrible and sweet than any I had ever been able to imagine."[29] In the South-west, Mabel Dodge continued in her roles as patron and social activist, and became "the most controversial and influential personality in the Four Cor-ners."[30] After building the "Big House" in Taos in 1920, she entertained visiting artists with the help of the Taos Indian Tony Luhan, her fourth husband. She also organized shows of Indian paintings in Manhattan galler-ies, worked to reform Pueblo schools and health care, and publicized the efforts of her fellow Anglos to change official policies of cultural assimilation. Unlike Florence and New York, places she selected primarily out of bore-dom or practicality, the Southwest seemed to promise a mystical connection with the land and its peoples. After visiting a medium who predicted that she would soon be surrounded by Indians, Luhan had a vision of her husband's disembodied head; in the vision, this head vanished and "a dark Indian face that affected her like 'medicine'" appeared.[31] She immediately set off to Santa Fe to join her third husband, the painter Maurice Sterne, and pushed north to Taos. In her own words, there she "was offered and accepted a spiritual therapy that was cleansing, one that provided a difficult and painful method of curing me of my epoch." Through an awakening consciousness "born and bred and developed in the whole body," she hoped to recover from the spiritual diseases spread by modern society.[32]

What Mabel Dodge Luhan felt she discovered in the Southwest was the possibility of leaving individual consciousness behind and of embracing a holistic understanding seemingly exemplified by the Pueblo people, but she also considered her own discovery of northern New Mexico to have political value. She came to believe that "we want *as a nation* to value the indian as we value our selves. We want to *consciously* love the wholeness and harmony of indian life, and to *consciously* protect it." She encouraged her guests to share and practice this belief.[33]

Luhan brought D. H. Lawrence to a ranch seventeen miles north of Taos in the hope that he would tell what she saw to be the "truth about America." With respect to the landscape Lawrence concurred. He saw "the false external America in the East, and the true, primordial, undiscovered America that was preserved, living, in the Indian bloodstream."[34] In an article titled "New Mexico," he wrote of the difference between seeing "the mucous-paper wrapping of civilization" promoted in films and by tourist boards, and touching the country, claiming that "in the magnificent fierce morning of New Mexico one sprang awake, a new part of the soul woke up suddenly, and the old world gave way to new."[35] Lawrence engaged the trope of a ruptured Western civilization and erased the Southwest's local history, imposing instead the blank slate of a new world. He claimed to find an inviolate landscape with neither history nor culture, a place where he sensed "the pristine something, unbroken, unbreakable."[36]

The poems Lawrence wrote in this period for *Birds, Beasts and Flowers,* as well as the story "Reflections on Death of a Porcupine," depict his intense confrontation with this natural wilderness. One of the most vivid descriptions of the Southwestern desert can be found at the end of *St. Mawr* (1924), when Lawrence shows us how the New England wife of a trader sees the land around her New Mexican ranch. The ranch gives her sexual energy, fills her with violence, intoxicates her; Lawrence depicts her passion through the light's savage animation of the landscape:

Past the column of that pine tree, the alfalfa field sloped gently down, to the circling guard of pine trees, from which silent, living barrier isolated pines rose to ragged heights at intervals, in blind assertiveness. Strange, those pine trees! In some lights all their needles glistened like polished steel, all subtly glittering with a whitish glitter among darkness, like real needles. Then again, at evening, the trunks would flare up orange-red, and the tufts would be dark, alert tufts like a wolf's tail touching the air. . . . But beyond the pine trees, ah, there beyond, there was beauty for the spirit to soar in. The circle of pines, with the loose trees rising high and ragged at intervals, this was the barrier, the fence to the fore-ground. Beyond was only distance, the desert a thousand feet below, and beyond.[37]

By constructing a classical landscape with foreground, middle ground, and horizon, and by drawing the reader's gaze relentlessly into the distance, Lawrence gestures toward a space of aesthetic and spiritual freedom that he calls "pure beauty, *absolute* beauty!" (*St. Mawr*, 153). This autonomous beauty is hostile to human presence and resists representation. For Lawrence, the Southwestern landscape was both an a priori modernist masterpiece (always beautiful without being theatrical, perfectly assembled but simple and natural) and a spiritual realm: "The landscape lived, and lived as the world of the gods" (155).

Lawrence's writings about Indians similarly engage in abstractions and idealize the purity of other races in an attempt to achieve personal and cultural transcendence. Just as the purebred horse in *St. Mawr* embodies a natural wild essence, so the Aztec gods personified by Ramon, Cipriano, and Kate in *The Plumed Serpent* (1926) simultaneously inhabit physical states of passion and a new world of pure spirit. By turning to the Americas to negate the constraining conditions of English culture—the effects of industrialism, class consciousness, and sexual repression—and by refusing any sustained contact with indigenous American cultures in the Southwest and Mexico, Lawrence effectively clears for himself a fictional space in which his obsessions could play themselves out.

The most prominent of imported Southwesterners, Lawrence typifies the pattern of escape, erasure, and invention repeated by Anglo writers throughout the modernist period. He translates the experience of place not from the facts of the land and cultural immersion but against models of decaying European culture. The protagonists of *St. Mawr* and *The Plumed Serpent,* Lou and Kate, are dissatisfied British women who seek sexual and spiritual fulfillment in non-Western cultures. In Lawrence's depiction of Lou and Kate, there may be elements of Mabel Dodge Luhan's experience and character, but the willed detachment of his female characters from any con-tact with the European world argues for the hypothetical and idealized na-ture of their encounters. And while Luhan and Lawrence shared concerns with spiritualism and the origins of human consciousness, Lawrence's New World aesthetics, founded on ideas of racial purity, must be seen as the region's most extreme articulations of modern primitivism.

Luhan's reach was so wide and her mystical promotion of the Southwest so successful that when Langston Hughes wrote "A House in Taos" in 1925, a poem that according to Arnold Rampersad was "the most 'modern' poem he had yet written," he had never set foot in New Mexico.[38] Hughes wrote the poem after attending a party in Greenwich Village with the poet Witter Bynner, who provided much of the gossip about Taos artists, and the rumors often centered around Luhan. Rampersad speculates that the three figures in Hughes's poem are Luhan, Tony Luhan, and the African-American writer Jean Toomer, whose public speeches about the teachings of the Russian mystic George Gurdjieff first attracted Luhan during a 1925 visit to New York. Certainly the house was Mabel's, and gossip must have conveyed her spiritual and sexual strivings.

Oliver La Farge's "Hard Winter," published in the *Saturday Evening Post* in 1933, constituted yet another attempt to capture Luhan's paradoxical ennui and erotic energy. Mabel appears in the story as the lone white woman at an Apache fiesta with her companion Juan, a Taos Indian like Tony. To the Apache Celestino, "she was girlish, and at the same time she was older than broad-hipped, drudging Apache mothers of the same years. . . . Plainly, she thought that Indians were very important, and she was enjoying herself playing Indian."[39] Celestino identifies her as one of a "special tribe" of white people always "fussing around Taos"; he is eager to "observe some of them at close range." So he travels for two days to visit her, and, though baffled by her society of artists who use him as a model for their paintings, allows her to seduce him, sexually and materially; to flaunt him, dressed in Indian finery, in Santa Fe; and to lure him with the promise of a trip to New York. A letter from Celestino's wife finally calls him home, where he arrives too late to move his family and sheep out of the danger of winter snow. By the end, when the family reaches a government camp, Celestino has lost his young son, almost the entire herd of sheep, and his wife's trust; when the white woman, who is never named, pulls up in a big sedan and fusses over him, he does not answer. Instead, as he looks at her and at the same time sees his wife preparing the tipi for him and their daughter, he begins to feel so much anger that he cannot speak. This final confrontation, in which the white woman speaks out of her own desire and the Indian man cannot speak because of his outrage, severely judges Luhan's failure to achieve any real connection with native groups.

Other portraits of Luhan explore the fluidity of her personality (as in Gertrude Stein's "Portrait of Mabel Dodge at the Villa Curonia" of 1912) or treat her "as a modernist symbol of the disintegration of Western culture" (as in painter Jacques-Émile Blanche's novel *Aymeris,* 1923).[40] Lawrence imagines that her urge to understand the "primitive" would result in complete self-destruction; he takes Luhan as his model for the unnamed "dazzling California girl" who submits herself to an alien language and allows herself to be sacrificed as a mystic object for Mexican Indians in his story "The Woman Who Rode Away." Finally, Austin's novel *Starry Adventure* (1931) mocks Luhan's cultural acquisitiveness, embodying her in the insatiable collector Eudora Ballatin. Each of these portraits reveals the identity of the Southwest's foremost cosmopolitan advocate to be a changeable, romantic, and thoroughly Euro-American invention. And because such advocates and interpreters projected their own desires onto their adopted land and culture, we could say the same of the cultural identity of the modernist Southwest.

Essence vs. Ethnology: Franz Boas and the Study of Culture

At the same time that Anglos such as Luhan romanticized the aesthetic and spiritual possibilities of the Southwest, anthropologists trained by Franz Boas worked to document the region's native Indian cultures. Once the "basic ethnographic mapping of the Southwest" had been accomplished, anthropologists could begin to focus on lesser-known tribes, conduct extensive studies of Indian languages and ceremonials, and investigate social organization and cultural patterns.[41] This scientific work applied the principles of ethnographic study and cultural relativism that Boas developed throughout his career. In the early essay "The Aims of Ethnology" (1889), Boas stressed the importance of leaving behind ethnocentric ways of feeling and thinking: "We must try to divest ourselves of these influences, and this is only possible by immersing ourselves in the spirit of primitive peoples whose perspective and development have almost nothing in common with our own."[42] Such immersion would enable "the careful and slow detailed study of local phenomena" confined to a "well-defined, small geographical area."[43]

Boas's belief in the individual's ability to feel the "spirit" of the observed culture was crucial to his formulation of ethnology's scientific method; in its early articulations, Boasian ethnology consisted of the firsthand observation and scientific analysis of culture, defined as "the totality of the mental and physical reactions and activities that characterize the behavior of the individuals composing a social group collectively and individually in relation to their natural environment, to other groups, to members of the group itself and each individual to himself."[44] During the 1920s Boas's refinement of fieldwork methodology, combined with more limited public support for field-work expeditions, shifted responsibility for the development and practice of ethnology from museum–affiliated researchers to university professionals; with the proliferation of academic ethnographers came a new generation of scientists trained in Boasian fieldwork and committed to the principles of cultural relativism. In the modernist Southwest, women scientists like Elsie Clews Parsons and Ruth Underhill combined such a belief in relativism with an "antimodernist feminism," simultaneously investigating cultural difference and resisting white, patriarchal authority.[45]

As George Stocking has explained, Boasian anthropology revealed some fundamental contradictions in theory and in practice. Throughout his career, Boas committed himself to the advancement of science and rational thought that led to cultural relativism. Yet Boas also belonged to a generation of postwar intellectuals who, disillusioned with the war, recoiled from consumer culture and traditional morality, and sought in their place a new basis for national culture; Stocking identifies Greenwich Village and Luhan's Southwestern salon as "Boasian milieux."[46] In Stocking's view, however, "any ethical and epistemological issues involved in the implicit opposition between what might be called the progressivist and the romantic anthropological attitudes never seemed a serious problem."[47] The attitude of progressivism dominated nineteenth-century science; its political application led to the belief in complete Indian assimilation behind the 1887 Dawes Act, and its social application in the early 1920s under the pressures of xenophobia and fears of immigration led to various "scientific" analyses of the origin and future implications of racial difference.[48] The attitude of romanticism, on the other hand, was "impelled by alienation toward an identification with the culturally exotic, seeking to *preserve* its 'otherness' as an affirmation of the possibility of cultural worlds more harmoniously fulfilling the potencies of the human spirit."[49] Such romanticism expressed itself with heightened urgency in 1920s New Mexico.

While Boas's teachings yielded many thorough linguistic and cultural studies, they also produced imaginative works meant to supplement scientific texts and correct romantic misconceptions. Some of his students rewrote their field experiences in fictional form for an anthology titled *American Indian Life* (1922). Intended for a general audience whose ideas were primarily shaped by James Fenimore Cooper's tales, this volume sought to depict the emotional life of the Indian unavailable in an ethnographic account.[50] Venturing that the function of biography in our own culture as "a clarifying form of description" might also work with respect to Indian lives, Parsons wrote "Wauyautitsa of Zuñi"; additional contributors to the volume included Alfred Kroeber, Edward Sapir, and Boas himself. Later students would write more complete narrative portraits, such as Underhill's *Autobiography of a Papago Woman* (1936), the first published life history of a Southwestern Indian woman, and Gladys Reichard's *Dezba: Woman of the Desert* (1939), a novel that weaves a composite portrait of a Navajo woman into a general tribal history.

The most popular supplement to traditional ethnography became the Native American autobiography, a genre Arnold Krupat calls the textual equivalent of the frontier because it is a "discursive ground" on which cultures interact.[51] Native American autobiographies extended the Boasian practice of ethnology: they sought to uncover universal truths through local observation, but they concentrated on the realm of emotion. As Edward Sapir wrote in the foreword to Walter Dyk's *Son of Old Man Hat: A Navaho Autobiography* (1938), the genre of autobiography—which he calls "the primitive case study"—arose in part out of a too-zealous application of cultural relativism. According to Sapir, the nonspecialist reader is often confused by an excess of detail and the seeming impersonality of the ethnologist who has taught himself to withhold "the recognition of universal modes of behavior, of universal feelings, of inescapable human necessities." He admits that the "conscious articulation of custom," like the *explication du texte,* might strike the man in the street as somewhat "inhuman." As a result, "there arises, partly under cover of orthodox ethnology, partly in unconcern of it, the primitive case history—biography or autobiography. One discovered that a primitive can talk, often prefers to talk, about his personal memories even where they do not seem to give the ethnologist chapter and verse for some important rubric in his filing cabinet."[52]

Clyde Kluckhohn observed in 1945 that anthropologists themselves might complete their study with a feeling that the data acquired scientifically somehow failed to produce an account true to the living culture they had observed.[53] In response, they would collect an autobiography, a genre that locates anthropologist and native between cultures and records the process by which informant, translator, and writer collaborate in textual production. Such autobiographies accommodate personal recollection, storytelling, and cultural history in a modernist composite narrative. While for anthropologists the autobiography became a means of combining scientific investigation and romantic identification with other ways of life, in the hands of Native American writers it would become the foundation for written storytelling.

Considered as both a scientific extension of Boasian ethnology and an emotional response against it, the genre of Native American autobiography revealed the continued Euro-American desire to capture the "spirit" of another culture. Nonetheless, Boas himself protested this trend in his last published paper. He argued that the reliability of these narratives was "doubtful," for they were "not facts but memories and memories distorted by the wishes and thoughts of the moment." If Goethe called his own autobiography a mixture of fiction and truth, Boas thought this confusion must be true of the recollections of all elderly persons. Boas's resistance to the new ethnographic genre attests to his commitment to arrive at the understanding of a culture through its unbiased study, "through a most intimate and long-continued life with the people and a perfect control of their language," though he admitted that these ideal conditions are "rarely attainable."[54]

In the wake of Clifford Geertz's persistent interrogation of the practice of anthropology, doubts like the ones Boas expressed seem tentative and too ready to compromise. Likewise, following the postmodern critiques of James Clifford, early twentieth-century ethnography seems troublingly unaware of its biases and partial truths. It is easy to pronounce these early efforts to combine scientific objectivity with romantic identification in fiction or in translations naive, ethnocentric, or scientifically unsound. But instead of reading them for purity—that is, seeking an accurate or "authentic" depiction of cultural patterns or ritual performance—as even their authors might ask us to do, we should consider how the "translations" of this transitional period express the desires of their writers to negotiate the demands of science and art, and reveal the difficulty of transcribing a "native voice." Not intended primarily to serve the historian, nor the bilingual interpreter, such translations often record the conditions of their own production and provide the raw materials for later, more complete literary works.

Searching for "American Rhythms"

Modernists in the Southwest rediscovered poetry's spoken power through Native American performances, and in response they produced texts that emphasize affective rhythm over linguistic accuracy, creative process over created form. Literary critics have read their translations as mere extensions of popular ethnographic studies like Natalie Curtis Burlin's *The Indians' Book* (1907), Nellie Barnes's "American Indian Verse: Characteristics of Style"

(1921), and Eda Lou Walton's *Dawn Boy: Blackfoot and Navajo Songs* (1926). Even as they consulted existing translations, musical values, and ceremonial contexts, Burlin and Walton advanced the notion that certain elements of the songs were untranslatable—much as ethnographers argued that the "essence" of a culture eluded scientific study. With an alarming combination of paternalism and assumed passivity, Burlin referred to herself as "the white friend [who] had come to be the pencil in the hand of the Indian," while Walton explained that her decision to interpret and "re-create" the songs, rather than merely translate them, came from her desire to promote "a truer understanding of the artistic value of Indian life and literature" and to be "true to the essence, the heart and spirit of the Indian poetic conception."[55] Both forms of "automatic writing" appropriate and thoroughly distort Indian art.

More rigorous studies accessible to literary translators included Washington Matthews's Navajo chant translations, James Mooney's "Sacred Formulas of the Cherokees," and Frances Densmore's transcriptions of Chippewa, Yaqui, Pueblo, and Papago (Tohono O'odham) music. As Michael Castro points out, "the ethnologists did not seem to think that the material they were translating had any particular relevance to the development of a new American poetry and identity. Rather, they saw themselves as either antiquarians or social scientists."[56] Regardless of their intended uses, these scholarly experiments with translation worked to communicate conceptions of artistic value very different from Euro-American beliefs in individual authorship and lyric conventions. They also provided the necessary foundation for modernist translators, who tended to shape Indian materials according to the contemporary aesthetic tastes for visual immediacy, direct language, and free verse.[57]

Popular interest in what Austin called Amerind poetry surged between 1905, when the *Atlantic Monthly* and a "widely read" editor scoffed at her translations, and 1918, when George Cronyn's anthology of Indian verse appeared. In 1917 *Poetry* magazine devoted an entire issue to "Aboriginal Literature," which included Indian song translations by Austin and other Anglo-American scholars of the Southwest. The collaboration required for these literary translations was mostly textual and rarely involved a native speaker. In her essay "The American Rhythm" (1923), Austin acknowledged "the help I have had from the ethnological studies of such scholars as Fletcher and Densmore, Goddard and Boas and Kroeber, Matthews and Cushing and Harrington," but mentioned no native singers.[58] Amy Lowell relied on the ethnographies of Boas and Matthews to produce the "Indianist" poetry in *Legends* and *Ballads for Sale,* while D. H. Lawrence derived his "Song of Huitzilopochtli" from a translation by D. G. Brinton.[59] Austin's theory and practice of song translation exemplify the contradictory ways that Anglo-Americans appropriated studies of the native cultures of the Southwest to invent a poetics they could call indigenous.

Austin claims the same autonomy for her translations in *The American Rhythm* that Benjamin claims in "The Task of the Translator," though she locates the common ground of the original and the translation not in a universal language but in the land itself. She argues that while rhythmic forms are always present in the environment, they must penetrate to a subconscious level where the body initiates movement before they can reach our consciousness and assume a formal shape, whether in writing, song, or dance. The most powerful rhythms are drawn from nature and from the body. At the same time that it sets in motion a process that yields a rhythmic phrase or gesture, the experience of nature also modifies the subconscious, inscribing "a track, a mold, by which our every mode of expression is shaped" (3). Austin reasons that this inscription might occur more easily on more "primitive" peoples, and speculates that the process could work on Anglo-Americans in reverse: aboriginal art could lead them back toward their own environments, and thus toward their own local sources of poetic inspiration. As for herself, she boasts that she can "listen to aboriginal verses on the phonograph in unidentified Amerindian languages, and securely refer them by their dominant rhythms to the plains, the deserts and woodlands that had produced them" (19). Both her understanding of "originals of whatever description" and her ability to overcome "the difficulty of language" derive from her experience of each distinct landscape.

Among the historical examples of an "American rhythm" is Lincoln's Gettysburg Address, which breaks into lines of verse as if on a "wilderness track." As Lincoln spoke, Austin maintains, "he fell unconsciously into the stride of one walking a woodland path with an axe on his shoulder" (16). Walt Whitman's poetry, too, bears the marks of his environment, but in Austin's view it reproduced urban rhythms, the "mere unpatterned noises of the street," not the sounds of the open road. Now, in the 1920s, she cites jazz as an example of the uninhibited expression "in musical intervals and accents" that might help to "unharness" the "traditional inhibition of response, indispensable to the formation of a democratic society out of such diverse materials as America has to work with" (168–69).[60] As she states explicitly in her essay on aboriginal literatures in *The Cambridge History of American Literature* (1931), she wants America to strive "for a state of things . . . in which all the literature will be the possession of all the people, and the distinction between 'popular' and real literature will cease to exist."[61]

Consistent with her promotion of a democracy of literary content is Austin's disavowal of her own claim to produce a definitive translation. She denies her authority "on things Indian, which I am not, as a translator, which I never pretended to be, and as a poet which I am only occasionally, and by induction" (*American Rhythm,* 37). About her translations she explains, "My method has been, by preference, to saturate myself in the poem, in the life that produced it and the environment that cradled that life, so that when the point of crystallization is reached, I myself give forth a poem which bears, I hope, a genetic resemblance to the Amerind song that was my point of contact" (37–38). Frank Cushing in fact made a similar translation claim: upon discovering an arrow, he aimed to understand its cultural origins once he had made an arrow himself. "If I would study any old, lost art, let us say, I must make myself the artisan of it—must by examining its products, learn both to see and to feel as much as may be the conditions under which they were produced and the needs they supplied or satisfied."[62] Like Austin, he protested against purely scientific study, and urged the readers of *American Anthropologist* to remember that "all anthropology is personal history; that even the things of past man were personal. . . . They must, therefore, be both treated and worked at, not solely according to ordinary methods of procedure or rules of logic, or to any given canons of learning, but in a profoundly personal mood and way" (309–10).

Austin argues that re-expression is possible without consulting the original form, claiming that "in the beginning, form interested me so little that I did not even undertake to record the original form of the songs I collected, stripping it off as so much husk, to get at the kernel of experience." This statement contains troubling echoes of Walton and Burlin, and arrogantly lays claim to a purely subjective mode of translation. She explains her highly unusual method as follows:

> I have naturally a mimetic temperament which drives me toward the understanding of life by living it. If I wished to know what went into the patterns of the basket makers, I gathered willows in the moon of white butterflies and fern stems when these were ripest. I soaked the fibers in running water, turning them as the light turned, and did my ineffectual

best to sit on the ground scraping them flat with an obsidian blade, holding the extra fibers between my toes. I made singing medicine as I was taught, and surprised the Friend-of-the-Soul-of-Man between the rattles and drums. Now and then in the midst of these processes I felt myself caught up in the collective mind, carried with it toward states of super-consciousness that escape the exactitudes of the ethnologist as the life of the flower escapes between the presses of the herbalist. So that when I say that I am not, have never been, nor offered myself, as an authority on things Amerindian, I do not wish to have it understood that I may not, at times, have succeeded in being an Indian. (41)

Most striking here is Austin's claim to Indian identity over literary authority: she argues that one can become an Indian by acting like one. The process of acquiring this identity begins in physical experience and leads toward the metaphysical, a state Austin figures as a collective unconscious. Whereas to assert authority with respect to a region or culture is to assert difference, to claim a common identity or sisterhood is to claim universality. Although Austin's sustained contact with the Southwest's native cultures informs particular "re-expressions," it is this process of imitating the relationship between the land and the native ways of life that shapes her "Amerind" poetry.

Despite the obvious problems with her idiosyncratic formulation of a "landscape line" as the mimetic key to translation, Austin's theory posed a serious challenge to the Euro-American literary orientation of her readers. Furthermore, the method does not always produce its intended results. Austin's "re-expressions" often lack expressive force; too many attempt to combine the economy of the lyric with the loose rhythm and implied ceremonial situation of ritual song, resulting in poems that are neither successfully translated into a new literary form nor adequately contextualized. The translations are best read as part of *The American Rhythm,* introduced by Austin's critical essay and supplemented by explanatory footnotes—in other words, in their own literary and cultural context. As Krupat explains, they may be "bad" translations but " 'good'—at least useful—as criticism."[63] One example of the modest success of Austin's method can be found in "Thunder Dance at San Ildefonso," a poem which selectively uses a condensed structure and incremental repetition to translate a ceremonial rain dance into a traditional lyric. Instead of retaining the basic structure of the original, Austin re-creates a ritualized performance in three short stanzas. Without providing a performative context, the poem seemingly retains the sequence of the dance: the first stanza states the purpose of the prayers, the second shows how the drums represent thunder, and the third describes the anticipated arrival of the rain. In the beginning of the first stanza, the stresses on the open vowel of calling and on the terms that modify "cloud"—dark, dun, eagle-feathered—link the singers with their desired object, grounding them against the scattered forms of clouds.

> We are calling on the dark cloud
> Calling on the dun cloud,
> On the eagle-feathered clouds
> From their mountain eyries.
> Come, cloud, come
> And bring the summer rain.

Though not initially stressed, the word "cloud" repeated in the first three lines builds residual force, so that by the time it is stressed in the center of line five, it assumes the full weight of the invocation. The equal distribution of stresses in the stanza's last two lines, from the single beat of each word in line five to the regular iambs of line six, both slows the pace of the song and leads it steadily toward its fulfillment.

The second stanza uses the repetitive structure of modifying phrases to achieve a series of substitutions that promote the efficacy of the song.

> Hear the thunder calling
> With the voice of many villages,
> With the sound of hollow drums,
> With the roll of pebbled gourds
> Like the swish of rushing rain.
> *Hoonah, hoonah,*
> The voice of the thunder
> Calling on the clouds to bring the summer rain.

Asking the audience to "hear the thunder calling," the poem evokes the thunder's rumble—only to replace it with the singer's voices, then with drumbeats, then with rattling gourds, and finally with sounds of rain. Like T. S. Eliot's prototypical modernist poem "The Waste Land," Austin's translation seems to figure the sterility of modern life in terms of an arid plain and dramatizes the longing for, in Eliot's words, "a damp gust / Bringing rain" and the sound of "Drip drop drip drop drop drop drop."[64] Austin's song, too, wills the progression from performance to storm. In line twelve the singers themselves assume the role of thunder, and Austin dramatizes this brief inhabitation of nature with a two-beat line and an exact repetition of the sound "*hoonah.*"

By mixing the previous techniques of repetition, the third stanza first builds suspense and then definitively satisfies the song's stated longing. The languid assonance of "slow," "low," and "hovering" and the added visual rhymes of "towns" and "down"; the fourfold repetition of "cloud"; the wide spaces in lines fifteen, sixteen, and twenty; and the increase in the number of feet per line from two to three to four all work to prolong the rain's arrival.

> Slow   cloud
> Low   cloud
> Wing-hovering cloud
> Over the thirsty fields,
> Over the waiting towns
> Low   cloud,   slow   cloud
> Let the rain down!
> Over the blossoming beans
> Over the tasseling corn.
> All day over the thirsty fields
> Let the rain down! (*American Rhythm,* 118–19)

When the singers finally demand the rain's release from the clouds in line twenty-one, their command conveys a cumulative authority: "Let the rain down!" And when they continue to describe the rainfall, they extend its reach temporally and geographically. In her notes to the song, Austin comments on the song's use of archaic words, "which renders the translation uncertain," but she also states that repetition is a common feature of Pueblo songs, "occurring with the frequency of Homer's 'wine-dark sea.'" In this translation, she has clearly decided to ignore the difficulties of recovering the meanings of archaic words and communicating a ceremonial situation in favor of the lyric mode. Austin applies a similar strategy to other songs clearly meant to be performed at ritual dances: "Song of the Basket Dancers" and "Rain Songs from the Rio Grande Pueblo" both impose a stanzaic structure and parallel syntax to suggest the progression and tone of a performance without relinquishing a cohesive lyric form.

To my ear, Austin's "re-expressions" work best when they carry out her professed emphasis on rhythm, or when they devise ways to suggest an extended oral performance and convey ceremonial language. A translation titled "Young Man's Song" mimics a call to a war god, indicating the length and emphasis of each utterance by means of vowel placement and punctuation. The first lines show the song's rhythmic play within a regular beat and use different vowels to convey a shift in the cry's tone: "Ah—ahou! Ahou—aou! / Hi! Hi! Hi! Hi-ah-ee—ah!" Variations on these sounds structure the entire song, culminating in the lines that release three quick cries against a final, elongated appeal: "Hi! Hi! Hi! / Ai . . ai . . ai . . ai . . ai . . ai . . i . . ee!" (94). Throughout the song Austin translates very few phrases, simply indicating the song's call to action ("Go we now") and intended result ("Many scalps / We shall bring returning"). The translation's emphasis on sound rather than language demands that the poem be chanted, and that the reader participate in the song's activity.

Those "re-expressions" which situate a song or narrative ceremonially, even if they fail to provide a full context, seem to ease the pressure on the translated form and permit a more precise reproduction of original elements. In a Paiute "Song of Victory" which the note claims to be "unintelligible without its accompanying dance," Austin combines translations of the song's chanted refrain with parenthetical instructions about the dance's enactment of the hunt. Again, the translated language is simple; it holds onto ritual repetitions regarding the actions of the hunt and the joy of the ensuing feast. In the "Kato Creation Myth," collected and translated first by Pliny Goddard, Austin gives an account of how all living things, from the round-horned elk to the blue heron, were destroyed by the flood, explaining that "in the original, the list of animals and birds is indefinitely extended to include all the species known to the reciter. When the list is exhausted, the narrative goes on" (148). In "Selections from the Tribal Rites of the Osage, Collected by Francis La Flesche," she indicates the sequence of a bear's search for a place to hibernate among trees and vines without reproducing the narrative of each encounter. Perhaps because they are clearly reworked from the texts of translators familiar with native traditions, these "re-expressions" successfully communicate the content of their tales in phrases that both complete each thought in preparation for the next and confirm the role of the speaker as a custodian and interpreter of tribal history. These examples show that while Austin's lyric "re-expressions" might appropriate a traditional Indian song for her own, obviously modernist ends, her reconstructions of ceremonial songs and narratives vary in style according to the nature of the original and her access to ethnographic information, and thus show a fuller understanding of the performative nature of oral poetry.

Like her sketches in *The Land of Little Rain,* Austin's entire translation project sought to redefine the regional writer's role from skilled fabricator or promoter to personally invested witness. As witness, this writer shifts the reader's responsibility from passive consumer to self-conscious observer of local customs. Her exercise in literary regionalism collects native art forms to construct a collective and rooted Southwestern culture implicitly opposed to the spiritual sterility and restlessness of cosmopolitan culture. While it gives us a historical perspective on the larger problem of translating verbal art, *The American Rhythm* proves that "impure" translations, whether modernist "re-expressions" or the hybrid story collections of Lummis and Cushing, can continue to build an audience for Native American and ethnopoetic writing.

Native American Writing and Postmodern Tasks of Translation

Since the 1970s, the challenge of translating and preserving oral traditions in Southwestern cultures has been taken up by Native American novelists, poets, and critics, not white ethnographers. Since they write about various native traditions in English, and out of extensive experience with Anglo-American culture, fiction writers like Scott Momaday and Leslie Marmon Silko necessarily begin with the problem of producing a translation and then construct the narrative form in which they want the translation to be read. Neither author relies exclusively on one tribal tradition; instead, each explores the means by which traditional histories acquire new meanings. For example, the central characters in Momaday's *House Made of Dawn* (1968) and Silko's *Ceremony* (1977), Abel and Tayo, both return to their reservations as U.S. veterans unable to articulate either their own tribal history or their war experience; though they listen passively to stories from a past that no longer carries meaning, for these young men speech is by necessity translation. Placed in the position of translators in search of informants, they must make do with the fragments of narrative and the songs at hand.

Whether or not one can produce a literary translation of a Native American song in the absence of a full cultural context continues to be debated. Dell Hymes and Dennis Tedlock have pioneered strategies for translating oral poetics out of rigorous ethnographic and linguistic study, attributing the lack of literary value in previous translations to inaccuracies of the dictation process, excessive emphasis on content, deafness to orality, and a too-rigid concept of the boundary between poetry and prose.[65] Both Lummis's efforts to find a general audience for story translations and Austin's attempts through song translation to remake poetic language suggest that fidelity to a translation ideal and communicability are often contradictory pursuits.

Anglo poets have tended to reverse the order of allegiance. Jerome Rothenberg, reflecting on his own versions of songs and stories from many oral traditions in *Technicians of the Sacred* (1968) and from Native American cultures in particular in *Shaking the Pumpkin* (1972), says that for him translation and poetics cannot be separated. While he values the way that translations of Native American songs raise issues of orality, the sacred, and imperial history, he also seeks to "cultivate the mystery" of the original, a mystery produced by "one's unknowing or cultural separation"; while he works to translate vocables and to reproduce the oral performance of a song, he is also self-consciously engaged in his own project of experimental poetics.[66] Brian Swann began *Song of the Sky*, his 1985 collection of song interpretations notable for their Apollinaire-like arrangements, by working with Natalie Curtis Burlin's word-by-word translations at the back of *The Indians' Book*. He explains that he attempted to "bring over" only "that small part of the originals which is accessible to me" (3) and to "utilize the silence of space" (6). Like Austin, both Swann and Rothenberg disclaim the role of translator and foreground their own interests as poets: Rothenberg's pragmatic and self-conscious practices of translation continue the modernist search for new poetic sounds, forms, and audiences, and Swann's intuitive translations hold on to the idea of "a common humanity" shared by poets and readers.

I agree with Arnold Krupat that Native American poetic texts currently provide the best examples of "anti-imperial translation" because they are able to "incorporate . . . alternate strategies, indigenous perspectives, or language usages that, literally or figuratively, make its 'English' on the page a translation in which the traces of the 'foreign tongue,' the 'Indian' can be discerned."[67] For proof of this claim, listen to the O'odham poet Ofelia Zepeda's opening poem in *Ocean Power* (1995). Like many recent translation experiments, Zepeda's poetry is itself a critical practice, and it proves the power of aesthetics to represent and produce locality. "With my harvesting stick I will hook the clouds," Zepeda begins the poem. "With my harvesting stick I will pull down the clouds. / With my harvesting stick I will stir the clouds." She continues, "With dreams of distant noise disturbing his sleep, / the smell of dirt, wet, for the first time in what seems like months. / The change in the molecules is sudden, / they enter the nasal cavity." This first half of the poem invokes the rain first in a traditional manner: through incremental and willed repetition, and through imagining that the harvesting stick often used to pick saguaro cactus fruit could reach the sky. But three O'odham lines of poetry—lines I cannot read—precede each of the first three English lines, reminding me that the poem translates an experience particular to O'odham culture. When English takes over the poem in the second stanza, so does a sleeping male subject, and a third, scientific observer, who tells us that rain produces a "change in the molecules" and specifies their physical effects on the body: "they enter the nasal cavity." Though many readers might know the smell of new rain, fewer can identity the smell and significance of the season's first rains in the desert; fewer still bring the experience of harvesting cactus fruit for survival. The unnamed man in the poem has what Geertz calls "local knowledge," the O'odham knowledge that attributes particular meaning to something as simple as a smell, knowledge that also produces "dry fear" in the throats of men at the first sight of the sea (83).

A full interpretation clearly requires intimate and extensive knowledge of both the original and the foreign language and culture. When poets translate their own work, they retain critical control over which elements of the original text will be elaborated and which will remain untranslated—and possibly protected from misunderstanding. While Austin's translations provide only a partial re-expression of Native American verbal art, Zepeda's work suggests that the questions raised by the production and reception of Anglo translations of the early twentieth century now structure Native American poetics. The contrast urges us to view Anglo translators of the modernist period, then, not as possessors of local knowledge, nor as authorities on regional culture, but as producers of an imagined locality and an invented art. If they knew "everything about Indians," as the Pueblo people joked about Austin, it was because they filled in substantial gaps with their own inventions and supplemented native poetry with their own dreams of translation.

5

Willa Cather and the Immeasurable Possession of Air

FROM HER FIRST TOUR of Europe in 1902 to her many travels in the American Southwest, Willa Cather asserted her fascination with unwritten regions. While in France she located a remote fishing village called Lavandou, seemingly unknown in the capital, invisible on ordinary maps, and "merely mention[ed]" in *Baedeker;* she and her companion, Isabelle McClung, chose it as their destination "chiefly because we could not find anyone who had ever been here, and because in Paris people seemed never to have heard of the place."[1] In Lavandou's conspicuous absence of aesthetic appeal, Cather found the subject that would preoccupy her fiction: the sense of relation that renders landscape a figure of epiphanic understanding, artistic autonomy, and imaginative possession. She wrote:

> Out of every wandering in which people and places come and go in long successions, there is always one place remembered above the rest because the external or internal conditions were such that they most nearly produced happiness. I am sure that for me that one place will always be Lavandou. Nothing else in England or France has given anything like this sense of *immeasurable possession* and *immeasurable content.* . . . No books have ever been written about Lavandou, no music or pictures ever came from here, but I know well enough that I shall yearn for it long after I have forgotten London and Paris. One cannot divine nor forecast the conditions that will make happiness; one only stumbles upon them by chance, in a lucky hour, at the world's end somewhere, and holds fast to the days, as to fortune or fame. (*Willa Cather in Europe,* 157–58; italics added)

The feeling of "possession" and "content" Cather finds along this patch of rocky coast acts as a substitute for the worldly power that other modernist writers sought in urban centers. With protective ambiguity, she refuses to specify whether this feeling is created by "external" or "internal" conditions because in her perception of place the two cannot be separated. She characterizes the village as "wretched" but "remembered," containing "nothing" but meaning more than all other European places. Cather asserts "immeasurable possession" of Lavandou *because* it will not yield its full meaning through a single comprehensive glance, and claims "immeasurable content" *because* its atmosphere has no significance when reduced to parts and names. In writing of the intuitive relation between place and consciousness while resisting its rational explication, Cather begins her romance with landscape.

Lavandou would not, of course, be the "one place" that produced happiness for Cather or for her readers. Cather's fiction provides seemingly easy access to many regions either in the early stages of settlement or long abandoned, places she would characterize in *Death Comes for the Archbishop* by their "newness" or "lightness" as "the bright edges of the world" (273). Cather's early critic Joseph Wood Krutch observed that she begins "not with an intellectual conviction, which is to be translated into characters and incidents, but with an emotional reaction which she endeavors to recapture in her works; and she completes the whole creative process without ever having, herself, imperilled the fresh richness of the emotion by subjecting it to analysis."[2] At the time of Krutch's review of *The Professor's House,* Cather had already written "The Novel Démeublé," stating that her aim was to do away with the props of the realist novel in order to focus on the feeling upon the page, to evoke "the inexplicable presence of the thing not named, of the overtone divined by the ear but not heard by it, the verbal mood."[3]

Debate about the value of Cather's fiction, however, has most often been concerned with the literal foundations of its emotional affect: its association with specific places, its historical settings, its encoding of sexual content. This debate has been further complicated by Cather's self-protective response to the criticism of the 1930s and 1940s, including her defense of "Escapism" in *Not Under Forty* (1936) and her subsequent withdrawal from public life, and by her tight control over biographical materials. But though Cather herself was eager to toss "all the meaningless reiterations concerning physical sensation" (*Willa Cather on Writing,* 42) out the window with the clumsy furniture of the realist novel, the response to her work has never quite been separated from either its regional specificity or the physical sensation it produces. Even Lionel Trilling, a critic notoriously hostile to Cather's perceived gentility, conceded that "perhaps few modern writers have been so successful with landscape."[4]

This chapter examines the basis of Cather's "success" with both Great Plains and Southwestern landscapes, and considers how this success has become intertwined with the author's narrative experiments, popularity, and critical status. Though Sharon O'Brien and Deborah Carlin have located Cather's value for readers and critics in the heroic myths of the Nebraska novels, they argue that she remains a not entirely canonical writer. "Because she "belongs to no school,'" Carlin explains, she "is especially subject to the revision, reification, and renunciation of widely disparate readerly contingents" (6). Considering the shifting critical foundations of Cather's position in the academy, it is not surprising that a reader like the *New Yorker* writer Joan Acocella might suggest, with aggressive regret, "Perhaps it is time for Cather to become a non-topic again, for the professional critics to give up and leave her books to those who care about them—her readers."[5] Readers care especially about novels like *O Pioneers!* (1913) and *My Ántonia* (1918) because they transform the work of everyday life into an art of American places; they assume that the ordinary spaces and routes through which life develops—the bare road and railroad track, the house, the tree behind the house, the field, the canyon—are meaningful when we make them so.

Yet, whether set in the Great Plains, the Southwest, Quebec, or Virginia, all of Cather's fiction emphasizes the aesthetic and social meanings of space, alternating between J. B. Jackson's two conceptions of landscape as "a portion of the earth's surface that can be comprehended at a glance" and a "three-dimensional, shared reality."[6] Perhaps readers embrace Cather's Southwestern novels less readily because the later works, rather than elevating the familiar, defamiliarize a landscape they have learned to view as exotic. Cather heightens the Southwest's strangeness to outsiders, preserving the region's capacity to transform while articulating its modes of native resistance. Readers have found *Death Comes for the Archbishop* (1927) challenging not only for its formal innovations but also, I believe, for its refusal to provide easy access to the region through picturesque scenery, masculine heroes, or Euro-American mysticism.

I analyze first how Cather develops a new landscape convention out of the interplay of external and internal conditions in the Nebraska novels because this technique is critical to her more complex representations of the Southwest. Then I consider how her middle and late novels *The Song of the*

Lark (1915), *The Professor's House* (1925), and *Death Comes for the Archbishop* (1927) construct the Southwest's visual and social landscapes around places where meaning eludes the observer or reader. The later novels articulate the gaps between outside and native perceptions through historic Southwestern sites at a time when the region's relentless commodification endangered its local histories and cultures, and they pose the question of whether those gaps can be transcended through the senses or the imagination. I locate the sources of Cather's strategies for representing Southwestern landscapes in the genre John McClure calls "late imperial romance" and in the logic of tourism, both manifestations of an antimodernist revolt against the evaluation of all territory according to its productive use. Focusing on Thea Kronborg's encounter with "The Ancient People" in *The Song of the Lark* and Tom Outland's discovery of Blue Mesa in *The Professor's House,* I examine Cather's formal solutions to the conflict between a premodern ideal and the culture of late capitalism, a conflict figured as the conceptual distance between native and nonnative points of view. Finally, I argue that the cultural and historical omissions necessary to achieve these solutions structure the narrative of *Death Comes for the Archbishop,* emerging through a series of confrontations that gesture toward native ways of knowing. In the transformation of the materials and forms through which Cather's fiction sustains the romance of the Southwest, we find the genealogy of a genre and the emergence of place as a mobile category of experience.

The Great Fact of the Land

In 1912 Cather traveled to Winslow, Arizona, to visit her brother Douglas. She already had a conception of the Southwest as the land where Coronado and his men searched for gold, the "queer place [with] nothing but cactus and desert for miles," and the realm of "the romance of the lone red rock and the extinct people."[7] She brought biblical and orientalist associations as well: "During the 1890s Cather considered desert landscapes to be sultry, foreign regions imbued with the 'oriental feeling' she found in the French literature she loved—Flaubert's *Salammbô* and Gaultier's *One of Cleopatra's Nights*."[8] While visiting Arizona she traveled to Colorado to climb among the cliff dwellings of Mesa Verde and "recovered from the conventional editorial point of view" developed while working at *McClure's*.[9] Rather than encourage her own interest in writing romantic fiction about the desert, this first visit to the Southwest seemed to strengthen her belief in writing of the world from the center of her own "parish." Her treatment of landscape, her incorporation of folk culture and legends, and her careful mapping of fictional settings, whether in the Great Plains or in New Mexico, all might be seen as translations of her observations in the Southwest into forms familiar to her. Although in the Southwest Cather "found, just at the point when her new life as writer was about to begin, a landscape which needed a new writing," first she created a writing out of the folk culture and landscape of her childhood, the Great Plains.[10] Like Sarah Orne Jewett and Robert Frost, both of whom she admired, Cather learned in the Southwest to tell universal stories with local details.

When she returned from the desert, Cather wrote "Prairie Spring," the poem that serves as the epigraph to O Pioneers! With its contrasts between the dark evening and a starry twilight, black soil and wild roses, tired men and desiring youth, silence and the songs drawn "out of the lips of silence," the poem plays the heavy surface of the land against the quick pulse of the life it produces. While the protagonist of "Prairie Spring" is "Youth," the crucial elements required to transform the land from a harsh, unresponsive field into a joyous place of song are "fierce necessity" and "sharp desire." To find language through "lips of silence" requires an acknowledgment of the raw power of a place—an acceptance of Whitman's "primitive elemental force" which Cather both admired and critiqued for being "limited to the physical"[11]—and the will to penentrate the land's resistance to aesthetic representation.

The early Nebraska novels set themselves the task of "creating a new convention" for landscape; as Edith Lewis asserts, "no one had ever found Nebraska beautiful until Willa Cather wrote about it" (17). Significantly, Cather described these novels "in the same terms she had used for poetry, as something intuitive, immediate, and unmistakable."[12] The creation of this new convention initiated a regionalist aesthetic that Cather would refine throughout the course of her career. When one of her novels "claims" a region, it articulates the interaction between the external conditions of a place, the response it evokes, and textual production; as Austin insisted but refused to recognize in Cather's work, the regional novel must be "of" the country. The relationship develops through sudden, internal realizations that are the opposite of rational understanding, much like Cather's almost violent realization that two stories, one about Swedish farmers and the other about Bohemian immigrants (whose inspiration "had come to her on the edge of a wheatfield in Red Cloud on her return from the Southwest"), belonged in one novel. According to Elizabeth Sargeant, she described this realization as "a sudden inner explosion and enlightenment"; with that explosion seemed to come "the inevitable shape" of the novel, which now "designs itself."[13] Such interruptions would often punctuate Cather's later narratives, creating an affinity between the external facts of a place, the internal creative process, and literary form.

O Pioneers! and My Ántonia present the land as the "great fact" that dominates the lives of those who live on it. They trace the contours of barely undulating plains and long grasses, a land severely lacking "human land-marks" (O Pioneers!, 12) where "between that earth and that sky" one tended to feel "erased, blotted out" (My Ántonia, 8). In O Pioneers!, as Alexandra Bergson and Carl Linstrum drive across the frozen fields toward their farms, the narrator observes that "the land wanted to be let alone, to preserve its own fierce strength, its peculiar, savage kind of beauty, its uninterrupted mournfulness" (9). Jim Burden, the east coast lawyer whose recollections of his Nebraska childhood constitute the narrative of My Ántonia, remembers that his first glimpse of the plains made him think there was "nothing to see; no fences, no creeks or trees, no hills or fields" (7); he explains that "on the farm the weather was the great fact, and men's affairs went on underneath it, as the streams creep under the ice" (116). Each of these descriptions subordi-nates the inhabitants of the region to their surroundings, and each novel as a whole poses the question of how to negotiate access to a country that seems hostile to the human eye and foreign to the imagination, whether that imagination be developed in the Old World or the east coast.

To argue that Cather derived the formal features of her novels from the land itself and her memory of it is not simply to mimic the critical terms of the author's own explanation of composition. To be sure, many critics have used Cather's defense of the lack of "sharp skeleton" in O Pioneers! to assert that her narratives merely imitate the land: "the land had no sculptured lines or features. The soil is soft, light, fluent, black, for the grass of the plains creates this type of soil as it decays. This influences the mind and memory of the author and so the composition of the story."[14] Or they have called atten-tion to Jim Burden's introduction to My Ántonia, which foregrounds the deliberate formlessness of the novel: "I didn't take time to arrange it; I simply wrote down pretty much all that [Ántonia's] name recalls to me" (2). But though it may be critical commonplace to read these novels as, somehow, "novels of the soil," few critics have explained how they transcribe the experience of place and produce their effects on the reader. Each novel juxtaposes a recollected linear narrative with lyrical moments of contact with the land that suspend narrative progression and expand to fill an entire sensory world. This structure represents not just the Great Plains itself but also the *process* of making sense of both a natural reality and a local culture.

In *O Pioneers!,* the lyrical moment in which the boundary between character and region dissolves is essential for several reasons. First, it supplies the motivation and shape for the Bergson plot: Alexandra fails to detect the relationship between her brother Emil and Marie Tovesky because she has dedicated herself to the land. Second, against the masculine conqueror it defines the character of the successful pioneer in affective terms, as one who loves and understands the land. Only Alexandra masters the Plains, and she does so because *she* yields to *them*. After a visit to the river farms, she returns to the Divide with a "radiant" face, sensing her own physical connection to the land as well as hope for the future: "She had never known before how much the country meant to her. The chirping of the insects down in the long grass had been like the sweetest music. She had felt as if her heart were hiding down there, somewhere, with the quail and the plover and all the little wild things that moved or buzzed in the sun. Under the long shaggy ridges, she felt the future stirring" (41). At this moment when Alexandra "had a new consciousness of the country, felt almost a new relation to it," she is granted visionary power: she feels the reality of the present and knows that the shape of the future rests with those attuned to the rhythms of the land. Under her hands, the land "woke up out of its sleep and stretched itself, and it was so big, so rich, that we suddenly found we were rich, just from sitting still" (69).

The depiction of Alexandra's work as a matter of sensation and still appreciation rewrites the terms of territorial possession. Moreover, these lyrical moments are essential to the "new convention" Cather constructs for communicating regional experience. Whereas at times the narrator presents the facts of the Plains in a realistic present tense, as if condensing the rhythms of everyday life into a measured narrative that could extend into the moment of reading, the lyrical moments focalized through characters in the novel offer the reader sensory access and an alternate temporality. Rather than positing one kind of representation as the truth against which the other is measured or proved false, these scenes demand that the reader shuttle between them.

My Ántonia further modifies the masculine Western tradition of asserting ownership over the land by portraying the Plains in motion. Jim Burden explains, "As I looked about me I felt that the grass was the country, as the water is the sea. The red of the grass made all the great prairie the colour of wine-stains, or of certain seaweeds when they are first washed up. And there was so much motion in it; the whole country seemed, somehow, to be running" (12). Then Jim extends his impression of a dynamic landscape, saying it looked "as if the shaggy grass were a sort of loose hide, and underneath it herds of wild buffalo were galloping, galloping" (13). He responds with fear and awe to the ability of this land to shift from the material to the immaterial under his gaze, and tries to preserve his distance. At other times the land seems to speak to this displaced observer with almost unbearable directness, through essence rather than appearance. Whereas in Virginia one could prepare for spring by heeding its signs, in Nebraska "there was only— spring itself; the throb of it, the light restlessness, the vital essence of it everywhere" (78); similarly, "the pale, cold light of the winter sunset did not beautify—it was like the light of truth itself" (111).

The novel forces the outsider to approach the land from a distance, then to live close to it, and finally to leave it behind and return imaginatively, in memory or in fiction. The crucial stage in this process of writing region is the middle one, the period when the land overtakes the body. In *My Ántonia,* such bodily possession first occurs just after Jim experiences the vastness of the land for the first time. He situates himself in the garden, leans against a pumpkin, and observes the local scene on a dramatically reduced scale: he picks ground-cherries; watches grasshoppers, gophers, and red bugs; listens to the wind blow through the grasses above; and feels the warm earth beneath.

> I kept as still as I could. Nothing happened. I did not expect anything to happen. I was something that lay under the sun and felt it, like the pumpkins, and I did not want to be anything more. I was entirely happy. Perhaps we feel like that when we die and become a part of something entire, whether it is sun and air, or goodness and knowledge. At any rate, that is happiness; to be dissoved into something complete and great. When it comes to one, it comes as naturally as sleep. (14)

This passage not only echoes Alexandra's feeling of place in *O Pioneers!* but also begins to apply it to the structure of the novel itself. A feeling of place suspends the progression of the story because nothing "happens," because character does not evolve and become "anything more." While the sensation may be immediate, the significance of this moment emerges only retrospectively, in narration. A similar urge to arrest the plot's progression occurs during a summer storm, when Jim and Ántonia observe thunderheads and lightning flashes from the roof of the chicken shed. To Jim the variegated sky appears as exotic as the most distant port, "like marble pavement, like the quay of some splendid sea-coast city, doomed to destruction." Clearly reaching for a descriptive language that will convey the strange power of the scene before him, Jim first scans his knowledge of foreign places before abandoning the imagined exotic for a more humble description: "the felty beat of the raindrops." Here the physical insistence of the storm concentrates the experience of the present; it makes everything "come close" and Ántonia wish that "no winter ever come again" (89–90).

Finally, the vision of the plow on the horizon, perhaps the dominant image of the novel, shows Cather's control over a descriptive technique that uses local details to bring together several registers of regional representation. The image embodies all the luminous moments of Jim's childhood on the Plains. Jim, Ántonia, Lena Lingard, Anna Hansen, and Tiny Soderball have taken a picnic to a riverbank where the elder trees are blooming, trees that from a distance look like pagodas to Jim; it is the last holiday he will take before leaving for college at Lincoln. Jim says that "for the first time it occurred to me that I should be homesick for that river after I left it" (149), just as the narrator in Cather's early story "The Enchanted Bluff" (1909) was homesick at the thought of leaving the Divide and going to a place "where there was nothing willful or unmanageable in the landscape, no new islands, and no chance of unfamiliar birds" (Willa Cather's Collected Short Fiction, 70). Jim remembers playing on the river's sandbars as a boy, much like the children in "The Enchanted Bluff," and, like them, he and the country girls conjure pictures of the legendary Southwest. While for the boys in the story the Enchanted Mesa remains a distant, unrealized dream, Jim incorporates the legend of Coronado into his own experience. Believing that Coronado traveled as far north as that very river, Jim describes the golden light playing off the water in such a way that the river seems to constitute its own "golden city." At this moment, the imagined reality of El Dorado meets—and even seems to produce—the real image of the plow. Magnified against the horizon by the angle of the sun, the typical tool of a Nebraska farm appears for an instant "heroic in size, a picture writing on the sun" (My Ántonia, 156). And just as suddenly as it appears, it sinks beneath the horizon, "back to its own littleness somewhere on the prairie" (156).

This moment, in which an individual epiphany acquires a symbolic significance fleeting in time but recoverable in memory, reveals Cather's mastery of the Nebraska landscape as a foundation for her modernist aesthetics of place. She links visionary moments to articulate an ideal relationship between individuals, their communities, and the places they inhabit. Alexandra Bergson's love of the soil and Jim Burden's vision of the plow both indicate the importance of external conditions, and especially premodern modes of production, to this vision. But internal conditions—the play of individual subjectivities and the imagined juxtaposition of the everyday and the fantastic—also shape Cather's regional conception. Though in each novel the land initially produces a response of disorientation and fear, sustained contact and sympathy cause the land to yield its own symbolic and writerly forms.

It is crucial to Cather's aesthetics that the arrangement of regional materials into landscape be provisional and momentary, made and dissolved by the perceiving consciousness. This process draws on the facts of a place without claiming full possession of them, and presents a transforming and curative vision of the relationship between the individual and nature. However, when Cather draws on the facts of a place which is not her native one in *The Song of the Lark, The Professor's House,* and *Death Comes for the Archbishop,* regional transcription becomes more complicated. We need to consider how each novel negotiates access to the region's past and to its present; evaluate the competing frames of reference which enable us to interpret local materials; and ask whether the imagined possession of a foreign region operates according to a different logic than the writing of a native one. In many ways Cather's Southwestern novels refigure the formal elements and themes common to Anglo writing in the Southwest, such as the narrative of discovery, the reinvention of a therapeutic landscape, and the translation of native stories. However, by elaborating the genre of late imperial romance, Cather's Southwestern novels revise the region's Anglo literary history and redefine the terms on which it can be possessed by imagination.

Spaces of American Romance

The elements of American romance were first articulated by Hawthorne in the preface to *The House of the Seven Gables* and the introduction to *The Marble Faun.* While both works allow the writer "a certain latitude, both as to its fashion and material," in the former Hawthorne achieves the atmospheric effects characteristic of romance through "the attempt to connect a by-gone time with the very Present that is flitting away from us" and the use of legend.[15] In the latter he relies in addition on the contrast implicit in cultural and geographic distance. To Hawthorne, contemporary America lacked such aesthetic opportunities, having "no shadow, no antiquity, no mystery, no picturesque and gloomy wrong, nor anything but a common-place prosperity, in broad and simple daylight. . . . Romance and poetry, like ivy, lichens, and wall-flowers, need Ruin to make them grow."[16] So Haw-thorne turned to Italy, where shadows played among the ruins and the foreign atmosphere obscured the boundaries between what exists and what is felt. In "affording a sort of poetic or fairy precinct, where actualities would not be so terribly insisted upon, as they are, and must needs be, in America," Italy provided for Hawthorne a solution to the contradiction between the work of "common-place prosperity" and the production of literature. It gave him the license to mix fact and imagination, local materials and idealized forms. Such a solution would not be found in America until the late nine-teenth century, when regional differences took the form of local color fic-tion, and into the twentieth, when the Southwest provided the raw materials for new forms of story translation, popular fiction, photographic portraits, and poetry.

Richard Brodhead has argued that regionalism of the late nineteenth century simultaneously performed the work of cultural elegy, told a story "of contemporary cultures and the relations among them" (121), and "rehearsed a habit of mental acquisitiveness strongly allied with genteel reading" (133). We can begin to read Cather's writing as part of this largely feminine literary history, as Judith Fetterley and Marjorie Pryse do in their anthology *American Women Regionalists*: Cather's "Old Mrs. Harris" concludes a survey of re-gionalist texts including work by Harriet Beecher Stowe, Celia Thaxter, Mary Wilkins Freeman, and Sarah Orne Jewett. But Brodhead's analysis ends in 1899, with the work of Charles Chesnutt, and the anthology's conception of regionalism ends in 1910, with all of Cather's mature work still ahead. Fetterley and Pryse explain that Cather "signals the beginning of a different historical moment from that which produced regionalism" (594). By the 1920s, regionalism of the old style had been supplanted by the local and folk representations of modernists like Sherwood Anderson and Jean Toomer; greater individual mobility, urbanization, immigration, and ethnographic study were also challenging the boundaries between regions, classes, races, and cultures. Cather's work signals the Southwestern culmination of a mod-ernist regionalism based on such an awareness of increasingly unstable social spaces and identities. Instead of naturalizing the relation between a geo-graphic place and a "knowable community," to use Raymond Williams's phrase, Cather heightens the differences between a place, its inhabitants, and the observer by organizing space through moments of individual sensation, scrutiny of artifacts, and scenes of cross-cultural contact.

The Song of the Lark, The Professor's House, and *Death Comes for the Archbishop* explore the ambivalent position of the regional outsider through a mixture of the material (texts, artifacts) and the immaterial (perception and experience). In testing the limits of an outsider's knowledge, these texts reveal the complexity of laying literary claim to any territory and constitute a significant revision of the romance genre. Moments of identification with ancient sites and artifacts in each novel correspond to romance's "poetic precinct." As opposed to the geography of narrative realism or local color writing, which can extend indefinitely, the space of romance detaches itself from its physical origins and from linear time to constitute a fulfilled present. As Jameson explains, "its inner-worldly objects such as landscape or village, forest or mansion—merely temporary stopping places on the lumbering coach or express-train itinerary of realistic representation—are somehow transformed into folds in space, into discontinuous pockets of homogeneous time and of heightened symbolic closure."[17] Like travel writing, which takes the form of a series of philosophical meditations and digressions on landscape and customs, local stories and people, the structure of romance demands spatial and temporal dissociation from the present space of writing. However, these folds must be read against the implied presence of a contrasting, realistic space in order to interpret them. In themselves, they function as fictions in which real cultural tensions are refracted; in contrast to the historical space that surrounds them, they function as assertions of aesthetic autonomy in a rationalized world.

Like the artisans of the Arts and Crafts movement or the collectors of premodern art that T. J. Jackson Lears terms "antimodernists," writers of late imperial romance protested against "the process of rationalization first described by Max Weber—the systematic organization of economic life for maximum productivity and of individual life for maximum personal achievement; the drive for efficient control of nature under the banner of improving human welfare; the reduction of the world to a disenchanted object to be manipulated by rational technique" (7). The American Southwest in the 1910s and 1920s was a place relatively untouched by rationalization, and Cather sought narrative means of resisting its manipulation and disenchantment. Her romances record the costs of both Western development and cultural imperialism, and suggest what might be saved through aesthetic experience.

At the time of the Mexican Cession of 1848 and the Gadsden Purchase of 1853, the final acts of continental conquest, the Southwest hardly seemed "the land of enchantment." Though under American jurisdiction, the territory still resisted American ideology until professionals aligned with national interests went to work in it.[18] Aiding economic and professional expansion into the region, as we have seen, were two critical developments: the technology of the railroad, and the official revision of Indian policy. In 1881, the Southern Pacific and the Atchison, Topeka, and Santa Fe railroads completed their Southwestern routes, opening the region to capital investment and tourism. And in 1887 the Dawes Severalty Act was passed with the official intention of forcing Indian "assimilation" through individual land allotment and Anglo education, and with the unofficial consequence of displacing Native Americans from their land, separating families, and arresting the transmission of tribal traditions and languages. This study has followed the various efforts that Anglo anthropologists, photographers, painters, and writers subsequently made to salvage the territory's "vanishing" cultures and translate their meanings for a national audience. Cather's fiction synthesizes the Southwest's late nineteenth-century cycle of conquest and anticipates that cycle's modern transformations.

Cather's engagement with the region recapitulates the Southwest's history and its appeal to armchair as well as actual tourists. Her own first response to the expansive Southwestern desert in 1912 combined fear and exhilaration: according to Hermione Lee, "the desert was intoxicating, but she was afraid of being consumed by it" (89). Soon, however, this ambivalent response began to be cast as natural appreciation. Edith Lewis's account of traveling there with Cather in 1915 portrays her response to the desert as entirely unforced, and therefore beyond speech. Lost and waiting for their guide to return, Cather and Lewis sat on a rock at the mouth of Cliff Canyon and "watched the summer twilight come on, the full moon rise up over the rim of the canyon." Lewis insists that Cather did not speak of the country but was "intensely alive" to it and "loved the Southwest for its own sake" (97). In her letter to *Commonweal* on the writing of *Death Comes for the Archbishop*, Cather also presented herself as an intrepid visitor making her way in the Southwest without a guide. "It was then much harder to get around than it is today," she insisted. "There were no automobile roads and no hotels off the main lines of railroad. One had to travel by wagon and carry a camp outfit. One travelled slowly, and had plenty of time for recollection" (*Willa Cather on Writing*, 4). In these recorded memories, Cather's affinity for the desert is made to seem absolute, free of any desire for economic or cultural possession. Though this experience of the Southwest was enabled by the area's rapid development and emerging tourist industry, its interpretation in Lewis's memoir or Cather's early fiction largely represses signs of modernization.

The writerly discovery of sites like Panther Canyon, Blue Mesa, and Stone Lips required extensive travel and research. Cather acquired her information about natural formations and local cultures from a variety of sources: to name a few, a brother of Richard Wetherill, one of two men who discovered the Mesa Verde ruins in 1888; her brother Douglas's friend in Winslow, Father Connolly; an exhibit at the American Museum of Natural History of cliff dweller artifacts; a Mexican guide named Julio; Tony Luhan; and books like Gustaf Nordenskiold's *The Cliff Dwellers of the Mesa Verde* (1893), Lummis's *Some Strange Corners of Our Country* (1892), and Reverend Howlett's *Life of the Right Reverend Joseph P. Machebeuf* (1908).[19] The range of Cather's Southwestern sources might be typical of the materials sought by an enthusiastic tourist of her time; had she been a controversial social figure rather than a writer, she might still have been invited to share the stimulation of Mabel Dodge Luhan's salon in Taos. But few Anglo inhabitants in the region, and even fewer tourists, attempted to assemble these materials into fiction in the 1920s. Cather's consistent interest in geographic and cultural materials prepared her to write about the Southwest as Hawthorne did about Europe: by mixing local facts with a foreign imagination. Instead of acting as a tourist or regional advocate, Cather began to extend the question posed by the narrator of *My Ántonia* and to play the role of imagined inhabitant; in her later fiction, she considers what would happen if one could be "dissolved into something complete and great," whether that "something" be a conscious abstraction like "knowledge" or history, or a physical abstraction like sun and air. She imagines that such dissolution would be most dramatic in the Southwest, where the promise of newness coexists with signs of ancient history.

The scenes of Southwestern discovery in *The Song of the Lark* and *The Professor's House* stage dramatic moments of dissolution into landscape and work like still centers in restless narratives, reconstructing the Southwest's prehistory while suspending the progression of individual and regional development that otherwise proceeds along a teleological axis. *The Song of the Lark* sets its imagined contact with the ancient cliff dwellers in Panther Canyon. Rather than emphasize the canyon's exoticism, however, the narrator stresses that it is a place "like a thousand others—one of those abrupt fissures with which the earth in the Southwest is riddled; so abrupt that you might walk over the edge of any one of them on a dark night and never know what had happened to you" (267). Like the plains "between that earth and that sky" where Jim Burden in *My Ántonia* feels "erased, blotted out" (8), the canyon challenges the observer to construct a human scale for measuring its meaning. The "Ancient People" did so, and the novel's heroine, Thea Kronborg, begins to establish her own relation to them by submitting her body to the forces of nature. Finally, "out of the stream of meaningless activity and undirected effort" (269) that constituted her daily life and established the realistic frame of the novel, Thea finds her thought converted to sensation: "She could become a mere receptacle for heat, or become a colour, like the bright lizards that darted about on the hot stones outside her door; or she could become a continuous repetition of sound, like the cicadas" (270). Here the body itself realizes Cather's conception of artistic creation as "whatever is felt on the page without being specifically named there" or "the inexplicable presence of the thing not named" (*Willa Cather on Writing,* 41).

Thea partially comprehends this strange and immense place by yielding to it with all of her senses, not just by observing it. As she follows the worn paths down to the sunny pool and swiftly moving stream at the very bottom of the canyon that suggests "a continuity of life that reached back into the old time" (*Song of the Lark,* 273), her senses transport her body from the modern urban world to its undeveloped edge, and her consciousness from the present to the ancient past. Yet the cliff city's meaning as an inhabited landscape cannot be fully grasped by a single outside observer; its geographic and sensory accessibility belies the difficulty of constructing a complete description of its inner life. Thea notices that "from the ancient dwelling there came always a dignified, unobtrusive sadness; now stronger, now fainter—like the aromatic smell which the dwarf cedars gave out in the sun—but always present, a part of the air one breathed" (271). The abandoned houses appear "like the buildings in a city block, or like a barracks" (267), lacking an informant who might interpret the scene. The water, scent, and architecture of Panther Canyon, the materials of another culture's memory, represent the human distance between the outside observer and the vanished native past.

It is the canyon's artifacts that survive the fleeting impressions of the body and hold out the possibility of imagined transport. The artifacts solve the problem of representing the affinity between an individual consciousness and a foreign region because they provide figures for the convergence of native, outside, and readerly perspectives. When Thea picks up the pottery left by the river, she momentarily inhabits not just the sublime Southwest but also its lost vernacular: the landscape as it was inhabited and used. If we keep in mind Geertz's assertion in *Local Knowledge* "that to study an art form is to explore a sensibility, that such a sensibility is essentially a collective formation, and that the foundations of such a formation are as wide as social existence and as deep" (99), we see that artifacts—and perhaps Cather's own narrative art—provide an outsider access to a native sensibility because they restore the vanished relation between a culture and its environment.

In a famous literary insult, Trilling mocked Cather's "mystical pots and pans" in *Shadows on the Rock;* he surely did so because they locate the value of art in terms of its everyday (and specifically bourgeois) gentility. Here Cather uses ancient pots not for their mystical aura but for their ability to redefine the aesthetics of landscape through patterns of local life. Exemplary is the "half a bowl with a broad band of white cliff-houses painted on black ground. They were scarcely conventionalized at all; there they were in the black border, just as they stood in the rock before her. It brought her centuries nearer to these people to find that they saw their houses exactly as she saw them" (*Song of the Lark,* 274). This fragment shows us how an outsider's experience of place and its native representation can come together, even as it insists that Anglo and native visions are not the same. To make meaning from the overpowering sensation of Southwestern spaces, Cather suggests, one must both allow the body to remove its defenses and find a means of aligning native and nonnative perspectives. In this novel, found artifacts perform that imagined alignment and thus construct the visionary link between native, outsider, and reader.

In *The Professor's House,* such a visionary link is displaced into the memory of the protagonist, Godfrey St. Peter. Like Thea's discovery of Panther Canyon, the discovery of Blue Mesa told in "Tom Outland's Story" opens a narrative space for forms of sensation dissociated from the ordinary rhythms of life. The mesa represents an absence of the modern world's complexity, artificiality, and commodification as it makes present Cather's "kingdom of art," an autonomous "world above the world" where even the air is filled with magic: "Soft, tingling, gold, hot with an edge of chill on it, full of the smell of piñons—it was like breathing the sun, breathing the color of the sky" (217). By imagining the Cliff City's Anglo discovery after years of abandonment and committing that discovery to memory, the novel both preserves the site as a continuing source of enchantment and protects it against scientific or commercial appropriation. Tom's story reinvigorates the

professor's body and mind, if not his heart: "Just when the morning bright-
ness of the world was wearing off for him, along came Outland and brought
him a kind of second youth" (234). While the early volumes of the professor's
massive study of the Spanish adventurers in North America suffered because
"he had not spent his youth in the great dazzling Southwest country which
was the scene of his explorers' adventures" (234), his work after Tom's arrival becomes properly "simple and inevitable." Tom embodies the ideal
interpenetration of place and experience required to re-enchant everyday
life and work.

Tom Outland's narrative bridges the distance of many centuries by eras-
ing any intervening traces, revealing the cost of re-enchantment to be the
loss of historical memory. While the air and water that surround the mesa are
so pure they exhilarate, its ancient culture is made pure through a fiction of
extinction. Furthermore, the mesa's setting and culture coalesce as landscape
only once the artifacts have been removed, sold by Tom's partner to a Ger-
man man eager to capitalize on the Indian curio market. Only when he is
standing on the ransacked mesa does Tom finally find it possible "to co-
ordinate and simplify, and that process, going on in my mind, brought with it
great happiness. It was possession" (226). Here possession refers to the place's
spiritual claim on Tom; now that the "other motives" luring him to the mesa
are removed, he explains, "I had my happiness unalloyed" (227). This passage
echoes Cather's description of Lavandou and reveals the foundation of
Southwestern romance as a mixture of positive sensory revelation and willful
erasure—all in the name of experiential possession.

Death Comes for the Archbishop

In *Death Comes for the Archbishop,* the history of the Southwestern landscape
does not vanish entirely between the conjured sensations of the past and the
rational pressures of the present. Archbishop Latour frames his experience
from the time the buffalo reigned to the arrival of the railroad, and the story of
his life spans two periods of great political and sociological change: 1848–58,
when the Mexican War ended and the Bishop first claimed his newly American New Mexican diocese; and 1859–88, when the Civil War pushed many
Americans west, the gold rush in Colorado began, and the government
exiled the Navajos from their sacred Canyon de Chelly to Bosque Redondo.
Joseph Urgo points out that while 1848 is a critical year for American
expansion, "Cather is not concerned with the usual talk of homesteads, forts,
Indian wars, and gold rushes." Instead, *Death Comes for the Archbishop* con-

cerns itself with "the way in which intellectual capital—ideas, spirituality, modes of thought—is carried from one place to the next" (172). By shifting the action into the recent past and depicting the relations between various Southwestern groups, the novel narrows the temporal and cultural gaps that separate the ideas and beliefs of outsiders and natives, only to prove the remaining fissures to be unimaginably deep. Though the novel's Southwest begins as pure aesthetic possibility, a "country waiting to be made into landscape" (95), its mixed modes of narration historicize the cycle of conflict through which that landscape will be produced. Here the imagination of Southwestern spaces becomes even more problematic, because though the process holds the potential for the moments of individual understanding and transcendence such as those evident in the earlier works, it also confronts the symbolic forms of cultural difference.

The novel depicts the history of perception as inextricable from the Southwest's history of conquest. One indication of this central concern lies in its use of two protagonists to show opposing points of view: Latour's belief that "his diocese changed little except in boundaries" repeatedly contrasts with the view of his companion Vaillant, who believes he "had been plunged into the midst of a great industrial expansion" (284). Another lies in its discontinuous structure as a series of encounters with Southwestern places, stories, and artifacts. In Judith Fryer Davidov's terms, the novel "works upon the reader as a series of sensations" mediated by words that dissolve the boundary between the vast space of the desert and "the intimacy of inner space."[20] Phyllis Rose has called its antinaturalistic structure "the most daring and innovative of Cather's works" (138) and has described the novel as "a series of stories so arranged as to blur the distinction between the past and the present, the miraculous and the mundane" (143). Through its protagonists, *Death Comes for the Archbishop* repeatedly records how ideological frameworks limit individual acts of perception; through its composite narrative, it defines the Southwest as a region of cultural conflict. Though formal strategies raise the possibility of uncontested discovery and "immeasurable possession" so attractive to the Euro-American imagination, they finally insist that sustaining this possibility will require the imposition of foreign modes of thought and the suppression of native ones.

The prologue of *Death Comes for the Archbishop* introduces us to a territory that resists visualization and habitation. From an elaborate garden on the fringes of Rome, the center of the Old World, we glimpse the prevailing view of the Southwest in 1848 as an utter wilderness. A discussion of the territory among European prelates produces no clear picture; instead, it reveals the tendency of each Cardinal to organize the world imperially, and to interpret the unknown region according to familiar paradigms. They cannot agree whether to call the region "*Le Mexique*" or "New Spain," much less generate interest in a territory "vague to all of them" (4). As Cardinal de Allande admits to the American missionary, "My knowledge of your country is chiefly drawn from the romances of Fenimore Cooper" (10). When the American tries to describe the New Mexican landscape, he speaks of its negativity, of the transportation routes it lacks, and of the canyons carved out of the earth's surface: "There are no wagon roads, no canals, no navigable rivers. Trade is carried on by means of pack-mules, over treacherous trails. The desert down there has a peculiar horror; I do not mean thirst, nor Indian massacres, which are frequent. The very floor of the world is cracked open" (7).

Even when described through the eyes of one who has seen it, and who might lay claim to it through the dual authority of church and nation, the region appears no easier to map than it did before. The "peculiar horror" of the desert lies in the strain it places on the mind to navigate it and on the spirit to keep faith in the journey; in a place where "the very floor of the world is cracked open," one might come close to traversing the boundary not just between past and present but also between the earthly world and the underworld. Whether approached in the imagination from a vast geographical or cultural distance (as the Europeans, the Americans who had just acquired the territory, and Cather's readers do), or in actuality from the United States (as the missionary does), the novel's Southwest defies landscape convention: it cannot be comprehended in a glance.

In Book One, the Southwestern territory continues to elude arrangement in terms of structures that might be familiar to the European imagination: religious belief, landscape, and individual memory. Latour's first venture into the desert might be read as an allegory of the European quest to colonize and civilize the New World, or as the beginning of a traditional romance. But the land which will confound the church's imperial mission immediately baffles the Bishop's sense of direction and the purpose of his quest. Lost in the desert, Latour attributes his trouble to the monotonous country itself, so "crowded with features, all exactly alike" (17). He describes the experience as a "geometrical nightmare," like Kant's mathematical sublime, and strains to compare the desert to a familiar landscape, likening the red sand hills to France's haycocks. Then, scrutinizing the shape of the hills, he claims they are "more the shape of Mexican ovens than haycocks—yes, exactly the shape of Mexican ovens, red as brick-dust." (17). Not surprisingly, even this forced comparison fails to reassure him. Soon he notices that the junipers which cover the hills, "a uniform yellowish green, as the hills were a uniform red," are also the shape of Mexican ovens.

In the equivalent of Dante's *selva oscura,* this pilgrim cannot find his way. The focus of the first scene then widens from the protagonist's point of view to an omniscient one, and as the narrator reveals to us details of the hero's appearance, she solemnly proclaims his identity: "The traveller was Jean-Marie Latour, consecrated Vicar Apostolic of New Mexico and Bishop of Agathonica *in partibus* at Cincinnati a year ago" (20). The arrival seems to conclude with triumph: Latour and his childhood friend and companion in the new territory, Father Vaillant, ride into Santa Fe together, "claiming it for the glory of God" (22). A religious and imperial victory? For the moment, perhaps. But the novel stresses that the Bishop and the reader have only just arrived, for the new territory has yet to submit to Roman Catholicism, and the most reliable map of it is still "in Kit Carson's brain" (76). As a new stage of imperial domination begins, the novel's Southwest resists the foreigner's claims of Christian mission and territorial conquest.

At the end of Book One, the disorienting effects of the desert's "peculiar horror" return in the enigmatic dream sequence of "A Bell and a Miracle." The dream introduces a new notion of place, suggesting that a knowledge of place might be not knowledge *about* it but what William James called "knowledge of its relations." Though individuals sense the relation between themselves and a thing that is not themselves, James thought that these relations rarely were fully conscious. He suggested terms like "psychic overtone" or "fringe" to designate the "unarticulated affinities" between two distinct things, and noted that "a tune, an odor, a flavor sometimes carry this inarticulate feeling" of deep familiarity.[21] In the dream, first the notes of a bell and then the scent of a flower bring the Bishop into relation with the real and imagined places of his past. On the edge of waking, he has "a pleasing delusion that he was in Rome" in the vicinity of St. John Lateran. An Ave Maria bell begins to toll:

> Full, clear, with something bland and suave, each note floated through the air like a globe of silver. Before the nine strokes were done Rome faded, and behind it he sensed something Eastern, with palm trees— Jerusalem, perhaps, though he had never been there. Keeping his eyes

closed, he cherished for a moment this sudden, pervasive sense of the East. Once before he had been carried out of the body thus to a place far away. It had happened in a street in New Orleans. He had turned a corner and come upon an old woman with a basket of yellow flowers; sprays of yellow sending out a honey-sweet perfume. Mimosa—but before he could think of the name he was overcome by a feeling of place, was dropped, cassock and all, into a garden in the south of France where he had been sent one winter in his childhood to recover from an illness. And now this silvery bell had carried him farther and faster than sound could travel. (43)

The dream begins at the center of the ancient world, travels to the "East" and to New Orleans, and then returns to a childhood garden in France, thus enacting a retreat from the present need to make sense of the world. It mingles the iconography of imperialism (the imagined possession of new territory) with scenes from childhood (naturally possessed in memory). As opposed to a strained, conscious interpretation of the territory, the Bishop's dream records affinities between places that he cannot consciously explain. Indeed, though the passage appears to emanate from the Bishop's stream of consciousness, it supplies language that would have been available to the speaker only in retrospect: the word "mimosa" escapes the Bishop's tongue, but is caught by the narrator. The dream's free indirect discourse provides narrative form for a knowledge of place that resists articulation and analysis.

Native knowledge of the region, however, remains exceedingly difficult for an outsider to obtain. For example, as Latour and his Pueblo guide Jacinto approach Ácoma in Book Three, the Bishop asks the name of the mesas that surround them.

> "No, I not know any name," he shook his head. "I know Indian name," he added, as if, for once, he were thinking aloud.
> "And what is the Indian name?"
> "The Laguna Indians call Snow-Bird mountain." He spoke somewhat unwillingly.
> "That is very nice," said the Bishop musingly. "Yes, that is a pretty name."
> "Oh, Indians have nice names too!" Jacinto replied quickly, with a curl of the lip. (90)

This exchange shows the guide's reluctance to reveal the language that would enable a cultural mastery of the desert, as well as a flash of disdain for the outsider who seeks such mastery. The common "breech from one mind to another" that William James identifies as "perhaps the greatest breech in nature" (231) is compounded by differences in culture and inequalities of power. Whereas the artifact performed an imagined alignment between foreigner and native in *The Song of the Lark,* here language and unmediated natural formations fail to perform such a reconciliation. Latour realizes, "There was no way in which he could transfer his own memories of European civilization into the Indian mind, and he was quite willing to believe that behind Jacinto there was a long tradition, a story of experience, *which no language could translate to him*" (92; emphasis added). Here each man sits alone with his own thoughts, and the silence between them actively contains the differences between their lives, their cultures, and their relations to the desert.

At Ácoma, the city embodies a historical sublime, a past that precedes Latour's historical imagination and thus cannot be translated into landscape, desire, or sequential narrative. The plain that lies below appears incomplete, "as if, with all the materials for world-making assembled, the Creator had desisted, gone away and left everything on the point of being brought together, on the eve of being arranged into mountain, plain, plateau" (95). When the Bishop celebrates a Mass, the members of the congregation appear to him as "antediluvian creatures" with "shell-like" backs, part of a civilization that precedes Christianity. As night falls, the terrifying vision of the ancient past inspired by the landscape returns, producing in the Bishop an urgent longing for his own "story of experience." Just as his first encounter with the desert unsettled his visual sense of space and his conversation with Jacinto undermined a geographical mastery predicated on naming, so these disorienting conditions threaten his historical sense. For this moment, he is "on a naked rock in the desert, in the stone age, a prey to the homesickness for his own kind, his own epoch, for European man and his glorious history of desire and dreams" (103). The barren landscape forces Latour to recognize the absence of his own relation to it, and to confront a frightening vision of a past and a place beyond the interpretation of the Western mind. The colonizing dreams that constitute European history and equate mobility with progress may seem "glorious" from a distance, but here the ancient and immobile stone dashes such dreams. They are merely private feelings, something for which an exile might feel "homesick." By insisting on the inaccessibility of native life, the narrative records the "peculiar horror" of absence described by the missionary to the Roman prelates: the place where "the very floor of the world"—and Western history—are cracked open.

"Stone Lips" further tests the limits of an outsider's ability to understand local history by evoking the spiritual mysteries of a Pueblo cave. Latour and Jacinto seek shelter from a storm in a stone cave, whose entrance the Bishop sees as an open mouth. Once inside, the Bishop recoils from the "glacial" air and "the fetid odor, not very strong but highly disagreeable" (127). He watches uneasily as his guide fashions plaster to cover a hole in the rear of the cave, and becomes dizzy from the vibrations of an underground river, which he hears as "one of the oldest voices of the earth" (130). The scene works with familiar tropes: the rock formation as symbol of sexuality (Panther Canyon) and inviolate history (Blue Mesa and Ácoma), the flowing water as symbol of the willed (and purified) relation between past and present (the canyon's stream and the "liquid crystal, absolutely colorless" water of the mesa's spring). However, fear of an unbridgeable gap between observer and place dominates the Bishop's response and prevents him from claiming imaginative possession. Later he asks an old trader to confirm some of the myths he has heard: that the Pecos keep one fire perpetually burning and have never shown it to white men; and that the tribe practices snake worship, including the sacrifice of babies to an enormous serpent. The trader, who fails to confirm or deny these stories, strengthens Latour's sense that "neither the white men nor the Mexicans in Santa Fé understood anything about Indian beliefs or the workings of the Indian mind" (133).

In the scenes above, the narrative first approaches and then recoils from places historically and spiritually vital to Pueblo groups in the region. Substituting dreams, bare rock, and air for artifacts, it emphasizes the failure of alignment between outsiders and natives, constructing a romance of absence rather than revelation. The region's stories and landscapes can be understood only through a dialectic of presence and absence, desire and use, of myth-making and local experience—just as fiction itself requires readers alternately to invest themselves in the imaginary and inhabit an active but uninterpreted reality.

The construction of the Santa Fe cathedral synthesizes this dialectic and articulates the novel's ambivalent claim to comprehend the totality of the Southwest. In its epiphanic conception, use of local materials, and mixed design, the cathedral seems to embody the protagonist's ambition to arrange the surrounding territory into an enchanted landscape whose mysteries he has learned to leave untouched. Still, its perception as a physical structure shifts with atmospheric changes and with the viewer's historical awareness. Yellow stone from the Sandia hills links the cathedral's material to the region's earliest imperial exploration, Coronado's search for the seven legendary cities of gold. But El Dorado proved to be a mirage, and the stone only seems to hold the promise of spiritual riches. It appears alternately like gold (the imperialist's dream) and sunlight (a sign of divine presence, and in Cather's terms, what an artist sees but can never fully represent). The Midi-Romanesque design of the cathedral's tall towers alludes to European monuments. At the same time, though, they imitate the "slender crag" of Shiprock, the sacred rock of the Navajo, and their architect proclaims that the kinship of building and setting was accidental, as if willed by a local spirit.

Satisfying Latour's hope to leave "a physical body full of his aspirations" (175), the cathedral appears both to have organic origins and to express the Western belief in progress: "the tawny church seemed to start directly out of those rose-coloured hills—with a purpose so strong that it was like action" (269). The building's apparent vacillation among material, spiritual, and aesthetic meanings indicates the instability of any single claim of possession. Just as ownership seems secure, it may slip into a dream; and just as one delimits an imagined territory, those who inhabit it may challenge its boundaries. Though founded on the idea of an imperial past and realized through the appropriation of local resources, the cathedral comes close to representing an open present. It brings together the many different residents of Santa Fe through the most transitory and immaterial means: the sound of its bell. Uniting the city in a moment of time rather than in space, the bell alone sustains the regional myth of tricultural harmony, speaking to "the Mexican population of Santa Fé," "all American Catholics," and the local Pueblo and Navajo peoples (297).

As the cathedral suggests, the process of comprehending Southwestern spaces as landscape in *Death Comes for the Archbishop* has become increasingly dissociated from its physical sources, whether natural, artifactual, or architectural. Buildings require foundations and walls, and narratives require language, but Cather tests the limits of both kinds of necessity, seeing how much material can be removed before the form collapses. By eliminating physical excess, the novel gestures toward an active equilibrium between an individual consciousness and a place, a balance that is aesthetic and ecological rather than imperial. The strongest examples of this equilibrium can be found in the representation of the usually intangible air, which becomes endowed with a palpable spiritual presence. While Latour meditates in the hogan of his

Navajo friend Eusabio at the end of the novel, at first he feels adrift because sand blows in through the walls and the door: "This house was so frail a shelter that one seemed to be sitting in the heart of a world made of dusty earth and moving air" (229). The active center of the world, its "heart," exists in and around his body, but not because he conceives himself to be its source. Imitating "the Indian manner to vanish into the landscape, not to stand out against it" (233), he allows himself to become part of the changing relations among the elements of landscape, an open vessel for the constant motion among sky, air, and sun.

Though the novel does not make such a connection explicit, it articulates the Navajo belief that the wind is the source of all life when it recognizes the force of air. The Navajo creation story tells how *Nílch'i* the Wind breathed life into the Holy People and transformed ears of corn into the first two humans. As Zolbrod translates "Gathering of the Clans," part of the *Diné bahane'*, "It was the wind that had given life to these two *Nihookáá' dine'é*, or five-fingered Earth Surface People as *Bilagáana* the White Man would identify them. . . . It is the very same wind that gives those of us who dwell in the world today the breath that we breathe. / The trail of that very same wind can actually be seen in our fingertips to this day. / That very same wind has likewise created our ancestors ever since. / That very same wind continues to blow inside of us until we die" (287). Cather may have read a written version of the creation story or learned of Navajo religion from one of her many guides. David Harrell's thorough study of the sources for *The Professor's House* does not cite Washington Matthews's versions of *Navajo Legends* (1897) or *The Night Chant* (1902), the most complete and accessible transcriptions of origin stories and ceremonial practices available in the 1920s, but Cather may have consulted either work before writing *Death Comes for the Archbishop*. She might also have read one of Matthews's more general articles in F. W. Hodge's *The Handbook of American Indians* (1907). In any case, it is likely that she combined some knowledge of native beliefs with her own impressions of the Southwest to arrive at the Navajo conception of air as an active being and its corollary of respect for the mysteries of the natural world.

The dissolution of boundaries between inside and outside, self and world, earth and sky achieves the interpenetration of natural and literary realms of experience that Cather developed throughout her critical definitions of fiction while dissociating the representation of place from its material and historical foundations. Praising Sarah Orne Jewett's "Pointed Fir" sketches in 1925, Cather wrote that they "are living things caught in the open, with light and freedom and air-spaces around them. They melt into the land and the life of the land until they are not stories at all, but life itself" (*Willa Cather on Writing,* 49). This vision of art as the heightened experience of life collapses the differences between regions, cultures, and classes in order to articulate the possibility of a literature that might elude commercial and critical classification. As it alternately records and erases the obstacles to perceiving newness, *Death Comes for the Archbishop* exerts a strenuous effort to efface the signs of development, preserve the mysteries of place, and defend the transcendence of art. At the same time, it imagines a space at once spiritual and aesthetic through the opening of the body to the environment.

Other modernists, like William James and Wallace Stevens, arrived at their own solutions to the problem of conceptualizing the mobile relation between memory, sensation, and place. James's analysis of the feelings that structure streams of thought and Stevens's poetics of climate and seasons suggest that the efforts to re-enchant American space in the early twentieth century did not entirely rely on the materials of undeveloped regions, nor on the literary modes of regionalism or romance. James could describe the spaces in between concrete reality and propose that we "say a feeling of *and,* a feeling of *of,* a feeling of *but,* and a feeling of *by,* quite as readily as we say a feeling of *blue* or a feeling of *cold*" (228), while Stevens could explain in "The American Sublime" (1936) that "the sublime comes down / To the spirit itself, / The spirit and space, / The empty spirit / In vacant space."[22] In the poem "Local Objects" (1955), Stevens envisions "a spirit without a foyer" who desires "the objects of insight, the integrations / Of feeling, the things that came of their own accord"; Cather likewise works to abstract the body into spirit and achieve structures of feeling without force. Stevens keeps seeking a "fresh name" to "keep [local objects] from perishing," and describes the moments of serenity that constitute beauty as "an absolute foyer beyond romance,"[23] just as Cather's Latour keeps seeking "new countries" like "the great grass plains or the sage-brush desert" (273) to preserve the sensation of an open consciousness.

The will to imagine space as an active relation drives both writers' search for names and countries that might evoke newness, even as it demands strategic omissions. It would seem that no one could measure, or take away, the possession of air, but we should remember that Southwestern air itself had become a commodity: a therapeutic substance and a source of rejuvenation for weary tourists. Nevertheless, writers like Stevens and Cather continued to use particular places as a means of figuring—and idealizing—

individual perception and social relations. For Cather especially, the natural and social spaces of the Southwest provided compelling models of integration between culture and the environment, and the antagonistic structure of romance provided a flexible genre in which the opposition between the culturally determined imagination of space and its local experience could be finessed.

Toward a Mobile Poetics of Place

The quest for a "fulfilled present" that would transcend the material consequences of rationalization and the violent history of cultural conflict structures Cather's Southwestern fiction and explains her appeal to different groups of readers. The integration of art and life depicted in these moments of fulfillment is fortuitous, not difficult; it does not advance an elitist view of art, though it may be possible only in the bourgeois realm of private life. The success of Cather's landscapes lies in their ability to make distant regions comprehensible through the senses and local histories part of a reality that can be shared by any reader. At the same time, the mixture of regional materials and romance in *The Song of the Lark, The Professor's House,* and *Death Comes for the Archbishop* reveals the difficulty of reading local landscapes from an outsider's perspective. Each novel shows how an individual's perception, culture, and memory combine to distort places already inscribed by native cultures. Each also seeks to imagine landscape as an open present in which the relation between individuals, cultures, and the environment can be intuited. "How many maps, in the descriptive or geographic sense, might be needed to deal exhaustively with a given space, to code and decode all the meanings and contents?" Henri Lefebvre asks.[24] Cather's fiction shows us that many are needed, but any one traveler will have a hard time finding them all.

The partial and transitory nature of the Southwestern places depicted in each text accounts for some of the difficulty in categorizing the fiction by subject or technique, and it raises additional problems of subject position and cultural appropriation. I have already suggested that Cather does not belong among regionalist writers of the late nineteenth century, much as she admired Jewett's work; nor does she seem to belong among canonized modernists, though her narrative experiments and "belief in the authenticity of private vision" could place her among them.[25] Cather's work in fact lies at the intersection of these two long-standing categories of late nineteenth and early twentieth century fiction. While the Southwestern novels in particular constitute a literary commitment to the exploration of local ways of life in a society divided by desires for mobility and for rootedness, they also address the larger economic and cultural conditions that produced the varieties of regionalism and modernism I have addressed throughout this study. These conditions promoted the development of the world's "bright edges" along with its metropolitan centers, as well as the apparent opposition between antimodernist and modernist ideologies. Like modernism, regionalism is an aesthetic response to the long and uneven process of development, but it privileges categories of space rather than time, and links the cultural production of local knowledge to the groups that occupy specific places.

While Cather's fiction explores the sources of local knowledge, it also seeks to transcend the particularities of place. In this way, it forces us to confront a question that regionalist and modernist texts continue to raise for postmodern readers and critics. We have learned all too well to recognize and privilege cultural difference, read this difference politically, and locate spaces of resistance. But can we go respectfully beyond a recognition of difference? Cather wrote of *Death Comes for the Archbishop,* "My book was a conjunction of the general and the particular, like most works of the imagination" (*Willa Cather on Writing,* 9). We tend to be more wary of a universal aesthetics and a universal science; to us the imagination no longer seems so free: as David Simpson explains, "the local and the particular are now commonly identified as determining the only subject positions that are ethically and epistemologically allowable" (118). I believe that these concepts, like the space of romance, must be read against our increasingly nuanced awareness of larger, fragmented worlds. Cather's Southwestern fiction anticipates our reluctance to claim too much penetration for unfamiliar places and cultures, but it also articulates our continued desire to translate their meaning, and to reach for more.

epilogue

On the Uses of Region in a Postregional World

IN THIS STUDY I HAVE explained how modern constructions of the Southwest as a rugged tourists' paradise, a space of masculine freedom, a site of aesthetic purity, a collection of indigenous art, or a location of native resistance projected foreign desires onto native places and animated Anglo dreams of cultural translation. Whether popular or literary, Anglo writing between 1880 and 1930 recorded both factual observation and a fascination with the unknowable. It proposed the most powerful regional monuments to be the artifacts of everyday life and those abandoned or inaccessible formations whose meaning could be recovered only in the imagination: the path to Ácoma, the cliff dwellings of Surprise Valley, New Mexico's ghost towns, the distant Shoshone Land, the hidden depths of Stone Lips.

Such dreams of translation and such fascination with the dead and the inaccessible can unwittingly do violence to the living, but they also pose the problem of whether we can really imagine native points of view. In our mobile, postregional society, we continuously confront and redefine the differences in perspective between outsiders and natives. Learning to apprehend an unfamiliar culture with all one's senses, to listen to its stories, and to recognize how one's own past shapes perception are skills that the Southwest's Anglo literature asks its readers to develop and apply to their own communities, wherever they may be.

While region was the spatial concept that guided most Anglo constructions of the Southwest in the early twentieth century, I suggested in my introduction that the term became tainted in the United States by the reactionary ideology of the 1930s Agrarians. More recently, the concept of "the local" has seemed to provide a more flexible and ideologically neutral alternative to geographical and geopolitical formations like region, nation, periphery, and colony. As it is put to current critical use, "the local" encodes an ethical or political position (refusal to make a grand claim, resistance to external forces of development) and connotes a positive alternative to restrictive senses of place (place as provincial, subjective, regional). However, "the local" runs the risk of functioning as a new idealization, or as the universal opposite of an ever-expanding "global"; for scholars of literature, it also carries a reactionary charge. In *The Academic Postmodern,* David Simpson explicitly identifies "the local" as a reaction formation against modernity. He begins his genealogy of the term in the late eighteenth century: the French Revolution intensified the rhetoric of localism, making "small, self-sufficient communities" a British national ideal. Wordsworth's Dove Cottage may thus be seen as one of the first icons of an "authentic localism" that still fuels Britain's "heritage industry," a pastoral myth sustained through its realization in a particular place. In American Studies, comparable icons would be Walden Pond, as Lawrence Buell has argued in *The Environmental Imagination;* Red Cloud, Nebraska (scene of Willa Cather's childhood); or perhaps Georgia O'Keeffe's house in Abiquiu, New Mexico. Like regionalism, this kind of localism is at once aesthetic and ideological, inseparable from the geography and temporality of modernity—that is, from the uneven nature of capitalist development. Rarely urban and often inhabited by "natives," this localism, too, is an illusory alternative to modernization that in fact preserves metropolitan and colonial hierarchies.

The literary histories of British localism and American regionalism have made me aware of how frequently spatial models are used to articulate utopian and nostalgic hopes, to advocate an idealized diversity, or to recover a lost way of life. If we were to investigate the histories of America's recent spatial formations such as the suburb, the Sunbelt, and the edge city, we would find that each emerged in response to particular economic and social pressures and each has since been reappropriated for new political purposes. Despite their obvious problems as analytical terms, however, I think that regions and localities deserve a critical place in American Studies. Regions and localities have distinct natural and cultural histories that can be more concretely apprehended than abstract formations like nationality or ethnicity, histories that are best told through an intensifying lens. The "close living" achieved in regional fiction, Raymond Williams argues, "seek[s] the substance of those finer-drawn, often occluded, relations and relationships" that constitute communal formations "in self-realization and in struggle."[1] As long as we resist reifying region or locality, a focus on local practices and relations helps us to contend with marginalized sectors of society and to break down polarizing distinctions. A critical regionalism thus could function as what Immanuel Wallerstein calls an "antisystematic movement," an experimental and mobile strategy that seeks alternatives to the dominant structure of the capitalist world-system.[2]

From a more modest, specifically literary perspective, the region's spatial framework opens a number of critical possibilities. Taking the region as a unit of study temporarily suspends traditional literary categories like period, genre, and value. It promotes what we might call *indiscriminate reading*: a shift from the question of what and what not to read to the question of how to make sense of a broad range of texts; the analysis of cultural function rather than literary hermeneutics; and the production of genuinely new kinds of interactions between literature and other disciplines. Such an approach would also prevent us from bracketing issues of race, gender, and ethnicity, since these issues are critical to the constitution of the writer's subject position. The difficulty lies in attributing proper significance and emphasis to the array of materials a region spreads before the critic. But having submitted oneself to the possibilities, one returns to the province of high literary culture with an altered eye, and to the practice of literary criticism with a recognition of one's obligation to tell, however imperfectly, the whole history.

Notes

Introduction

1. Berman, *Everything Solid Melts into Air,* 15.

2. Brodhead, *Cultures of Letters,* 121.

3. For a discussion of regionalism "as an attempt to revive some particularly nationalistic ideals," see Dainotto, " 'All the Regions Do Smilingly Revolt.' "

4. Mumford, *The Story of Utopias,* in *The Lewis Mumford Reader,* 221.

5. Davidson, "Regionalism and Nationalism in American Literature," in his *Still Rebels, Still Yankees, and Other Essays,* 271. Dorman provides thorough accounts of aesthetic regionalism between the wars and of regionalism's ideological instability in *The Revolt of the Provinces.*

6. Francaviglia, "Elusive Land: Changing Geographic Images of the Southwest," in *Essays on the Changing Images of the Southwest,* ed. Francaviglia and Narrett, 9.

7. For a full account of colonialism's rhetorical repertoire, see Spurr, *The Rhetoric of Empire.*

8. I use the notion of trajectory in Bourdieu's sense, as "the series of positions successively occupied by the same writer in the successive states of the literary field" (189). Bourdieu, "Principles for a Sociology of Cultural Works," in his *The Field of Cultural Production.*

9. Jameson, "Reification and Utopia in Mass Culture," in his *Signatures of the Visible,* 14.

10. Venuti, "Translation, Community, Utopia," in *The Translation Studies Reader,* ed. Venuti, 471.

11. To consider fully the effects of these texts on either the region's native communities or contemporary practices of translation and photography would require a much broader study than this one. For a brilliant example, see Womack, *Red on Red: Native American Literary Separatism.*

12. Saldívar, *Border Matters,* 13.

13. Limón, *American Encounters,* 4.

14. Kaplan, " 'Left Alone with America,' " 17.

15. V. Turner, "Dewey, Dilthey, and Drama," in *The Anthropology of Experience,* ed. Turner and Bruner, 41–42.

16. See also Clifford's *The Predicament of Culture* and his "Introduction: Partial Truths," in *Writing Culture,* ed. Clifford and Marcus.

17. Geertz, "Found in Translation," in his *Local Knowledge,* 44.

18. S. Ortiz, Introduction to *Speaking for the Generations,* ed. Ortiz.

19. de Vaca, *Cabeza de Vaca's Adventures in the Unknown Interior of America,* 120.

20. Fontana, "Church and Crown," 459.

21. Clifford, *Routes,* 23.

22. While Myrick's study of New Mexico's railroads emphasizes the construction of main routes, branch lines, and spurs to serve coal, silver, copper, and lumber industries, Babcock and Weigle's survey of the Fred Harvey Company shows how Southwestern railroads both developed and were put to use by the new industry of tourism. See Myrick, *New Mexico's Railroads,* and Babcock and Weigle, eds., *The Great Southwest of the Fred Harvey Company and the Santa Fe Railway.*

23. See McWilliams, *Southern California,* and Starr, *Material Dreams,* for accounts of these westward migrations.

24. Nugent, "The People of the West," 43.

25. Lavender, *The Southwest,* 268.

26. To see how corporate organization transformed these communities, see Deutsch, *No Separate Refuge,* and White, *"It's Your Misfortune and None of My Own,"* ch. 10.

27. Robbins, *Colony and Empire,* 63.

28. D. Harvey, *The Condition of Postmodernity,* 271.

29. Pomeroy, *In Search of the Golden West,* 69.

30. Poling-Kempes, *The Harvey Girls,* 169.

31. For a complete account and analysis of such tours, see Weigle, "Southwest Lures."

32. Lummis, *Mesa, Cañon and Pueblo,* 7.

33. Soja, *Postmodern Geographies,* 107.

34. A common source for the widely applied concept of cultural "invention" is Hobsbawm and Ranger, eds., *The Invention of Tradition.*

35. Nugent, "The People of the West," 36.

36. Jameson, *Postmodernism,* 307.

37. In addition to D. Harvey, *The Condition of Postmodernity,* Soja, *Postmodern Geographies,* and Geertz, *Local Knowledge,* see Appadurai, *Modernity at Large,* and Friedman, *The Lexus and the Olive Tree.*

38. Lippard, *The Lure of the Local,* 7.

Chapter 1. Charles Lummis's Tasks of Translation

1. Pomeroy, *The Pacific Slope,* 388.

2. Quoted in Apostol, *El Alisal.* By 1895, the magazine's circulation in

southern California far exceeded the combined sales of Eastern magazines such as *Harper's, Century, Scribner's, McClure's,* and *Cosmopolitan,* and San Francisco's *Overland Monthly.* Its distribution soon became national (with the most concentrated audiences in the Arizona Territory, New York, Massachusetts, and New Mexico). For a full account of *Land of Sunshine's* publication history, see Bingham, *Charles F. Lummis: Editor of the Southwest.*

3. Starr, *Americans and the California Dream,* 401, 398.

4. Padget, "Travel, Exoticism, and the Writing of Region," 448.

5. Byrkit, "Land, Sky, People," 356–57.

6. "Sunshine or *Noir?*," ch. 1 of M. Davis's *City of Quartz.* For a discussion of "mission mania" in the context of southern California's late nineteenth-century expansion, see Deverell, "Privileging the Mission over the Mexican," in *Many Wests,* ed. Steiner and Wrobel, 235–58.

7. Byrkit, Introduction to Lummis, *Letters from the Southwest,* xxi, xxiv.

8. See Lears, *No Place of Grace,* and Cotkin, *Reluctant Modernism,* respectively. Lears uses the term "antimodernism" to describe patterns of dissent from dominant culture. That Lummis's efforts also worked to turn the Southwest itself into an object to be consumed by tourists was a irony typical of many such half-conscious "antimodern" attempts: as Lears argues, antimodernism "promoted an accommodation to new modes of cultural hegemony while it preserved an eloquent edge of protest" (301).

9. Higginson to Lummis, 26 April 1888, Charles Fletcher Lummis Papers, MS 39, Special Collections, University of Arizona Library.

10. Holmes to Lummis, 16 September 1879, Charles Fletcher Lummis Papers, MS 39, Special Collections, University of Arizona Library.

11. Whitman to Lummis, 29 January 1884, Charles Fletcher Lummis Papers, MS 39, Special Collections, University of Arizona Library.

12. Lummis, "As I Remember," Charles Fletcher Lummis Papers, MS 39, Special Collections, University of Arizona Library.

13. The railroad also indirectly paid his way. The promise of employment at the *Los Angeles Times* indicated the rapid growth of southern California and an emerging pattern of large-scale migration that would peak in the 1920s. Without the critical technology of the railroad, such migration would have been limited to the hardy few willing to cross the Rockies and the desert, rather than the multitudes pursuing "material dreams." It was this aspiring, middle-class audience of actual and potential migrants that would buy Lummis's regional romances. See Starr, *Material Dreams.*

14. In his memoir "As I Remember," Lummis recalls that he hesitated when his friend Frederick Webb Hodge of the Smithsonian Institution met his train in Washington "with a message to come to the White House immediately as lunch

was waiting." Wearing his "travel corduroys and pretty dusty," he telephoned first—and was urged to come directly.

15. Byrkit, "Land, Sky, People," 345.

16. Weigle and White, eds., *The Lore of New Mexico*, 49–51.

17. Because of the scale of the view, the panorama is the genre of landscape that inspires "the feelings of extension, immensity and infinitude (in short, of the romantic sublime)." Sayre claims in "Surveying the Vast Profound" that "this collective, anonymous and sovereign gaze permeates American culture throughout the last half of the nineteenth century" (725, 736).

18. Lummis, *Letters from the Southwest*, 62.

19. The geographer Clarence Dutton, for example, had already called the Canyon "by far the most sublime of all earthly spectacles" and named the approach from Kaibab "Point Sublime." To emphasize the difficulty of apprehending the Canyon, Anglo writers frequently compensated with excess verbiage, and Theodore Roosevelt was no exception: "to none of the sons of men is it given to tell of the wonder and splendor of sunrise and sunset in the Grand Canyon of the Colorado," he proclaimed. See *Grand Canyon: An Anthology*, ed. Babbitt, 62, 202.

20. Greenblatt, *Marvelous Possessions*, 20.

21. Warner, "The Heart of the Desert," 403.

22. Lummis, Introduction to Bandelier, *The Delight Makers*, xiii–xiv.

23. Long embroiled in disputes over land tenure and suffering from crops lost to floods, Laguna at this time began to look for alternatives to agriculture for sustenance. With other local Indians, African-Americans, and Asian immigrants, Laguna men worked a difficult stretch of desert track for the Santa Fe Railroad. The Laguna people made a special oral arrangement with the Santa Fe Railroad: in exchange for the "unmolested" progress of the railroad through Laguna territory, the company would hire as many Laguna men as wanted to work on the system. For a discussion of this agreement and a transcript of interviews with Laguna elders who recall it, see Peters, "Watering the Flow: Laguna Pueblo and the Santa Fe Railroad, 1880–1942," in *Native Americans and Wage Labor*, ed. Littlefield and Knack, 177–97. In "Organized Labor: Race, Radicalism, and Gender," Kern argues that such an informal arrangement may have survived because of the dominance of Hispanic workers on the line and the nonunion status of New Mexican railway workers through 1906. See *Essays in Twentieth-Century New Mexico History*, ed. DeMark, 149–68.

24. Hinsley, "Zunis and Brahmins," in *Romantic Motives*, ed. Stocking, 175.

25. Heib, "Elsie Clews Parsons in the Southwest," in *Hidden Scholars*, ed. Parezo, 63.

26. Deacon, *Elsie Clews Parsons*, 223.

27. For example, Parsons wrote a fictional account, "Waiyautitsa of Zuñi,

New Mexico," that appeared in *Scribner's Monthly* in 1919 to illustrate "the differentiation of the sexes at Zuñi." See Parsons, *Pueblo Mothers and Children.*

28. A. Ortiz, "The Dynamics of Pueblo Cultural Survival," 304. Along with the desire for dramatic change, the ideological and class position of the observer or scholar has distorted our historical understanding of the Southwest's non-Anglo communities.

29. Briggs and Bauman, " 'The Foundation of All Future Researches,' " 482.

30. Stocking, *Race, Culture and Evolution,* 227.

31. Conn, *Museums and American Intellectual Life, 1876–1926,* 4. For a dissenting perspective, see Hinsley's review in *Winterthur Portfolio.*

32. Clemens, *Native American Verbal Art,* 4–5.

33. Matthews, unsigned article in *Field and Stream,* 1884, quoted in *Washington Matthews: Studies in Navajo Culture, 1880–1894,* ed. Halpern and McGreevey, 217.

34. Benjamin, "The Task of the Translator," in *The Translation Studies Reader,* ed. Venuti, 15.

35. Matthews to Lummis, 31 May 1901, Braun Research Library, MS 1.1.3023B. Courtesy of the Southwest Museum, Los Angeles.

36. Lummis to Matthews, 5 September 1879, Braun Research Library, MS 1.1.3023A. Courtesy of the Southwest Museum, Los Angles.

37. See Zolbrod, "On the Multicultural Frontier with Washington Matthews," 81.

38. Songs from his translation of the chant were included in one of the first anthologies of Native American verbal art, *The Path on the Rainbow,* ed. Cronyn; were re-interpreted by Mary Austin in her *American Rhythm;* and now appear in the most canonical texts: Library of America's two-volume compilation of nineteenth-century American poetry and the Norton anthologies of American and world literature. Matthews's entire study of the *Night Chant* ceremonial has been re-issued by the University of Utah Press, and his manuscripts and methodology are the subject of Halpern and McGreevy's *Washington Matthews: Studies in Navajo Culture 1880–1894.* If publication history is any indication, there is now no shortage of readers for this once-neglected text.

39. The Zunis have passed on stories of Cushing's residence among them. As Barbara Tedlock recounts in *The Beautiful and the Dangerous,* some Zunis say that when Cushing "got initiated as a Bow Priest, he went out across Oak Wash to a Navajo hogan and took a scalp" (176) rather than producing his own; yet others keep reprints of Cushing's *Zuni Fetishes* on their coffee tables—a sign that might indicate Cushing's role in preserving cultural memory, or might just serve as a necessary reminder to any visitor that, in Tedlock's words, "all educated Zunis already knew what asses ethnographers could be" (118).

40. Lummis, "The White Indian," 8.

41. Hinsley, "Life on the Margins." See also his "Zunis and Brahmins"; "Ethnographic Charisma and Scientific Routine"; and *Savages and Scientists;* and Hinsley and Wilcox, eds., *The Southwest in the American Imagination.*

42. Gish, Introduction to Lummis, *Pueblo Indian Folk-Stories,* xviii.

43. For a description of factions within Isleta, see Sando, 181–92. Citing an unpublished article by Theodore S. Jojola, Padget observes that Lummis's associations with the Abeitas and with local traders and missionaries "suggest the degree to which Lummis associated with the Pueblo 'progressives,'" those who sought contact with outsiders. Among these "progressives" were the Isleta people who traveled to Los Angeles every year between 1895 and 1903 at Lummis's invitation. See Padget, 446.

44. Parsons, "Isleta, New Mexico," 207. Candelaria Chavez, who had much contact with whites, defended the book to the tribal chiefs on the grounds that it was "written 30 years or more ago" and, more important, that the stories were "not very important stories."

45. For example, on 27 September 1891 the diary reports 278 blueprints made; on 28 September, 359. On 11 October of the same year, it claims "escribo 500 w de Lo Not Poor" (an article published in *Scribner's*) and 302 blueprints, commenting matter-of-factly, "Imprimo muchos retratos. Trabajo mucho con retratos." The yield for such labor was not always high, but it added up. Eight blueprints sold for $1.00, compared with $2.90 for thirteen pieces of Ácoma pottery and $6.00 for a "first class" Ácoma serape. At the end of each diary is a ledger listing the pieces Lummis submitted for periodical and book publication, the name of the magazine or publisher, the status of the piece, and the monies paid. Though many articles were rejected in the first round, most eventually made their way into print. (*St. Nicholas* published almost all the chapters of *Some Strange Corners of Our Country* before its appearance in book form; when American Century Company rejected *A Tramp across the Continent,* Scribner's accepted it.) Braun Research Library, MS 1. Courtesy of the Southwest Museum, Los Angeles.

46. Lummis's best-selling postcards included "a macabre view of prehistorical Peruvian skulls as well as a shot of Pizarro's tomb." Houlihan and Campbell, "Lummis as a Photographer," in *Charles F. Lummis: The Centennial Exhibition Commemorating His Tramp across the Continent,* ed. Moneta, 29.

47. Clark to Lummis, 12 June 1891, Charles Fletcher Lummis Papers, MS 39, Special Collections, University of Arizona Library.

48. The Penitentes were a devout Catholic group which practiced flagellation and staged a crucifixion during Holy Week. When Lummis learned of the crucifixion, he resolved to photograph it, despite warnings that he would be killed for doing so. He struck a deal with the chief brother of the Penitentes, and, protected by his friend Chavez's son Ireneo, on Good Friday set up his tripod,

thus becoming the "first to bring the astonishing practices to the notice of the world" (127). He captured the images unharmed (though the subsequent capture of a scourge prompted a member to shoot him through his hat and calf). "The Penitente Brothers," in his *The Land of Poco Tiempo.* For accounts claiming that Lummis had three friends hold the Penitentes at gunpoint to obtain the pictures, see the essays by Materassi and Traugott in *La terra incantata dei Pueblo,* ed. Traugott, Secco, and Materassi.

49. Lummis, "As I Remember," quoted in Houlihan and Houlihan, *Lummis in the Pueblos,* 3.

50. See Babcock's "First Families: Gender, Reproduction, and the Mythic Southwest," in *The Great Southwest of the Fred Harvey Company,* ed. Babcock and Weigle, 207–17, for a discussion of how Lummis's writing and photography shaped the myth of Native American women.

51. Howells to Lummis, 29 October 1900, Charles Fletcher Lummis Papers, MS 39, Special Collections, University of Arizona Library.

52. Krupat, *Ethnocriticism,* 71.

53. D. Tedlock, *The Spoken Word and the Work of Interpretation,* 35–36.

54. D. Tedlock, *Finding the Center,* 75–84.

55. Wiget, too, shows in his analysis of Helen Sequaptewa's Hopi Coyote story that "what the story is—an artistic creation that both expresses and defines a genre—is formally only available in performance" (317). For Wiget, videotapes of storytelling constitute the best primary texts. See Wiget's "Telling the Tale: A Performance Analysis of a Hopi Coyote Story," in *Recovering the Word,* ed. Krupat and Swann, 297–336.

56. Basso's study of the Western Apache, *Wisdom Sits in Places,* confirms the importance of geographical names to the articulation of a worldview in the native Southwest, and suggests that strangers need to learn an unfamiliar landscape, just as they would an unfamiliar language, if they hope to gain access to a native point of view.

57. Parsons, *Tewa Tales,* 296.

58. Another transcription of a Hopi Coyote tale by a native, bilingual story-teller also presents the exchange between Coyote and, in this case, Cicada Woman, as similarly formal, as if to convey that they really are strangers, and perhaps to suggest a certain wariness between them. Out hunting, Coyote hears the sobs of a cicada mourning for the loss of her children, recently eaten by Sparrow Hawk. The translation from the Hopi reads, "Coyote greeted her. 'Is that you around here? You are really singing a beautiful song,' she complimented Cicada." When Cicada protests that she is not singing but crying, Coyote persists: "Still, your chanting is very pleasant. Why don't you teach me that tune?" (107). Malotki and Lomatuway'ma, eds., *Hopi Coyote Tales.*

59. Gish, *Beyond Bounds,* 5.

60. Scribner to Lummis, 23 April 1891, Charles Fletcher Lummis Papers, MS 39, Special Collections, University of Arizona Library.

61. Lummis to Ellsworth, 15 July 1909, Charles Fletcher Lummis Papers, MS 39, Special Collections, University of Arizona Library.

62. Zolbrod, *Reading the Voice,* 64.

63. Parker distinguishes between particular translation practices, which in the case of Hymes and Tedlock "has led to exceptionally good translations" (141) and the canonical value recently accorded to such translations. Since "every storytelling, written, audiotaped, videotaped, watched live, or performed by ourselves, is always already mediated" (162), it is a mistake to privilege a single approach to translation. See Parker, "Text, Lines, and Videotape."

64. The multiple versions of this story anticipate the translation strategies of Boas, who frequently juxtaposed interlinear and "free" story texts in his ethnographies. Lummis believed that the technique had "never been done in any popular book." Lummis to Ellsworth, 8 April 1910, Charles Fletcher Lummis Papers, MS 39, Special Collections, University of Arizona Library.

65. Venuti, 473.

66. Welsh, "Lummis and Ethnography," in *Charles F. Lummis,* ed. Moneta, 37.

67. Quoted in Fiske and Lummis, *Charles F. Lummis: The Man and His West,* 167.

68. Lummis, Introduction to his *Spanish Songs of Old California.*

69. Lummis, "New Mexican Folk Songs," 720.

70. Koegel, "Hispanic Music in Nineteenth-Century California."

71. Like Lummis, Farwell conceived of the recovery of indigenous music as the proper development of the nation's resources, "both racial and territorial." Whereas the ethnologist has "found another world" in the "subjective life of the Indian," according to Farwell "the opportunity—the privilege—the need—of its ideal representation in terms comprehensible to all, falls to art." Farwell, "Toward American Music."

72. James, *Overland Monthly* (11 May 1923), quoted in Fiske and Lummis, 106.

73. D. Harvey, *The Condition of Postmodernity,* 303–04.

74. Lummis to Abbott, 19 September 1922, MS 1.2.545. Braun Research Library. Courtesy of the Southwest Museum, Los Angeles.

75. Abbott to Lummis, 21 September 1922; Lummis's reply undated, MS 1.2.545, Braun Research Library. Courtesy of the Southwest Museum, Los Angeles.

76. Lummis to Abbott, 2 September 1922, MS 1.2.545, Braun Research Library. Courtesy of the Southwest Museum, Los Angeles.

77. Lummis to Abbott, n.d., MS 1.2.545, Braun Research Library. Courtesy of the Southwest Museum, Los Angeles.

78. Hansen, review of *Mesa, Cañon and Pueblo,* in the *Chicago Daily News,* from a copy collected in Lummis's scrapbook, Braun Research Library. Courtesy of the Southwest Museum, Los Angeles.

79. "Southwest's Charms Conveyed Again in Book by C. F. Lummis," review of *Mesa, Cañon and Pueblo* in the *El Paso Times,* 25 October 1925. Elizabeth Shipley Sargeant's generally positive evaluation for the *New York Herald Tribune* also noted the dulling effects of Lummis's consistently cheerful tone. "Beyond Man's Power to Spoil," *New York Herald Tribune,* 6 December 1925.

80. Review in *El Palacio* 19 (1 October 1925): 155.

Chapter 2. Incomprehensible Brotherhood in Zane Grey's Borderlands

1. Tompkins, *West of Everything,* 37.

2. L. C. Mitchell, *Westerns: Making the Man in Fiction and Film,* 27.

3. For descriptions of Grey's formula, see Ronald, *Zane Grey,* and Kimball, *Ace of Hearts.*

4. White, *"It's Your Misfortune and None of My Own,"* 620.

5. D. Harvey, *The Condition of Postmodernity,* 226.

6. Tatum, "The Problem of the 'Popular' in the New Western History," 164.

7. Jameson objects that the "popular" is an obsolete term: "the 'popular' as such no longer exists, except under very specific and marginalized conditions (internal and external pockets of so-called underdevelopment within the capitalist world system); the commodity production of contemporary or industrial mass culture has nothing whatsoever to do, and nothing in common, with older forms of popular or folk art." In my reading, Tatum's use of the term "popular" is not nostalgic, but corresponds to Jameson's conception of "mass culture." Jameson, "Reification and Utopia in Mass Culture," in his *Signatures of the Visible,* 15.

8. See D. Harvey, *The Condition of Postmodernity,* 16.

9. D. Harvey, *Spaces of Hope,* 173.

10. Anderson, *The Origins of Postmodernity,* 134.

11. Limón, *American Encounters,* 105.

12. Jameson argues that while mythic texts mediate conflict, utopian texts doubly cancel and thus neutralize the initial contradiction. See "Of Islands and Trenches," in his *The Ideologies of Theory,* vol. 2, 75–101.

13. Robbins, *Colony and Empire,* xii.

14. James Steele, *To Mexico by Palace Car* (1886), quoted by Brown in *The Material Unconscious,* 79.

15. D. Harvey, *The Condition of Postmodernity,* 177.

16. Williams, *The Politics of Modernism,* 46; Grey, *The Rainbow Trail,* 152.

17. Bourdieu, "The Market of Symbolic Goods," in his *The Field of Cultural Production*, 127.

18. Bourdieu's literary field is characterized by "the struggle for the monopolistic power to impose the legitimate categories of perception and appreciation"—that is, the battle between dominant figures who seek continuity and those who struggle to achieve "recognition (in both senses) of one's *difference* from other producers." *"The Production of Belief: Contribution to an Economy of Symbolic Goods," in Bourdieu's The Field of Cultural Production,* 106.

19. Bourdieu, "The Market of Symbolic Goods," 128.

20. In *Westerns,* Lee Mitchell locates the "aesthetic habits" of the genre in "its rhythm of landscape and narrative adventure; its concentration of a male body, beaten and convalescent; its investigation of the fragile balance between restraint and violence" (260).

21. Gruber, *Zane Grey,* 77.

22. See ibid., 45–85 (chs. 10–12).

23. Hamilton, *Western and Hard-Boiled Detective Fiction in America,* 55–56.

24. Brodhead, *Cultures of Letters,* 117.

25. Slotkin, *Gunfighter Nation,* 194.

26. One advertisement for International Correspondence Schools pictures a man gazing at three closed doors, one with the title Chief Draughtsman, another with Superintendent of Works, and the third with Office Manager written on it; the caption is "What Position Do You Want?" Other correspondence courses promise to teach subscribers shorthand, law, art, ventriloquism, or real estate, how to run an automobile, or how to curb liquor and drug use. See *Popular Magazine,* 10 June 1915.

27. Three films based on Grey's novels were made in 1918: *Riders of the Purple Sage, The Rainbow Trail,* and *The Border Legion.* Forty-six books were subsequently adapted, many several times and some featuring Grey himself. *The Heritage of the Desert* and *The Rainbow Trail* were adapted for film three times, and *Riders of the Purple Sage* was adapted four times between 1918 and 1996.

28. For a thorough discussion of the periodical market and popular Westerns, see Bold, *Selling the Wild West.*

29. As Bourdieu makes the point in his discussion of Weber's sociology of religion, "Competition for religious power owes its specificity (particularly in relation to the competition that takes place in the political field, for example) to the fact that what is at stake is the *monopoly of the legitimate exercise of the power to modify, in a deep and lasting fashion, the practice and world-view of lay people,* by imposing on and inculcating in them a particular *religious habitus*" (emphasis in original). "Legitimation and Structured Interests in Weber's Sociology of Religion," in *Max Weber, Rationality, and Modernity,* ed. Lash and Whimster, 126.

30. Martínez, *Border People,* xviii.

31. Weber, "The Protestant Sects and the Spirit of Capitalism" (1906), in his *From Max Weber,* 302–22; White, 309.

32. "The surface veneer of capitalism," David Harvey observes in *The Condition of Postmodernity,* "depends on a deep substratum of coerced cooperations and collaborations to ensure a framework for the free market and open trade" (181).

33. Folsom, ed., *The Western,* 173.

34. Arrington and Bitton, *The Mormon Experience,* 15.

35. Arrington, Fox, and May, *Building the City of God,* 203.

36. Ibid., 12.

37. Lamar, *The Far Southwest 1846–1912,* 411.

38. Arrington and Bitton, 178, 177.

39. Brigham Young, from remarks of 6 April 1869, reported in *Deseret News Weekly,* 26 May 1869, quoted in Arrington, Fox, and May, 99.

40. Arrington, Fox, and May, 101.

41. Foster, *Women, Family, and Utopia,* 193.

42. Ibid., 189.

43. In "Zane Grey and the Mormon Question," Handley locates the popularity of *Riders of the Purple Sage* in its "implicit nostalgia for Mormon peculiarity" and, more generally, in its nostalgia for the West's vanishing cultural differences.

44. The importance of access to nature in determining character is evident in Grey's variations on this formula. At times he introduces a cosmopolitan female outsider analogous to the male hero—women like Madeline in *The Light of Western Stars* (1924) or Marian in *The Vanishing American* (1925)—who likewise must be initiated into the West's strenuous demands by a native man in order to reap the land's physical and spiritual rewards and to share its unchecked power.

45. Jameson, "Of Islands and Trenches," 95.

46. Jameson, "Reification and Utopia in Mass Culture," 30.

47. Martínez, *Troublesome Border,* 5.

48. Herzog, *Where North Meets South,* ch. 3.

49. Salas, "Sonora: The Making of a Border Society, 1880–1910," 434.

50. Evans, "Yaquis vs. Yanquis," 364.

51. See Spicer, *The Yaquis,* ch. 5, for discussions of how Porfirian development affected the Yaqui Valley and of Yaqui involvement with revolutionary leaders.

52. Hu-DeHart, *Yaqui Resistance and Survival,* 161–62.

53. Oles, *South of the Border,* 51.

54. Hu-DeHart, 8. She argues that "deportation illustrates some of the contradictions that arose out of the limits of Porfirian growth," specifically the lack of industrialization that might have "absorbed its displaced, dispossessed rural population, such as the Yaquis, into a modern work force" (198).

Chapter 3. A Little History of Southwestern Photography

1. Benjamin, "Little History of Photography," in his *Selected Writings,* vol. 2, 507–30.

2. Lefebvre describes "qualitative spaces" as spaces of leisure opposed to the dominant tendency of assimilation, and names their qualities: "sun, snow, sea." The "qualities of space" he identifies in the Mediterranean also apply to the Southwest: "No sooner does the Mediterranean coast become a space offering leisure activities to industrial Europe than industry arrives there; but nostalgia for towns dedicated to leisure, spread out in the sunshine, continues to haunt the urbanite of the super-industrialized regions. Thus the contradictions become more acute—and the urbanites continue to clamor for a certain 'quality of space.'" Lefebvre, *The Production of Space,* 353.

3. In an essay on the history of photography's obsolescence, Rosalind Krauss calls attention to the difference between Benjamin's position in 1931, the date of "Little History of Photography," and in 1936, the date of his more famous "The Work of Art in the Age of Mechanical Reproduction." "In 1931 Benjamin was still interested in the *history* of photography, which is to say in photography as a medium with its own traditions and its own fate," Krauss explains. By the time of the later essay, photography had already become a theoretical object, a figure for "mechanical reproduction in all its modern, technological guises" that is "both source and symptom of a full-scale demise of this aura across all of culture." See Krauss, "Reinventing the Medium."

4. J. B. Jackson, "Seeing New Mexico," in his *A Sense of Place,* 18, 23.

5. Snyder, "Territorial Photography," 185.

6. Szarkowski, *Photography Until Now,* 117.

7. Naef and Wood, *The Era of Exploration,* 73.

8. Goetzmann and Goetzmann, *The West of the Imagination,* 167. See also Current, *Photography and the Old West.*

9. C. S. Peirce first differentiated icon, index, and symbol in 1940; for discussions of the application of Peirce's theory to photography, see Wright, "Photography: Theories of Realism and Convention," and Pinney, "The Parallel Histories of Anthropology and Photography," both in *Anthropology & Photography 1860–1920,* ed. Edwards.

10. Hambourg, "Carleton Watkins: An Introduction," in *Carleton Watkins: The Art of Perception,* ed. Nickel, 12.

11. Nickel, "An Art of Perception," in *Carleton Watkins,* ed. Nickel, 32.

12. Hambourg, "Carleton Watkins: An Introduction," 16.

13. Hales, *William Henry Jackson and the Transformation of the American Landscape,* 76. Hales provides a thorough analysis of Jackson's extensive career, from his independent beginnings in Omaha in the 1860s to his extensive participation in government surveys in the 1870s (including his 1877 *Descriptive Catalog of Photo-*

graphs of North American Indians); his entrepreneurial efforts, commissions for the Denver and Rio Grande Railroad, and collaborations with newspaper, magazine, and promotional publishers in the 1880s; his views of Eastern states, Mexico, and the 1893 Chicago Fair; and his work with Rand McNally and the Detroit Photographic Company at the turn of the century.

14. Bush and Mitchell, eds., *The Photograph and the American Indian,* xvi.

15. For example, the caption beneath a photograph Lummis took at Taos pueblo and published in *Mesa, Cañon and Pueblo* reads, "Taos—The Ceremonial Runners (one starting forward to smash my camera)" (313). The foreword to the volume boasts of Lummis's ability to overpower his subject: "In the old days, among the Indians, I was largely the 'ice-breaker'—and long, difficult, and sometimes dangerous years I had, to 'break' them to the camera. They believed that the photograph was taken not only of them but *from* them; and that, with enough prints, they would waste away to nothingness" (ix).

16. Many writers have provided thorough accounts and provocative analyses of American expositions. For example, see Hinsley, "The World as Marketplace," in *Exhibiting Cultures,* ed. Karp and Lavine; Rydell, *All the World's a Fair* and *World of Fairs;* Schlereth, *Cultural History and Material Culture;* and Moses, *Wild West Shows and Images of American Indians, 1883–1933.*

17. Others in the "Eight" were George Wharton James, Lummis, Frederick Monsen, and Adam Clark Vroman. Bush and Mitchell, *The Photograph and the American Indian,* xxiii. Many Colorado-based photographers—such as J. L. Clinton, W. G. Chamberlain, W. H. Jackson, and F. A. Nims—also worked in New Mexico at this time. See Coke, "Pictures of New Mexico's Land and People" in his *Photography in New Mexico.*

18. Tydeman's "New Mexico Tourist Images" identifies the "Pueblo-centrism of Indian Detours" as "an attempt to limit the tourist's view of New Mexico's multiculturalism" (205). See *Essays in Twentieth-Century New Mexico History,* ed. DeMark, 199–212. In *Imagining Indians in the Southwest,* Dilworth also discusses this issue at length, arguing in particular that the Hopi were just primitive enough to provide Anglos with an instructive contrast. For this reason, the Hopi Snake Dance and its many representations "became a spectacle that defined and displayed the cultural differences between the 'primitive' Hopis and 'civilized' Americans" (22), thus enacting a domestic orientalism.

19. Although Wittick apparently earned the trust of the Hopi elders, he of course still remained an outsider, and his death ironically fulfilled the prediction of the Snake Priest that, without proper initiation, "Death shall come to you from the fangs of our little brothers." (Wittick had intended the fatal rattlesnake to be a gift for his Hopi friends.) Quoted in Broder, *Shadows on Glass,* 36.

20. Vroman observed that in 1895 about forty people, including artists, journalists, and "ladies," gathered at First Mesa for the dance; by 1897 he esti-

mated the crowd of whites at about two hundred. The Hopis repeatedly tried to limit the intrusion: in 1902 they confined the photographers at Oraibi to one area; after 1910 they restricted photography during the Snake Dance; and in 1971 the community at Mishongnovi barred all whites from viewing the ceremony. Webb and Weinstein, *Dwellers at the Source.*

21. Houlihan discusses this issue when reflecting on museum exhibits of Native American art. He notes that many displays concentrate on the history of turquoise in terms of the jewelry valued by Anglos rather than the substance and mythical values of the stone itself. Houlihan, "The Poetic Image and Native American Art," in *Exhibiting Cultures,* ed. Karp and Lavine, 209.

22. Vroman's collection included works by early explorers like Cabeza de Vaca, Fray Marcos de Niza; Bandelier's papers; illustrated books by George Catlin; journals such as *American Ethnology and Archaeology* and *American Anthropologist; National Geographic;* many accounts of the Hopi snake dance; and Lummis's *The Spanish Pioneers.* A bibliography of the collection has been compiled by Stephen Dow Beckham from research conducted at the Pasadena Public Library.

23. Mahood argues in *Photographer of the Southwest* that Vroman "avoided the sentimental, the contrived and the obvious," choosing instead to work "simply, directly, and sympathetically" (9–10).

24. Webb and Weinstein, 207.

25. Because Monsen could carry the small camera unobtrusively, he claimed to approach his subjects gradually, "to gain their friendship and so coax them by imperceptive degrees to forget to be watchful and conscious in the presence of a stranger." Monsen, "The Destruction of Our Indians."

26. Davidov, *Women's Camera Work,* 119.

27. For the most complete account of Curtis's method, see Lyman, *The Vanishing Race and Other Illusions.*

28. For a discussion of the project's financing and audience, see Goetzmann, "The Arcadian Landscapes of Edward S. Curtis," in *Perpetual Mirage,* ed. Castleberry, 83–91.

29. The "orotone" process involved a special treatment after printing on a glass plate. Curtis apparently "seal[ed] the back of the image with a viscous mixture of powdered gold pigment and banana oil" and promoted the results "as being 'full of life and sparkle as an opal.'" Each 11 x 14 framed print typically cost fifteen dollars. K. F. Davis, ed., *An American Century of Photography,* 25.

30. In a letter dated 26 October 1941, Adams wrote to Beaumont and Nancy, "I photographed the White House Ruins from almost the identical spot and time of the O'Sullivan picture!! Can't wait to see what I got." Adams, *Letters and Images 1916–1984,* 132.

31. Adams, *Examples: The Making of 40 Photographs,* 127–29.

32. O'Keeffe to Strand, 30 June 1917, Paul Strand Collection, Center for Creative Photography, Tucson, AZ.

33. Strand, "What Was '291'?," 5. Typescript © Aperture Foundation Inc. Paul Strand Archive, in Stieglitz Archives, Yale Collection of American Literature, Beinecke Rare Book and Manuscript Library, New Haven, CT

34. Strand, "The Art Motive in Photography," 615.

35. Seligman, "291: A Vision through Photography," in *America and Alfred Stieglitz,* ed. Frank, 121.

36. Strand, "What Was '291'?," 6.

37. For example, Strand told Beaumont Newhall that Stieglitz's "equivalents" were "cloud photographs and nothing else." Unpublished interview with Newhall, 1959, quoted in Rathbone, "Paul Strand: The Land & Its People," 3.

38. Quoted in Hambourg, ed., *Paul Strand Circa 1916,* 25.

39. O'Keeffe to Strand, 12 June 1917, Strand Collection, Center for Creative Photography, Tucson, AZ.

40. Adams, *Photographs of the Southwest,* viii.

41. Strand to Stieglitz, 27 August 1930, © Aperture Foundation Inc., Paul Strand Archive, in Steiglitz Archives, Yale Collection of American Literature, Beinecke Rare Book and Manuscript Library, New Haven, CT.

42. Jay B. Nash (director, Indian Emergency Conservation Work, U.S. Department of the Interior, Office of Indian Affairs, Washington) to Strand, 24 May 1933. Strand Coll., Scrapbook 2, Center for Creative Photography, Tucson.

43. Strand to Nash, 31 May 1933, © Aperture Foundation Inc., Paul Strand Archive, in Strand Coll., Center for Creative Photography, Tucson. Strand's reluctance here, however, does follow an earlier disappointment at organizing a project around Native Americans in the Southwest, for in the same letter he refers to an application he had made to the Heye Museum to photograph and film Indians. "[N]othing happened because of 'lack of funds,'" he reported to Nash.

44. Strand to Stieglitz, 20 September 1926, © Aperture Foundation, Inc., Paul Strand Archive, in Stieglitz Archives, Yale Collection of American Literature, Beinecke Rare Book and Manuscript Library, New Haven, CT.

45. Strand to Stieglitz, 13 September 1926, © Aperture Foundation, Inc., Paul Strand Archive, in Stieglitz Archives, Yale Collection of American Literature, Beinecke Rare Book and Manucript Library, New Haven, CT.

46. Adams to Stieglitz, 21 September 1937, in Adams, *Letters and Images,* 98.

47. Strand to Stieglitz, 22 August 1931, © Aperture Foundation, Inc., Paul Strand Archive, in Stieglitz Archives, Yale Collection of American Literature, Beinecke Rare Book and Manuscript Library, New Haven, CT.

48. Jameson, "Transformations of the Image," in his *The Cultural Turn,* 101.

49. T. S. Eliot, "East Coker" 1–4, the second of "Four Quartets," in his *The Complete Poems and Plays 1909–1950,* 123.

50. Quoted by Krauss, 293.

51. McMurtry, "Inventing the West," 24.

52. Appadurai, *Modernity at Large,* 4.

53. Harris, *Red White Blue and God Bless You,* 12.

54. J. B. Jackson, *Discovering the Vernacular Landscape,* 148.

55. J. B. Jackson, "Roads Belong in the Landscape," in his *A Sense of Place,* 190.

Chapter 4. Unconsummated Intimacies in Mary Austin's Southwest

1. Pearce, *Mary Hunter Austin,* 101.

2. Jameson, "Reification and Utopia in Mass Culture," in his *Signatures of the Visible,* 25–26.

3. Austin to Eve Douglas, 27 August 1903, Charles Fletcher Lummis Papers, MS 297, Special Collections, University of Arizona Library.

4. For a complete account of Austin's early periodical career, which I have summarized here, see Langlois, "A Fresh Voice from the West."

5. Lummis to Austin, 24 November 1904, in Pearce, ed., *Literary America, 1903–1934: The Mary Austin Letters,* 19.

6. Later Lummis criticized Austin's activism in New Mexico and her treatment of the Southwest in *The Land of Journey's Ending* (1924)—surely anxious responses to Austin's infringement on his own authority in the region. See Stineman, *Mary Austin: Song of a Maverick,* 63–67.

7. Austin, "Regionalism in American Fiction" (1932), in *Beyond Borders: The Selected Essays of Mary Austin,* 131.

8. *Literary America,* 16–17.

9. Langlois, 29.

10. Perry, "The Short Story," 246.

11. See, for example, Reed, "The Desert."

12. Turner, "The Problem of the West" and "Contributions of the West to American Democracy"; Jordan, "California and Californians."

13. Bashford, "The Literary Development of the Pacific Coast," 4.

14. Monroe, "Arizona," 780–81.

15. In "The Forests of Yosemite Park," Muir recounted Emerson's 1871 visit to the famed Mariposa grove; unfortunately, Muir was unable to persuade Emerson's companions to relinquish their custodianship for one night so that Muir could take him camping in the grove. Muir pronounced the failed expedition a "sad commentary on culture and the glorious transcendentalism" (506).

16. Muir, "The Wild Parks and Forest Reservations of the West," 15.

17. Fox, *The American Conservation Movement,* 116–17.

18. A journalist for the *Brooklyn Eagle* compared the two naturalists in terms of their affective claims to different parts of the Sierra Mountains: "What John Muir has done for the Western slopes of the Sierras, Austin does in a more tender and intimate way for the eastern slopes." Quoted in Riley, " 'Wimmin Is Everywhere,' " 15.

19. Trilling, *Sincerity and Authenticity,* 2, 5.

20. Muir, *My First Summer in the Sierra,* 21, 132, 110.

21. Fetterley and Pryse point out in *American Women Regionalists* that Austin "tak[es] Seyavi as her model and mirror. . . . Like her regionalist predecessors, Austin explored the meaning of women's lives—both Indian and white women—in her writing; she locates in their lives the source of creative power" (566).

22. Stineman, 178.

23. D. Harvey, *The Condition of Postmodernity,* 11.

24. Hegeman, *Patterns for America,* 26–27.

25. Rudnick, *Utopian Vistas,* 24.

26. Taos and Santa Fe were comparable to the artists' colonies at Woodstock, New York; Provincetown, Gloucester, and Cape Cod, Massachusetts; New Hope, Pennsylvania; and Carmel and Monterey, California, all of which encouraged the pursuit of indigenous American subjects. See Eldredge, "The Faraway Nearby."

27. Luhan always wanted to know "the Heads of Things, Heads of Movements, Heads of Newspapers, Heads of all kinds of groups of people"—she was a "Species of Head Hunter, in fact." Luhan, *Intimate Memories: Movers and Shakers,* quoted in Crunden, *American Salons,* 387.

28. Austin, on the other hand, could not make sense of New York. In "the web of city life, the cross-ties and interweavings which brought all class into coalition," she could discern only disorganized "whorls of social contact and activity" (Crunden, 352). Her experience in Manhattan between 1910 and 1917 also required that she confront the issue of race as she did not in the Southwest. She recounts with pride her divided response at meeting James Weldon Johnson and his wife. First they seemed partly white to her, and attractive; then she noticed his black hand against a white dinner plate; finally, her inner voice denied seeing any difference in the colors of their skin. Just as when she walked in the streets of Harlem, first fearing the approach of black men walking toward her with a "jungle stride" and then ceasing to see the blackness, or when she attended a dinner for W. E. B. DuBois and, sitting between Walter Hampden and Countee Cullen, kept "not seeing their blackness," on this occasion Austin's changing perception leads her to conclude that one learns to see racial difference—and that one can choose not to see it. However, these experiences do not prevent her from

denouncing the excessive influence of urban, Jewish critics like Waldo Frank on American literary life. See Austin, *Earth Horizon,* and "New York: Dictator of American Criticism."

29. Luhan, *Edge of Taos Desert,* 298.

30. Waters, *Masked Gods,* 131.

31. A few weeks later, Maurice appealed to her to come and "Save the Indians, the art—culture—reveal it to the world!" He compared the possibility to "That which . . . others are doing for the Negroes" and felt that "there is somehow a strange relationship between yourself and the Indians." Rudnick, Mabel Dodge Luhan, 142.

32. Luhan, *Edge of Taos Desert,* 298, 314.

33. Luhan to Austin, December 1922, in *Literary America,* 172–73. Luhan insisted that the publicity surrounding the bill was "invaluable," and continued in the letter, "That it is began [*sic*] in politics does not prevent its being channelled into aesthetics. Please get busy and write—write. . . . Don't you *want* to write about indians? Any magazine will publish things about them now."

34. Lawrence, *D. H. Lawrence and New Mexico,* 5–6. In many respects Luhan was disappointed: Lawrence referred to her as a "culture carrier"; Frieda Lawrence refused to allow Luhan to collaborate with her husband on a novel; and Lawrence could never quite commit himself to New Mexico. Luhan wrote to Austin, "My dear! D. H. Lawrence turns out to be completely disconcerted by the indians! He got all his ideas about them from reading Fenimore Cooper one winter. He says its all wrong! He is quite put out about it!" Luhan to Austin, 28 November 1922, Mary Austin Papers, Huntington Library, San Marino, CA.

35. Lawrence, "New Mexico," in *D. H. Lawrence and New Mexico,* 96.

36. Lawrence, letter to Harriet Monroe, in *D. H. Lawrence and New Mexico,* 9.

37. Lawrence, *St. Mawr,* in *The Later D. H. Lawrence,* 152–53.

38. Rampersad, *The Life of Langston Hughes, Vol I: 1902–1941,* 121.

39. La Farge, *Yellow Sun, Bright Sky,* 28.

40. Rudnick, *Mabel Dodge Luhan,* 42.

41. See Babcock and Parezo, eds., *Daughters of the Desert,* ch. 2. The authors show that "both as an alternative to masculine, industrial civilization and as an exotic but safe 'laboratory' for the young science of anthropology, the Southwest became an important place for women" (7)—notably, Matilda Coxe Stevenson, Elsie Clews Parsons, Ruth Bunzel, Gladys Reichard, Frances Densmore, and Natalie Curtis Burlin.

42. Boas, "The Aims of Ethnology," in *A Franz Boas Reader,* 71.

43. Boas, "The Limitations of the Comparative Method of Anthropology," *Science* 4 (1896): 903–04, quoted by Stocking in his *Race, Culture and Evolution,* 211.

44. Boas, *The Mind of Primitive Man,* 149.

45. For an analysis of the congruence of cultural relativism and feminism in the Southwest, see Jacobs, *Engendered Encounters,* ch. 3.

46. Stocking, "Ideas and Institutions in American Anthropology," in his *The Ethnographer's Magic,* 162. According to Stocking, Ruth Benedict's *Patterns of Culture* (1934) marked the culmination of this romanticism.

47. Stocking, "Anthropology as *Kulturkampf,*" in his *The Ethnographer's Magic,* 97.

48. See Hoxie, *A Final Promise,* especially ch. 4.

49. Stocking, "Ideas and Institutions in American Anthropology," 160.

50. Edited by Parsons and introduced by Kroeber, *American Indian Life* claimed to weave facts into narrative in the method of a historical novel, inventing nothing and emphasizing the history rather than the romance.

51. Significantly, Krupat distinguishes these texts from earlier autobiographies by Indians, such as Charles Eastman's *Indian Boyhood* (1902), which required the native author to have an Anglo-European education—and thus to be already alienated from his or her traditional culture. Krupat, introduction to *Native American Autobiography: An Anthology.*

52. Sapir, foreword to *Son of Old Man Hat: A Navaho Autobiography Recorded by Walter Dyk,* vi.

53. For an overview of collaborative autobiographies and a thorough analysis of their methodological difficulties, see Kluckhohn, "The Personal Document in Anthropological Science."

54. Boas, "Recent Anthropology II."

55. Burlin, *The Indians' Book,* xxi; and Walton, *Dawn Boy,* viii–ix.

56. Castro, *Interpreting the Indian,* 7–8.

57. For discussions of the modernist context for the translation of Native American materials, see Carr, *Inventing the American Primitive;* Rudnick, "Re-Naming the Land: Anglo Expatriate Women in the Southwest," in *The Desert Is No Lady,* ed. Norwood and Monk, 10–26; and Ruppert, "Discovering America: Mary Austin and Imagism," in *Studies in American Indian Literature,* ed. Allen, 243–58.

58. Austin, *The American Rhythm,* 2d ed., 64.

59. Bierhorst, "Incorporating the Native Voice: A Look Back from 1990," in *On the Translation of Native American Literatures,* ed. Swann, 60.

60. "Praising the impeccably crafted art of Harlem's great song-and-dance man Bill ('Bojangles') Robinson, in *The Nation* [Austin] remarked that 'the eye filmed and covered by 5,000 years of absorbed culture' is cleared by the 'rhythm' of Robinson's flying feet. In her view, Bojangles represented 'the great desiderium of modern art, a clean shortcut to areas of enjoyment long closed to us by the accumulated rubbish of the culture route.'" Douglas, *Terrible Honesty,* 93.

61. Austin, "Non-English Writings II: Aboriginal," 611.

62. Cushing, "The Arrow," 310.

63. Krupat, *Ethnocriticism,* 194.

64. Eliot, "The Waste Land," lines 394–95, 358, in *The Complete Poems and Plays, 1909–1950,* 48–49.

65. See, for example, Hymes, "Discovering Oral Performance and Measured Verse in American Indian Narrative"; and D. Tedlock, *The Spoken Word and the Work of Interpretation.*

66. See Rothenberg, " 'We Explain Nothing, We Believe Nothing,' " in *On the Translation of Native American Literatures,* ed. Swann, 64–79.

67. Krupat, *The Turn to the Native,* 38.

Chapter 5. Willa Cather and the Immeasurable Possession of Air

1. Cather, *Willa Cather in Europe,* 154.

2. Krutch, "Second Best: *The Professor's House,* " repr. in *Willa Cather and Her Critics,* ed. Schroeter, 55.

3. Cather, *Willa Cather on Writing,* 41–42.

4. Trilling, "Willa Cather," repr. in Schroeter, 153, 155.

5. Acocella, "Cather and the Academy," 71. See also Acocella's more expansive treatment in her *Willa Cather and the Politics of Criticism.*

6. J. B. Jackson, *Discovering the Vernacular Landscape,* 3, 8.

7. Cather, "The Enchanted Bluff," in *Willa Cather's Collected Short Fiction,* ed. Faulkner, 75, 77.

8. O'Brien, *Willa Cather: The Emerging Voice,* 406.

9. Cather, "My First Novels [There Were Two]," in *Willa Cather on Writing,* 92.

10. Lee, *Willa Cather: Double Lives,* 89.

11. Cather, "Whitman," *Nebraska State Journal* (19 January 1896): 9, repr. in her *The Kingdom of Art,* 351–53.

12. Slote, introduction to Cather, *April Twilights* (1903), xiv.

13. Sergeant, *Willa Cather: A Memoir,* 126.

14. Ibid., 107.

15. Hawthorne, *The House of the Seven Gables,* in *Nathaniel Hawthorne: Novels,* 351.

16. Hawthorne, *The Marble Faun,* in *Nathaniel Hawthorne: Novels,* 854–55.

17. Jameson, *The Political Unconscious,* 112.

18. deBuys, *Enchantment and Exploitation,* 163.

19. See Harrell, *From Mesa Verde to The Professor's House;* Lewis, *Willa Cather Living,* 101; Sargeant, 122–23; Lee, 88–89; and Lewis, 142, respectively.

20. Fryer, *Felicitous Space,* 313, 318.

21. W. James, *The Principles of Psychology,* 244.

22. Stevens, *Collected Poems,* 131.

23. Stevens, *Opus Posthumous,* 137–38.

24. Lefebvre, *The Production of Space,* 85.

25. Urgo, *Willa Cather and the Myth of American Migration,* 183.

Epilogue

1. Williams, "Region and Class in the Novel," in his *Writing in Society,* 238.

2. Wallerstein, "What Can One Mean by Southern Culture" and "The Modern World-System as a Civilization," in his *Geopolitics and Geoculture.*

Bibliography

Manuscript Sources

Charles Fletcher Lummis Papers. Special Collections, University of Arizona Library, Tucson.

Charles Fletcher Lummis Papers. Braun Research Library, Southwest Museum, Los Angeles.

Mary Austin Papers. Huntington Library, San Marino, CA.

Strand Collection. Center for Creative Photography, Tucson, AZ.

Stieglitz Archives. Yale Collection of American Literature, Beinecke Rare Book and Manuscript Library, New Haven, CT.

Vroman, Adam Clark. Diary, Summer 1895. Huntington Library, San Marino, CA.

Photography Sources

Adam Clark Vroman Collection. Pasadena Public Library, Pasadena, CA.

Center for Southwest Research. University of New Mexico, Albuquerque.

Center for Western Americana. Beinecke Rare Book and Manuscript Library, Yale University, New Haven, CT.

Charles Fletcher Lummis Collection. University of Arizona Library, Tucson.

Photography Archives. Museum of New Mexico, Santa Fe.

Seaver Center for Western History Research. Los Angeles County Museum of Natural History, Los Angeles.

Strand Collection. Center for Creative Photography, University of Arizona, Tucson.

Yale Collection of Western Americana. Beinecke Rare Book and Manuscript Library, New Haven, CT.

Published Sources

Acocella, Joan. "Cather and the Academy." *New Yorker,* 27 November 1995, 65–71.

——. *Willa Cather and the Politics of Criticism.* Lincoln: University of Nebraska Press, 2000.

Adams, Ansel. *The American Wilderness*. Ed. Andrea G. Stillman. Boston: Little, Brown, 1990.

——. *Examples: The Making of 40 Photographs*. Boston: Little, Brown, 1983.

——. *Letters and Images, 1916–1984*. Ed. Mary Street Alinder and Andrea Grey Stillman. Boston: Little, Brown, 1988.

——. *Photographs of the Southwest*. Boston: Little, Brown, and New York Graphic Society, 1976.

Aiken, Susan Hardy, Ann Brigham, Sallie A. Marston, and Penny Waterstone, eds. *Making Worlds: Gender, Metaphor, Materiality*. Tucson: University of Arizona Press, 1998.

Allen, Paula Gunn. *Off the Reservation: Reflections on Boundary-Busting, Border-Crossing, Loose Canons*. Boston: Beacon Press, 1998.

——. *The Sacred Hoop: Recovering the Feminine in American Indian Traditions*. Boston: Beacon Press, 1992.

——, ed. *Studies in American Indian Literature*. New York: Modern Language Association, 1983.

Anderson, Eric. *American Indian Literature and the Southwest: Contexts and Dispositions*. Austin: University of Texas Press, 1999.

Anderson, Perry. *The Origins of Postmodernity*. New York: Verso, 1998.

Anzaldúa, Gloria. *Borderlands / La Frontera*. San Francisco: Spinsters / Aunt Lute, 1987.

Apostol, Jane. *El Alisal: Where History Lingers*. Los Angeles: Historical Society of Southern California, 1994.

Appadurai, Arjun. *Modernity at Large: The Cultural Dimensions of Globalization*. Minneapolis: University of Minnesota Press, 1996.

Arrington, Leonard J., and Davis Bitton. *The Mormon Experience: A History of the Latter-Day Saints*. 2d ed. Urbana: University of Illinois Press, 1992.

Arrington, Leonard J., Feramorz Y. Fox, and Dean L. May. *Building the City of God: Community and Cooperation among the Mormons*. 2d ed. Urbana: University of Illinois Press, 1992.

Austin, Mary. *The American Rhythm*. 2d ed., 1930. Repr. New York: Cooper Square Publishers, 1970.

——. *Beyond Borders: The Selected Essays of Mary Austin*. Ed. Reuben J. Ellis. Carbondale: Southern Illinois University Press, 1996.

——. *Earth Horizon*. Boston: Houghton Mifflin, 1932.

——. *The Land of Little Rain*. 1903. Repr. Albuquerque: University of New Mexico Press, 1974.

——. *Literary America, 1903–1934: The Mary Austin Letters*. Ed. T. M. Pearce. Westport, CT: Greenwood Press, 1979.

——. "New York: Dictator of American Criticism." *Nation* (July 1920): 129–30.

——. "Non-English Writings II: Aboriginal." In *The Cambridge History of American Literature*. Vol. 4. New York: Macmillan, 1931. 610–34.

——. *Starry Adventure*. Boston: Houghton Mifflin, 1931.

——. *Stories from the Country of Lost Borders*. Ed. Marjorie Pryse. New Brunswick, NJ: Rutgers University Press, 1987.

Babbitt, Bruce, ed. *Grand Canyon: An Anthology*. Flagstaff, AZ: Northland Press, 1978.

Babcock, Barbara. "Pueblo Cultural Bodies." *Journal of American Folklore* 107, no. 423 (1994): 40–54.

Babcock, Barbara, and Nancy J. Parezo, eds. *Daughters of the Desert: Women Anthropologists and the Native American Southwest, 1880–1980*. Albuquerque: University of New Mexico Press, 1988.

Babcock, Barbara, and Marta Weigle, eds. *The Great Southwest of the Fred Harvey Company and the Santa Fe Railway*. Tucson: University of Arizona Press, 1996.

Babcock, Barbara, and Joseph Wilder, eds. "Inventing the Southwest: Region as Commodity." *Journal of the Southwest* 32, no. 4 (1990). Special issue.

Bancroft, H. H. *Arizona and New Mexico, 1530–1888*. San Francisco: History Company, 1889.

——. *The Book of the Fair: Columbian Exposition, 1893*. 4 vols. Chicago: Bancroft, 1893.

Bandelier, Adolph. *The Delight-Makers*. 1890. Repr. New York: Dodd, Mead, 1942.

——. *The Southwestern Journals*. 4 vols. 1884. Repr. ed. Charles H. Lange and Carroll L. Riley. Albuquerque: University of New Mexico Press, 1966–84.

Barclay, Donald A., James H. Maguire, and Peter Wild, eds. *Into the Wilderness Dream: Exploration Narrative of the American West, 1500–1805*. Salt Lake City: University of Utah Press, 1994.

Bashford, Herbert. "The Literary Development of the Pacific Coast." *Atlantic Monthly* 92 (July 1903): 1–9.

Basso, Keith. *Wisdom Sits in Places: Landscape and Language among the Western Apache*. Albuquerque: University of New Mexico Press, 1996.

"The Beginnings of Literature." Unsigned review of Charles F. Lummis, *The Man Who Married the Moon*. *The Critic*, 9 March 1895.

Benedict, Burton. *Anthropology of World's Fairs: San Francisco's Panama Pacific International Exposition of 1915*. Berkeley: Scholar Press, 1983.

Benjamin, Walter. "The Task of the Translator." Trans. Harry Zohn. In *The Translation Studies Reader*. Ed. Lawrence Venuti. New York: Routledge, 2000. 15–25.

——. *Walter Benjamin: Selected Writings*. Vol. 1: *1913–1926*. Ed. Marcus Bullock and Michael W. Jennings. Cambridge, MA: Belknap Press of Harvard University Press, 1996.

———. *Walter Benjamin: Selected Writings*. Vol. 2: *1927–1934*. Ed. Michael W. Jennings, Howard Eiland, and Gary Smith. Cambridge, MA: Belknap Press of Harvard University Press, 1999.

Berman, Russell. *Everything Solid Melts into Air: The Experience of Modernity*. New York: Penguin Books, 1988.

Bierhorst, John, ed. *Four Masterworks of American Indian Literature*. Tucson: University of Arizona Press, 1974.

Bingham, Edwin R. *Charles F. Lummis: Editor of the Southwest*. 1955. Repr. Westport, CT: Greenwood Press, 1973.

Bloom, Edward A., and Lillian D. Bloom. *Willa Cather's Gift of Sympathy*. Carbondale: Southern Illinois University Press, 1962.

Boas, Franz. *A Franz Boas Reader*. Ed. George W. Stocking Jr. Chicago: University of Chicago Press, 1974.

———. *Keresan Texts*. New York: American Ethnological Society, 1928.

———. *The Mind of Primitive Man*. 1911. Repr. New York: Collier, 1963.

———. *Race, Language and Culture*. New York: Macmillan, 1946.

———. "Recent Anthropology II." *Science* 98 (1943): 334–37.

Bold, Christine. *Selling the Wild West: Popular Western Fiction, 1860 to 1960*. Bloomington: Indiana University Press, 1987.

Bourdieu, Pierre. *The Field of Cultural Production: Essays on Art and Literature*. Ed. Randal Johnson. New York: Columbia University Press, 1993.

———. "Legitimation and Structured Interests in Weber's Sociology of Religion." Trans. Chris Turner. In *Max Weber, Rationality, and Modernity*. Ed. Scott Lash and Sam Whimster. London: Allen and Unwin, 1987. 119–36.

———. *The Rules of Art: Genesis and Structure of the Literary Field*. Trans. Susan Emanuel. Stanford, CA: Stanford University Press, 1995.

Bradshaw, Michael. *Regions and Regionalism in the United States*. Jackson: University Press of Mississippi, 1988.

Briggs, Charles, and Richard Bauman. "'The Foundation of All Future Researches': Franz Boas, George Hunt, Native American Texts, and the Construction of Modernity." *American Quarterly* 51 (1999): 479–528.

Broder, Patricia Janis. *Shadows on Glass: The Indian World of Ben Wittick*. Savage, MD: Rowman & Littlefield, 1990.

Brodhead, Richard. *Cultures of Letters: Scenes of Reading and Writing in Nineteenth-Century America*. Chicago: University of Chicago Press, 1993.

Brown, Bill. *The Material Unconscious: American Amusement, Stephen Crane, and the Economies of Play*. Cambridge, MA: Harvard University Press, 1996.

Buell, Lawrence. *The Environmental Imagination: Thoreau, Nature Writing, and the*

Formation of American Culture. Cambridge, MA: Harvard University Press, 1995.

Burlin, Natalie Curtis. *The Indians' Book*. New York: Harper and Brothers, 1907.

Bush, Alfred L., and Lee Clark Mitchell, eds. *The Photograph and the American Indian*. Princeton, NJ: Princeton University Press, 1994.

Byrkit, James. "Land, Sky, People: The Southwest Defined." *Journal of the Southwest* 34, no. 3 (1992): 257–387.

Calderón, Héctor, and Saldívar, José, eds. *Criticism in the Borderlands: Studies in Chicano Literature, Culture, and Ideology*. Durham, NC: Duke University Press, 1991.

Calvin, Ross. *Sky Determines: An Interpretation of the Southwest*. 1948. Repr. Albuquerque: University of New Mexico Press, 1965.

Carlin, Deborah. *Cather, Canon, and the Politics of Reading*. Amherst: University of Massachusetts Press, 1992.

Carr, Helen. *Inventing the American Primitive: Politics, Gender and the Representations of Native American Literary Traditions, 1789–1936*. New York: New York University Press, 1996.

Castleberry, May, ed. *Perpetual Mirage: Photographic Narratives of the Desert West*. New York: Whitney Museum of American Art and Harry N. Abrams, 1996.

Castro, Michael. *Interpreting the Indian: Twentieth-Century Poets and the Native American*. Albuquerque: University of New Mexico Press, 1983.

Cather, Willa. *April Twilights*. Revised edition. Lincoln: University of Nebraska Press, 1968.

——. *Death Comes for the Archbishop*. 1927. Repr. New York: Vintage Books, 1990.

——. *The Kingdom of Art*. Ed. Bernice Slote. Lincoln: University of Nebraska Press, 1967.

——. *My Ántonia*. 1918. Repr. Boston: Houghton Mifflin, 1988.

——. *O Pioneers!* 1913. Repr. Boston: Houghton Mifflin, 1988.

——. *The Professor's House*. 1925. Repr. New York: Vintage Books, 1990.

——. *The Song of the Lark*. 1915. Repr. Boston: Houghton Mifflin, 1988.

——. *Willa Cather in Europe*. Repr. New York: Alfred A. Knopf, 1956.

——. *Willa Cather on Writing*. Repr. New York: Alfred A. Knopf, 1962.

——. *Willa Cather's Collected Short Fiction*. Ed. Virginia Faulkner. Lincoln: University of Nebraska Press, 1970.

Cawelti, John G. *Adventure, Mystery, and Romance: Formula Stories as Art and Popular Culture*. Chicago: University of Chicago Press, 1976.

Cheyfitz, Eric. *The Poetics of Imperialism: Translation and Colonization from The Tempest to Tarzan*. Expanded edition. Philadelphia: University of Pennsylvania Press, 1997.

Clark, T. J. *Farewell to an Idea: Episodes from a History of Modernism*. New Haven, CT: Yale University Press, 1999.

Clemens, William M. *Native American Verbal Art*. Tucson: University of Arizona Press, 1996.

Clifford, James. *The Predicament of Culture: Twentieth-Century Ethnography, Literature, and Art*. Cambridge, MA: Harvard University Press, 1988.

——. *Routes: Travel and Translation in the Late Twentieth Century*. Cambridge, MA: Harvard University Press, 1997.

Clifford, James, and George Marcus, eds. *Writing Culture: The Poetics and Politics of Ethnography*. Berkeley: University of California Press, 1986.

Cohen, Michael P. *The Pathless Way: John Muir and the American Wilderness*. Madison: University of Wisconsin Press, 1984.

Coke, Van Deren. *Photography in New Mexico: From the Daguerrotype to the Present*. Albuquerque: University of New Mexico Press, 1979.

——. *Taos and Santa Fe: The Artist's Environment, 1882–1942*. Albuquerque: University of New Mexico Press, 1963.

Comer, Krista. *Landscapes of the New West*. Chapel Hill: University of North Carolina Press, 1999.

——. "Literature, Gender Studies, and the New Western History." *Arizona Quarterly* 53, no. 2 (1997): 99–134.

Conn, Steven. *Museums and American Intellectual Life, 1876–1926*. Chicago: University of Chicago Press, 1998.

Cotkin, George. *Reluctant Modernism: American Thought and Culture, 1880–1900*. New York: Twayne, 1992.

Cronon, William, George Miles, and Jay Gitlin, eds. *Under an Open Sky: Rethinking America's Western Past*. New York: W. W. Norton, 1992.

Cronyn, George W., ed. *The Path on the Rainbow: An Anthology of Songs and Chants from the Indians of North America*. New York: Boni and Liveright, 1918.

Crunden, Robert M. *American Salons: Encounters with European Modernism, 1885–1917*. New York: Oxford University Press, 1993.

Current, Karen. *Photography and the Old West*. Fort Worth, TX: Amon Carter Museum of Western Art, 1978.

Curtis, Edward. *The North American Indian*. New York: Johnson Reprint, 1970.

Cushing, Frank. "The Arrow." *American Anthropologist* 8 (1895): 307–49.

——. "My Adventures in Zuñi." *Century Illustrated Magazine* 25 (June 1882, February 1883): 191–207, 500–11; 26 (May 1883): 28–47.

——. *The Nation of the Willows*. Flagstaff, AZ: Northland Press, 1965.

——. *Zuñi Breadstuff*. New York: Museum of the American Indian / Heye Foundation, 1920.

——. *Zuñi Folk Tales*. 1901. Repr. Tucson: University of Arizona Press, 1992.

Dainotto, Roberto Maria. " 'All the Regions Do Smilingly Revolt': The Literature of Place and Region." *Critical Inquiry* 22 (Spring 1996): 486–505.

Darnell, Regina Diebold. "The Development of American Anthropology 1879–1920: From the Bureau of Ethnography to Franz Boas." Ph.D. dissertation, University of Pennsylvania, 1969.

Davidov, Judith Fryer. *Women's Camera Work: Self / Body / Other in American Visual Culture.* Durham, NC: Duke University Press, 1998.

Davidson, Donald. *Still Rebels, Still Yankees, and Other Essays.* Baton Rouge: Louisiana State University Press, 1957.

Davis, Keith F., ed. *An American Century of Photography: From Dry Plate to Digital.* Kansas City, MO: Hallmark Cards and Harry N. Abrams, 1995.

Davis, Mike. *City of Quartz.* New York: Vintage Books, 1992.

Deacon, Delsey. *Elsie Clews Parsons: Inventing Modern Life.* Chicago: University of Chicago Press, 1997.

deBuys, William. *Enchantment and Exploitation: The Life and Hard Times of a New Mexico Mountain Range.* Albuquerque: University of New Mexico Press, 1985.

de Certeau, Michel. *The Practice of Everyday Life.* Berkeley: University of California Press, 1984.

de la Garza, Rodolfo O., and Jesús Velasco. *Bridging the Border: Transforming Mexico-U.S. Relations.* New York: Rowman and Littlefield, 1997.

Deloria, Philip. *Playing Indian.* New Haven, CT: Yale University Press, 1998.

Delpar, Helen. *The Enormous Vogue of Things Mexican: Cultural Relations Between the United States and Mexico, 1920–1935.* Tuscaloosa: University of Alabama Press, 1992.

DeMark, Judith Boyce, ed. *Essays in Twentieth Century New Mexico History.* Albuquerque: University of New Mexico Press, 1994.

Deutsch, Sarah. *No Separate Refuge: Culture, Class, and Gender on the Anglo-Hispanic Frontier in the American Southwest, 1880–1940.* New York: Oxford University Press, 1987.

de Vaca, Álvar Nuñez Cabeza. *Cabeza de Vaca's Adventures in the Unknown Interior of America.* Trans. and ed. Cyclone Covey. Albuquerque: University of New Mexico Press, 1961.

Dilworth, Leah. *Imagining Indians in the Southwest: Persistent Visions of a Primitive Past.* Washington, DC: Smithsonian Institution Press, 1996.

Dippie, Brian W. *The Vanishing American: White Attitudes and U.S. Indian Policy.* Lawrence: University Press of Kansas, 1982.

Dobie, Frank. *Guide to Life and Literature in the Southwest.* Dallas: Southern Methodist University Press, 1952.

Dorman, Robert. *The Revolt of the Provinces: The Regionalist Movement in America, 1920–1945.* Chapel Hill: University of North Carolina Press, 1993.

Douglas, Ann [Wood]. "The Literature of Impoverishment: The Women Local Colorists in America, 1865–1914." *Women's Studies* 1 (1972): 3–40.

——. *Terrible Honesty: Mongrel Manhattan in the 1920s*. New York: Farrar, Straus and Giroux, 1995.

Dyk, Walter. *Son of Old Man Hat: A Navaho Autobiography Recorded by Walter Dyk*. 1938. Repr. Lincoln: University of Nebraska Press, 1967.

Edwards, Elizabeth, ed. *Anthropology and Photography, 1860–1920*. New Haven, CT: Yale University Press, 1992.

Eldredge, Charles. "The Faraway Nearby." In *Art in New Mexico, 1900–1945: Paths to Santa Fe and Taos*. Ed. Charles Eldredge, Julie Schimmel, and William H. Treuttner. Washington, DC: National Museum of American Art and Abbeville Press, 1986. 147–80.

Eliot, T. S. *The Complete Poems and Plays, 1909–1950*. New York: Harcourt Brace Jovanovich, 1971.

Entrikin, J. Nicholas. *The Betweenness of Place: Towards a Geography of Modernity*. Baltimore: Johns Hopkins University Press, 1991.

Etulain, Richard. *Reimagining the Modern American West: A Century of Fiction, History, and Art*. Tucson: University of Arizona Press, 1996.

Evans, Sterling. "Yaquis vs. Yanquis: An Environmental and Historical Comparison of Coping with Aridity in Sonora." *Journal of the Southwest* 40, no. 3 (1998): 363–96.

Evers, Larry, and Felipe S. Molina. *Yaqui Deer Songs*. Tucson: Sun Tracks and University of Arizona Press, 1987.

Faris, James C. *The Nightway: A History and a History of the Documentation of a Navajo Ceremonial*. Albuquerque: University of New Mexico Press, 1990.

Farwell, Arthur. "Toward American Music." *Out West* 20 (May 1904): 456–57.

Fender, Stephen. *Plotting the Golden West: American Literature and the Rhetoric of the California Trail*. New York: Cambridge University Press, 1981.

Fetterley, Judith, and Marjorie Pryse, eds. *American Women Regionalists, 1850–1910: A Norton Anthology*. New York: W. W. Norton, 1992.

Fewkes, J. Walter. "A Suggestion as to the Meaning of the Moki Snake Dance." *Journal of American Folklore* 4 (April–June 1891): 129–38.

Fiske, Turbesé Lummis, and Keith Lummis. *Charles F. Lummis: The Man and His West*. Norman: University of Oklahoma Press, 1975.

Fitzgerald, F. Scott. *The Great Gatsby*. 1925. Repr. New York: Macmillan, 1980.

Fleming, Robert E. *Charles F. Lummis*. Boise, ID: Boise State University Press, 1981.

Folsom, James K., ed. *The Western: A Collection of Critical Essays*. Englewood Cliffs, NJ: Prentice-Hall, 1979.

Fontana, Bernard. "Church and Crown." *Journal of the Southwest* 32, no. 4 (1990): 451–61.

Foster, Lawrence. *Women, Family, and Utopia: Communal Experiments of the Shakers, the Oneida Community, and the Mormons*. Syracuse, N.Y.: Syracuse University Press, 1991.

Fox, Stephen. *The American Conservation Movement: John Muir and His Legacy*. Madison: University of Wisconsin Press, 1985.

Fraenkel, Jeffrey, ed. *Carleton E. Watkins: Photographs, 1861–1874*. San Francisco: Fraenkel Gallery and Bedford Arts, 1989.

Francaviglia, Richard, and David Narrett, eds. *Essays on the Changing Images of the Southwest*. College Station: Texas A&M University Press, 1994.

Frank, Waldo, ed. *America and Alfred Stieglitz*. Garden City, NY: Doubleday, Doran, 1934.

Friedman, Thomas. *The Lexus and the Olive Tree*. New York: Farrar, Straus and Giroux, 1999.

Fryer, Judith. *Felicitous Space*. Chapel Hill: University of North Carolina Press, 1986.

Gaard, Greta, and Patrick D. Murphy, eds. *Ecofeminist Literary Criticism: Theory, Interpretation, Pedagogy*. Chicago: University of Illinois Press, 1998.

Gaede, Marnie, ed. *Camera, Spade, and Pen: An Inside View of Southwestern Archaeology*. Tucson: University of Arizona Press, 1980.

Geertz, Clifford. *After the Fact*. Cambridge, MA: Harvard University Press, 1995.

——. *Available Light*. Princeton, NJ: Princeton University Press, 2000.

——. *The Interpretation of Cultures*. New York: Basic Books, 1971.

——. *Local Knowledge: Further Essays in Interpretive Anthropology*. New York: Basic Books, 1983.

——. *Works and Lives: The Anthropologist as Author*. Stanford, CA: Stanford University Press, 1988.

Gilman, Benjamin Ives. *Hopi Songs. Journal of American Ethnology and Archaeology*, vol. 5 (1908). Repr. New York: AMS Press, 1977.

Gilpin, Laura. *The Pueblos: A Camera Chronicle*. New York: Hastings House, 1941.

Gish, Robert. *Beyond Bounds: Cross-Cultural Essays on Anglo, American Indian & Chicano Literature*. Albuquerque: University of New Mexico Press, 1996.

Goddard, Pliny Earle. *Navajo Texts*. Anthropological Papers 24. New York: American Museum of Natural History, 1933.

Goetzmann, William H. *Exploration and Empire: The Explorer and Scientist in the Winning of the American West*. New York: Alfred A. Knopf, 1966.

Goetzmann, William H., and William N. Goetzmann. *The West of the Imagination*. New York: W. W. Norton, 1986.

Gonzales-Berry, Erlinda, ed. *Pasó por Aquí: Critical Essays on the New Mexican Literary Tradition, 1542–1988*. Albuquerque: University of New Mexico Press, 1989.

Graulich, Melody, and Elizabeth Klimasmith, eds. *Exploring Lost Borders: Critical Essays on Mary Austin*. Reno: University of Nevada Press, 1999.

Green, Jesse, ed. *Cushing at Zuni: The Correspondence and Journals of Frank Hamilton Cushing, 1879–1884*. Albuquerque: University of New Mexico Press, 1990.

Green, Jonathan, ed. *Camera Work: A Critical Anthology*. New York: Aperture, 1973.

Greenblatt, Stephen. *Marvelous Possessions: The Wonder of the New World*. Chicago: University of Chicago Press, 1991.

Greenough, Sarah. *Paul Strand: An American Vision*. Washington, DC: Aperture Foundation and the National Gallery of Art, 1990.

Grey, Zane. *Desert Gold*. 1913. Repr. Roslyn, NY: Walter J. Black, 1941.

——. *The Heritage of the Desert*. 1910. Repr. New York: Grosset & Dunlap, 1916.

——. *The Light of Western Stars*. New York: Harper and Brothers, 1924.

——. *The Rainbow Trail*. 1915. Repr. New York: Pocket Books, 1961.

——. *Riders of the Purple Sage*. 1912. Repr. New York: Penguin Books, 1990.

——. *The Vanishing American*. New York: Harper and Brothers, 1925.

Griffith, James. *A Shared Space: Folklife in the Arizona-Sonora Borderlands*. Logan: Utah State University Press, 1995.

Groth, Paul, and Todd Bressi, eds. *Understanding Ordinary Landscapes*. New Haven, CT: Yale University Press, 1997.

Gruber, Frank. *Zane Grey*. New York: World Publishing Company, 1970.

Haile, Father Berard. *Origin Legend of the Navaho Enemy Way: Text and Translation*. New Haven, CT: Yale University Press, 1938.

——. *Origin Legend of the Navajo Flintway: Text and Translation*. Chicago: University of Chicago Press, 1943.

Hales, Peter B. *William Henry Jackson and the Transformation of the American Landscape*. Philadelphia: Temple University Press, 1988.

Halpern, Katherine Spencer, and Susan Brown McGreevy, eds. *Washington Matthews: Studies in Navajo Culture, 1880–1894*. Albuquerque: University of New Mexico Press, 1997.

Hambourg, Maria Morris, ed. *Paul Strand Circa 1916*. New York: Metropolitan Museum of Art and Harry N. Abrams, 1998.

——. *The Waking Dream: Photography's First Century*. New York: Harry N. Abrams, 1993.

Hamilton, Cynthia. *Western and Hard-Boiled Detective Fiction in America: From High Noon to Midnight*. New York: Macmillan, 1987.

Handley, William. "Zane Grey and the Mormon Question." *Arizona Quarterly* 54, no. 1 (2001): 1–33.

Harrell, David. *From Mesa Verde to The Professor's House*. Albuquerque: University of New Mexico Press, 1992.

Harris, Alex. *Red White Blue and God Bless You: A Portrait of Northern New Mexico.* Albuquerque: University of New Mexico Press, 1992.

Harvey, David. *The Condition of Postmodernity.* Cambridge, MA: Blackwell, 1990.

——. *Spaces of Hope.* Berkeley: University of California Press, 2000.

Harvey, Fred. *The Great Southwest Along the Santa Fe.* Kansas City, MO: Fred Harvey, 1921.

Hawthorne, Nathaniel. *Nathaniel Hawthorne: Novels.* Ed. Millicent Bell. New York: Library of America, 1983.

Hegeman, Susan. *Patterns for America: Modernism and the Concept of Culture.* Princeton, NJ: Princeton University Press, 1999.

Henderson, Alice Corbin. *Red Earth.* Chicago: Ralph Seymour, 1920.

——, ed. *The Turquoise Trail: An Anthology of New Mexican Poetry.* Boston: Houghton Mifflin, 1928.

Herzog, Lawrence A. *Where North Meets South: Cities, Space, and Politics on the U.S.–Mexico Border.* Austin: Center for Mexican American Studies and University of Texas Press, 1990.

Higham, John. *Strangers in the Land: Patterns of American Nativism, 1860–1925.* 2d ed. New Brunswick, NJ: Rutgers University Press, 1988.

Hinsley, Curtis M., Jr. "Authoring Authenticity." *Journal of the Southwest* 32, no. 4 (1990): 463–78.

——. "Ethnographic Charisma and Scientific Routine: Cushing and Fewkes in the American Southwest." In *Observers Observed: Essays on Ethnographic Fieldwork.* Ed. George Stocking Jr. Madison: University of Wisonsin Press, 1983. 53–69.

——. "Life on the Margins: The Ethnographic Poetics of Frank Hamilton Cushing." *Journal of the Southwest* 41, no. 3 (1999): 371–82.

——. Review of *Museums and American Intellectual Life, 1876–1926* by Steven Conn. *Winterthur Portfolio* 34 (Winter 1999): 272–74.

——. *Savages and Scientists: The Smithsonian and the Development of American Anthropology, 1846–1910.* Washington, DC: Smithsonian Institution Press, 1981.

——. "Zunis and Brahmins: Cultural Ambivalence in the Gilded Age." In *Romantic Motives: Essays on Anthropological Sensibility.* Ed. George Stocking Jr. Madison: University of Wisconsin Press, 1989. 169–207.

Hinsley, Curtis M., Jr., and David R. Wilcox, eds. *The Southwest in the American Imagination: The Writings of Sylvester Baxter, 1881–1889.* Tucson: University of Arizona Press, 1996.

Hobsbawm, Eric, and Terence Ranger, eds. *The Invention of Tradition.* New York: Cambridge University Press, 1993.

Hollander, John, ed. *American Poetry: The Nineteenth Century.* Volume 2. New York: Library of America, 1993.

Hollon, W. Eugene. *The Southwest: Old and New.* New York: Alfred A. Knopf, 1961.

Horgan, Paul. *The Heroic Triad: Essays in the Social Energies of Three Southwestern Cultures.* New York: Holt, Rinehart and Winston, 1970.

Houghland, Willard, ed. *Mary Austin: A Memorial.* Santa Fe: Laboratory of Anthropology, 1944.

Houlihan, Patrick T., and Betsy E. Houlihan. *Lummis in the Pueblos.* Flagstaff, AZ: Northland Press, 1986.

Howard, June. "Unraveling Regions, Unsettling Periods: Sarah Orne Jewett and American Literary History." *American Literature* 68 (1996): 365–84.

Howard, Sam, Enrique D. Lamadrid, and Miguel Gandert. *Pilgrimage to Chimayo.* Santa Fe: Museum of New Mexico Press, 1999.

Howlett, Rev. W. J. *Life of the Right Reverend Joseph P. Machebeuf.* 1908. Repr. Denver: Regis College Press, 1987.

Hoxie, Frederick E. *A Final Promise: The Campaign to Assimilate the Indians, 1880–1920.* New York: Cambridge University Press, 1995.

Hu-DeHart, Evelyn. *Yaqui Resistance and Survival: The Struggle for Land and Autonomy, 1821–1910.* Madison: University of Wisconsin Press, 1984.

Hughes, Langston. *The Collected Poems of Langston Hughes.* Ed. Arnold Rampersad. New York: Vintage Classics, 1995.

Hyde, Anne Farrar. *An American Vision: Far Western Landscape and National Culture, 1820–1920.* New York: New York University Press, 1990.

Hymes, Dell. "Discovering Oral Performance and Measured Verse in American Indian Narrative." *New Literary History* 8 (1977): 431–57.

Inness, Sherrie A., and Diana Royer, eds. *Breaking Boundaries: New Perspectives on Women's Regional Writing.* Iowa City: University of Iowa Press, 1997.

Jackson, John Brinckerhoff. *Discovering the Vernacular Landscape.* New Haven, CT: Yale University Press, 1984.

——. *Landscape in Sight.* Ed. Helen Lefkowitz Horowitz. New Haven CT: Yale University Press, 1997.

——. *A Sense of Place, a Sense of Time.* New Haven, CT: Yale University Press, 1994.

Jackson, Peter. *Maps of Meaning.* New York: Routledge, 1999.

Jacobs, Margaret D. *Engendered Encounters: Feminism and Pueblo Cultures, 1879–1934.* Lincoln: University of Nebraska Press, 1999.

James, George Wharton. *New Mexico, the Land of the Delight Makers.* Boston: The Page Company, 1920.

James, Harry C. *Pages from Hopi History.* Tucson: University of Arizona Press, 1974.

James, William. *The Principles of Psychology.* 1890. Repr. Cambridge, MA: Harvard University Press, 1983.

Jameson, Fredric. *The Cultural Turn: Selected Writings on the Postmodern, 1983–1998.* New York: Verso, 1998.

——. *The Ideologies of Theory: Essays, 1971–1986,* Vol. 2. Minneapolis: University of Minnesota Press, 1988.

——. *The Political Unconscious: Narrative as a Socially Symbolic Act.* Ithaca, NY: Cornell University Press, 1981.

——. *Postmodernism or, The Cultural Logic of Late Capitalism.* Durham, NC: Duke University Press, 1991.

——. *Signatures of the Visible.* New York: Routledge, 1992.

Jensen, Merrill, ed. *Regionalism in America.* Madison: University of Wisconsin Press, 1951.

Jordan, David, ed. *Regionalism Reconsidered: New Approaches to the Field.* New York: Garland, 1994.

Jordan, David Starr. "California and Californians." *Atlantic Monthly* 82 (December 1898): 793–801.

Kant, Candace C. *Zane Grey's Arizona.* Flagstaff, AZ: Northland Press, 1984.

Kaplan, Amy. " 'Left Alone with America': The Absence of Empire in the Study of American Culture." In *Cultures of United States Imperialism.* Ed. Amy Kaplan and Donald E. Pease. Durham, NC: Duke University Press, 1993. 3–21.

——. "Nation, Region, and Empire." In *The Columbia History of the American Novel.* Ed. Emory Elliott. New York: Columbia University Press, 1991. 240–66.

Karp, Ivan, and Stephen D. Lavine, eds. *Exhibiting Cultures: The Poetics and Politics of Museum Display.* Washington, DC: Smithsonian Institution Press, 1991.

Kimball, Arthur G. *Ace of Hearts: The Westerns of Zane Grey.* Fort Worth: Texas Christian University Press, 1993.

Kluckhohn, Clyde. "The Personal Document in Anthropological Science." In *The Use of Personal Documents in History, Anthropology, and Sociology.* Ed. Louis Gottschalk, Clyde Kluckhohn, and Robert Angell. New York: Social Sciences Research Council, 1945. 79–173.

Kluckhohn, Clyde, and Leland C. Wyman. *An Introduction to Navajo Chant Practice.* Menasha, WI: American Anthropological Association, 1940.

Koegel, John. "Hispanic Music in Nineteenth-Century California: The Lummis Collection of Cylinder Recordings at the Southwest Museum." Master's thesis for the Claremont Graduate School, 1992. Braun Research Library, The Southwest Museum.

Kolodny, Annette. "The Integrity of Memory: Creating a New Literary History of the United States." *American Literature* 57 (1985): 291–307.

——. *The Land Before Her: Fantasy and Experience of the American Frontier.* Chapel Hill: University of North Carolina Press, 1984.

——. *The Lay of the Land: Metaphor as Experience and History in American Life and Letters*. Chapel Hill: University of North Carolina Press, 1975.

Kowalewski, Michael. "Writing Place: The New American Regionalism." *American Literary History* 6 (1994): 171–83.

——, ed. *Reading the West: New Essays on the Literature of the American West*. New York: Cambridge University Press, 1996.

Krauss, Roslind E. "Reinventing the Medium." *Critical Inquiry* 25 (1999): 289–305.

Kroeber, Karl, ed. *American Indian Persistence and Resurgence*. Durham, NC: Duke University Press, 1994.

Krupat, Arnold. *Ethnocriticism: Ethnology, History, Literature*. Berkeley: University of California Press, 1992.

——. *The Turn to the Native: Studies in Criticism and Culture*. Lincoln: University of Nebraska Press, 1996.

——. *The Voice in the Margin: Native American Literature and the Canon*. Berkeley: University of California Press, 1989.

——, ed. *Native American Autobiography: An Anthology*. Madison: University of Wisconsin Press, 1994.

Krupat, Arnold, and Brian Swann, eds. *Recovering the Word: Essays on Native American Literature*. Berkeley: University of California Press, 1987.

La Farge, Oliver. *The Enemy Gods*. New York: Literary Classics, 1937.

——. *Laughing Boy*. Boston: Houghton Mifflin, 1929.

——. *Yellow Sun, Bright Sky: The Indian Country Stories of Oliver La Farge*. Ed. David L. Caffey. Albuquerque: University of New Mexico Press, 1988.

Lamar, Howard Roberts. *Far Southwest, 1846–1912: A Territorial History*. New Haven, CT: Yale University Press, 1966.

Langlois, Karen. "A Fresh Voice from the West: Mary Austin, California, and American Literary Magazines, 1892–1910." *California History* 69 (1990): 22–35.

Lavender, David. *The Southwest*. New York: Harper & Row, 1980.

Lawrence, D. H. *D. H. Lawrence and New Mexico*. Ed. Keith Sagar. Salt Lake City: Gibbs M. Smith, 1982.

——. *The Later D. H. Lawrence*. New York: Alfred A. Knopf, 1952.

Lears, T. J. Jackson. *No Place of Grace: Antimodernism and the Transformation of American Culture, 1880–1920*. Chicago: University of Chicago Press, 1981.

Lee, Hermione. *Willa Cather: Double Lives*. New York: Vintage Books, 1991.

Lefebvre, Henri. *The Production of Space*. Trans. Donald Nicolson-Smith. Cambridge, MA: Blackwell, 1991.

——. *Writings on Cities*. Trans. and ed. Eleonore Kofman and Elizabeth Lebas. Cambridge, MA: Blackwell, 1996.

Lensink, Judy Nolte, ed. *Old Southwest / New Southwest: Essays on a Region and Its Literature*. Tucson, AZ: Tucson Public Library, 1987.

Lewis, Edith. *Willa Cather Living: A Personal Record*. New York: Alfred A. Knopf, 1953.

Limerick, Patricia Nelson. *Desert Passages: Encounters with the American Deserts*. Albuquerque: University of New Mexico Press, 1985.

——. *The Legacy of Conquest: The Unbroken Past of the American West*. New York: W. W. Norton, 1987.

Limón, José E. *American Encounters: Greater Mexico, the United States, and the Erotics of Culture*. Boston: Beacon Press, 1998.

Lippard, Lucy. *The Lure of the Local: Senses of Place in a Multicentered Society*. New York: New Press, 1997.

Littlefield, Alice, and Martha C. Knack, eds. *Native Americans and Wage Labor*. Norman: University of Oklahoma Press, 1996.

Luckert, Karl W., with Johnny C. Cooke. *Coyoteway: A Holyway Healing Ceremonial*. Tucson: University of Arizona Press, 1979.

Luhan, Mabel Dodge. *Edge of Taos Desert: Escape to Reality*. 1937. Repr. Albuquerque: University of New Mexico Press, 1987.

Lummis, Charles Fletcher. "The Artist's Paradise." *Land of Sunshine* 28 (June 1908): 236–37.

——. *Bullying the Moqui*. Prescott, AZ: Prescott College Press, 1968.

——. "Catching Our Archaeology Alive." *Out West* 22 (January 1905): 35–45.

——. *The Enchanted Burro: Stories of New Mexico and South America*. Chicago: Way and Williams, 1897.

——. *The King of the Broncos and Other Stories of New Mexico*. New York: Charles Scribner's Sons, 1897.

——. *The Land of Poco Tiempo*. 1893. Repr. Albuquerque: University of New Mexico Press, 1952.

——. *Letters from the Southwest, September 20, 1884 to March 14, 1885*. Ed. James W. Byrkit. Tucson: University of Arizona Press, 1989.

——. *The Man Who Married the Moon, and Other Pueblo Indian Folk-Stories*. New York: The Century Company, 1894.

——. *Mesa, Cañon and Pueblo*. New York: The Century Company, 1925.

——. "New Mexican Folk-Songs." *Cosmopolitan* 13 (1892): 720–29.

——. *A New Mexico David and Other Stories and Sketches of the Southwest*. New York: Charles Scribner's Sons, 1891.

——. *Pueblo Indian Folk-Stories*. 1910. Repr. Lincoln: University of Nebraska Press, 1992. Reprint of *The Man Who Married the Moon*.

——. *Some Strange Corners of Our Country*. New York: The Century Company, 1892.

——. *The Spanish Pioneers*. Chicago: A. C. McClurg, 1893.

——. *A Tramp across the Continent*. New York: Charles Scribner's Sons, 1892.

——. "The White Indian." *Land of Sunshine* 12 (1900): 8–17.

Lummis, Charles Fletcher, and Arthur Farwell. *Spanish Songs of Old California*. Los Angeles: Charles F. Lummis, 1923.

Lyman, Christopher M. *The Vanishing Race and Other Illusions: Photographs of Indians by Edward S. Curtis*. New York: Pantheon Books, 1982.

Mahood, Ruth I., ed. *Photographer of the Southwest: Adam Clark Vroman, 1856– 1916*. Los Angeles: Ward Ritchie Press, 1961.

Malotki, Ekkehart, and Michael Lomatuway'ma, eds. *Hopi Coyote Tales*. Lincoln: University of Nebraska Press, 1984.

Marcus, George E, ed. *Rereading Cultural Anthropology*. Durham, NC: Duke University Press, 1992.

Marcus, George E., and Michael Fischer, eds. *Anthropology as Cultural Critique: An Experimental Moment in the Sciences*. Chicago: University of Chicago Press, 1986.

Mark, Joan. *Four Anthropologists: An American Science in Its Early Years*. New York: Science History Publications, 1980.

Martínez, Oscar J. *Border People: Life and Society in the U.S.–Mexico Borderlands*. Tucson: University of Arizona Press, 1994.

——. *Troublesome Border*. Tucson: University of Arizona Press, 1988.

Marx, Leo. *The Machine in the Garden: Technology and the Pastoral Ideal in America*. New York: Oxford University Press, 1964.

Masayevsa, Victor, Jr., and Erin Younger, eds. *Hopi Photographers, Hopi Images*. Tucson: Sun Tracks and University of Arizona Press, 1983.

Matthews, Washington. *Navajo Legends*. 1897. Repr. Salt Lake City: University of Utah Press, 1994.

——. *The Night Chant, a Navajo Ceremony*. Memoirs of the American Museum of Natural History, 6. New York: The Museum, 1902.

May, Stephen. *Zane Grey: Romancing the West*. Athens: Ohio University Press, 1997.

McClure, John A. *Late Imperial Romance*. New York: Verso, 1994.

McLuhan, T. C. *Dream Tracks: The Railroad and the American Indian, 1890–1930*. New York: Harry N. Abrams, 1985.

McMurtry, Larry. "Inventing the West." *New York Review of Books* 47, no. 13 (2000): 24–29.

McWilliams, Carey. *Southern California: An Island on the Land*. 1946. Repr. Salt Lake City: Peregrine Smith Books, 1973.

Meinig, D. W. *Southwest: Three Peoples in Geographical Change, 1600–1970*. New York: Oxford University Press, 1971.

"*Mesa, Cañon and Pueblo,* by Charles F. Lummis." Review. *El Palacio,* 1 October 1925, 55.

"*Mesa, Cañon and Pueblo,* by Charles F. Lummis." Review. *El Paso Times,* 25 October 1925.

Michaels, Walter Benn. *Our America: Nativism, Modernism, and Pluralism.* Durham, NC: Duke University Press, 1995.

Miller, Angela. *The Empire of the Eye: Landscape Representation and American Cultural Politics, 1825–1875.* Ithaca, NY: Cornell University Press, 1993.

Miller, George, and Dorothy Miller. *Picture Postcards in the United States, 1893–1918.* New York: Clarkson N. Potter, 1976.

Mitchell, Frank. *Navajo Blessingway Singer: The Autobiography of Frank Mitchell, 1881–1967.* Ed. Charlotte J. Frisbie and David P. McAllester. Tucson: University of Arizona Press, 1978.

Mitchell, Lee Clark. *Westerns: Making the Man in Fiction and Film.* Chicago: University of Chicago Press, 1996.

———. "White Slaves and Purple Sage: Plotting Sex in Zane Grey's West." *American Literary History* 6 (1994): 234–64.

———. *Witnesses to a Vanishing America: The Nineteenth-Century Response.* Princeton, NJ: Princeton University Press, 1981.

Mitchell, W.J.T. *Iconology.* Chicago: University of Chicago Press, 1986.

Mohl, Raymond A., ed. *Searching for the Sunbelt: Historical Perspectives on a Region.* Knoxville: University of Tennessee Press, 1990.

Momaday, N. Scott. *House Made of Dawn.* New York: Harper & Row, 1968.

Moneta, Daniel P., ed. *Charles F. Lummis: The Centennial Exhibition Commemorating His Tramp across the Continent.* Los Angeles: Southwest Museum, 1985.

Monroe, Harriet. "Arizona." *Atlantic Monthly* 89 (June 1902): 780–89.

Monsen, Frederick. "The Destruction of Our Indians." *The Craftsman* 11 (March 1907).

Moses, L. G. *Wild West Shows and the Images of American Indians, 1883–1933.* Albuquerque: University of New Mexico Press, 1996.

Muir, John. "The Forests of Yosemite Park." *Atlantic Monthly* 85 (April 1900): 493–507.

———. *The Mountains of California.* 1894. Repr. New York: The Century Company, 1913.

———. *My First Summer in the Sierra.* 1911. Repr. New York: Penguin Books, 1987.

———. "The Wild Parks and Forest Reservations of the West." *Atlantic Monthly* 81 (January 1898): 15–28.

Mumford, Lewis. *The Culture of Cities.* New York: Harcourt Brace Jovanovich, 1938.

——. *The Golden Day: A Study in American Experience and Culture*. New York: Boni and Liveright, 1926.

——. *The Lewis Mumford Reader*. Ed. Donald L. Miller. Athens: University of Georgia Press, 1995.

Murphy, John J., ed. *Critical Essays on Willa Cather*. Boston: G. K. Hall, 1984.

Murray, David. *Forked Tongues: Speech, Writing and Representation in North American Indian Texts*. London: Pinter Books, 1991.

Myrick, David. *New Mexico's Railroads: A Historical Survey*. Revised edition. Albuquerque: University of New Mexico Press, 1990.

Naef, Weston J., and James N. Wood. *The Era of Exploration: The Rise of Landscape Photography in the American West, 1860–1885*. Buffalo, NY, and New York: Albright-Knox Gallery and Metropolitan Museum of Art, 1975.

Nash, Roderick. *Wilderness and the American Mind*. New Haven, CT: Yale University Press, 1967.

Newhall, Beaumont. *Photography: Essays and Images*. New York: Museum of Modern Art, 1980.

Nickel, Douglas R., ed. Carleton *Watkins: The Art of Perception*. San Francisco: San Francisco Museum of Modern Art and Harry N. Abrams, 1999.

Nordenskiold, Gustaf. *The Cliff Dwellers of the Mesa Verde*. Trans. D. Lloyd Morgan. 1893. Repr. New York: AMS Press, 1973.

Noriega, Chon A., ed. *From the West: Chicano Narrative Photography*. San Francisco: The Mexican Museum, 1995.

Norman, Dorothy. *Alfred Stieglitz: Introduction to an American Seer*. New York: Duell, Sloan, and Pearce, 1960.

Norwood, Vera, and Janice Monk, eds. *The Desert Is No Lady: Southwestern Landscapes in Women's Writing and Art*. New Haven, CT: Yale University Press, 1987.

Novak, Barbara. *Nature and Culture: American Landscape and Painting, 1825–1875*. New York: Oxford University Press, 1980.

Nugent, Walter. "The People of the West." In *The Twentieth-Century West*. Ed. Gerald D. Nash and Richard Etulain. Albuquerque: University of New Mexico Press, 1989. 35–70.

O'Brien, Sharon. "Becoming Noncanonical: The Case Against Willa Cather." *American Quarterly* 40 (1988): 110–26.

——. *Willa Cather: The Emerging Voice*. New York: Oxford University Press, 1987.

Odum, Howard, and Harry Estill Moore. *American Regionalism: A Cultural-Historical Approach to National Integration*. New York: Henry Holt, 1938.

Oles, James. *South of the Border: Mexico in the American Imagination, 1914–1947*. Washington, DC: Smithsonian Institution Press, 1993.

Ortiz, Alfonso. "The Dynamics of Pueblo Cultural Survival." In *North American*

Indian Anthropology: Essays on Society and Culture. Ed. Raymond J. DeMaillie and Alfonso Ortiz. Norman: University of Oklahoma Press, 1994. 296–305.

Ortiz, Simon, ed. *Speaking for the Generations: Native Writers on Writing.* Tucson: University of Arizona Press, 1998.

Orvell, Miles. *The Real Thing.* Chapel Hill: University of North Carolina Press, 1989.

Packard, Gar, and Maggy Packard. *Southwest 1880 with Ben Wittick, Pioneer Photographer of Indian and Frontier Life.* Santa Fe, NM: Packard Publications, 1970.

Padget, Martin. "Travel, Exoticism, and the Writing of Region: Charles Fletcher Lummis and the 'Creation' of the Southwest." *Journal of the Southwest* 37, no. 3 (1995): 421–49.

Palmquist, Peter E. *Carleton E. Watkins: Photographer of the American West.* Albuquerque: University of New Mexico Press and Amon Carter Museum, 1983.

Paredes, Américo. *Folkore and Culture on the Texas-Mexican Border.* Ed. Richard Bauman. Austin: Center for Mexican American Studies and University of Texas Press, 1993.

——. *A Texas-Mexican Cancionero: Folksongs of the Lower Border.* Austin: University of Texas Press, 1976.

——. *"With His Pistol in His Hand": A Border Ballad and Its Hero.* Austin: University of Texas Press, 1958.

Parezo, Nancy J., ed. *Hidden Scholars: Women Anthropologists and the Native American Southwest.* Albuquerque: University of New Mexico Press, 1993.

Parker, Robert. "Text, Lines, and Videotape: The Ideology of Genre and the Transcription of Traditional Native American Oral Narrative as Poetry." *Arizona Quarterly* 53, no. 3 (1997): 141–69.

Parsons, Elsie Clews. *American Indian Life.* New York: B. W. Huebsch, 1922.

——. "Isleta, New Mexico." In *Forty-seventh Annual Report of the Bureau of American Ethnology.* Washington, DC: U.S. Government Printing Office, 1932. 195–466.

——. *Pueblo Mothers and Children: Essays.* Ed. Barbara Babcock. Santa Fe, N.M.: Ancient City Press, 1991.

——. *Tewa Tales.* New York: American Folklore Society, 1926.

Pearce, T. M. *The Beloved House.* Caldwell, ID: Caxton Printers, 1940.

——. *Mary Hunter Austin.* New York: Twayne, 1965.

——, ed. *America in the Southwest.* Albuquerque: University of New Mexico Press, 1933.

Pearce, T. M., and A. P. Thomason, eds. *Southwesterners Write.* Albuquerque: University of New Mexico Press, 1946.

Perry, Bliss. "The Short Story." *Atlantic Monthly* 90 (August 1902): 241-52.

Pilkington, William T. *My Blood's Country: Studies in Southwestern Literature.* Fort Worth: Texas Christian University Press, 1973.

Poling-Kempes, Lesley. *The Harvey Girls: Women Who Opened the West.* New York: Paragon House, 1989.

Pomeroy, Earl. *In Search of the Golden West: The Tourist in Western America.* Lincoln: University of Nebraska Press, 1957.

———. *The Pacific Slope: A History of California, Oregon, Washington, Idaho, Utah, and Nevada.* New York: Alfred A. Knopf, 1965.

Powell, Lawrence Clark. *Southwest Classics: The Creative Literature of the Arid Lands.* Los Angeles: Ward Richie Press, 1974.

Pratt, Mary Louise. *Imperial Eyes: Travel Writing and Transculturation.* New York: Routledge, 1992.

Rabb, Jane M., ed. *Literature and Photography: Interactions, 1840–1990.* Albuquerque: University of New Mexico Press, 1995.

Rampersad, Arnold. *The Life of Langston Hughes, Vol. I: 1902–1941.* New York: Oxford University Press, 1986.

Rathbone, Belinda. "Paul Strand: The Land & Its People." *The Print Collector's Newsletter* 21, no. 1 (1990): 1–5.

Reed, Verner Z. "The Desert." *Atlantic Monthly* 90 (August 1902): 166–72.

Reeve, Kay Aiken. *Santa Fe and Taos, 1898–1942: An American Cultural Center.* El Paso: Texas Western Press, 1982.

Reichard, Gladys A. *Dezba: Woman of the Desert.* New York: J. J. Augustin, 1939.

Ricoeur, Paul. *Lectures on Ideology and Utopia.* Ed. George H. Taylor. New York: Columbia University Press, 1986.

Riley, Glenda. " 'Wimmin Is Everywhere': Conserving and Feminizing Western Landscapes, 1870–1940." *Western History Quarterly* 29 (Spring 1998): 4–23.

Robbins, William G. *Colony and Empire: The Capitalist Transformation of the American West.* Lawrence: University Press of Kansas, 1994.

Robinson, Cecil. *No Short Journeys.* Tucson: University of Arizona Press, 1992.

Robinson, Will H. *Under Turquoise Skies: Outstanding Features of the Story of America's Southwest from the Days of the Ancient Cliff-Dwellers to Modern Times.* New York: Macmillan, 1928.

Roemer, Kenneth. "The Nightway Question in American Literature." *American Literature* 66 (1994): 817–29.

Ronald, Ann. *Zane Grey.* Boise, ID: Boise State University Press, 1975.

Rosaldo, Renato. *Culture & Truth: The Remaking of Social Analysis.* Boston: Beacon Press, 1989.

Rose, Phyllis. "Modernism: The Case of Willa Cather." In *Modernism Reconsidered.* Ed. Robert Kiely. Cambridge, MA: Harvard University Press, 1983. 123–45.

Rosenbaum, Robert J. *Mexicano Resistance in the Southwest*. Dallas: Southern Methodist University Press, 1998.

Rosowski, Susan J. *The Voyage Perilous: Willa Cather's Romanticism*. Lincoln: University of Nebraska Press, 1986.

———. "Willa Cather's Ecology of Place." *Western American Literature* 30, no. 1 (1995): 37–51.

Rudnick, Lois Palken. *Mabel Dodge Luhan: New Woman, New Worlds*. Albuquerque: University of New Mexico Press, 1984.

———. *Utopian Vistas: The Mabel Dodge Luhan House and the American Counterculture*. Albuquerque: University of New Mexico Press, 1996.

Rydell, Robert W. *All the World's a Fair: Visions of Empire at American International Exhibitions, 1876–1916*. Chicago: University of Chicago Press, 1984.

———. *World of Fairs: The Century of Progress Exposition*. Chicago: University of Chicago Press, 1993.

Salas, Miguel Tinker. "Sonora: The Making of a Border Society, 1880–1910." *Journal of the Southwest* 34, no. 4 (1992): 429–56.

Saldívar, José David. "Américo Paredes and Decolonization." In *Cultures of United States Imperialism*. Ed. Amy Kaplan and Donald E. Pease. Durham, NC: Duke University Press, 1993. 291–311.

———. *Border Matters*. Berkeley: University of California Press, 1997.

Sando, Joe. *Pueblo Nation: Eight Centuries of Pueblo History*. Santa Fe, NM: Clear Light Publishers, 1992.

Sandweiss, Martha, ed. *Photography in Nineteenth-Century America*. New York and Fort Worth, TX: Harry N. Abrams and The Amon Carter Museum, 1991.

Sarber, Mary A. *Charles F. Lummis: A Bibliography*. Tucson: Graduate Library School, University of Arizona, 1977.

Sargeant, Elizabeth Shepley. "Beyond Man's Power to Spoil." *New York Herald Tribune*, 6 December 1925.

———. *Willa Cather: A Memoir*. Philadelphia: Lippincott, 1953.

Sayre, Henry M. "Surveying the Vast Profound." *The Massachusetts Review* 24 (1983): 723–42.

Schlereth, Thomas J. *Cultural History and Material Culture: Everyday Life, Landscapes, Museums*. Charlottesville: University Press of Virginia, 1992.

Schroeter, James, ed. *Willa Cather and Her Critics*. Ithaca, NY: Cornell University Press, 1967.

Sekaquaptewa, Helen. *Me and Mine: The Story of Helen Sekaquaptewa as Told to Louise Udall*. Tucson: University of Arizona Press, 1969.

Shoumatoff, Alex. *Legends of the American Desert: Sojourns in the Greater Southwest*. New York: Alfred A. Knopf, 1997.

Silko, Leslie Marmon. *Ceremony*. 1977. Repr. New York: Penguin Books, 1986.

——. *Gardens in the Dunes*. New York: Simon and Schuster, 1999.

Simmons, Marc. *Witchcraft in the Southwest: Spanish and Indian Supernaturalism on the Rio Grande*. Flagstaff, AZ: Northland Press, 1974.

Simonson, Harold P. *Beyond the Frontier: Writers, Western Regionalism and a Sense of Place*. Fort Worth: Texas Christian University Press, 1989.

Simpson, David. *The Academic Postmodern and the Rule of Literature: A Report on Half-Knowledge*. Chicago: University of Chicago Press, 1995.

Slotkin, Richard. *The Fatal Environment: The Myth of the Frontier in the Age of Industrialization, 1800–1890*. New York: Atheneum, 1985.

——. *Gunfighter Nation: The Myth of the Frontier in Twentieth-Century America*. New York: Atheneum, 1992.

——. *Regeneration through Violence: The Mythology of the American Frontier, 1600–1860*. Middletown, CT: Wesleyan University Press, 1973.

Smith, Henry Nash. *Virgin Land: The American West as Symbol and Myth*. Cambridge, MA: Harvard University Press, 1950.

Smith, Neil. *Uneven Development: Nature, Capital and the Production of Space*. London: Basil Blackwell, 1984.

Snyder, Joel. "Territorial Photography." In *Landscape and Power*. Ed. W.J.T. Mitchell. Chicago: University of Chicago Press, 1994. 175–201.

Soja, Edward. *Postmodern Geographies: The Reassertion of Space in Critical Social Theory*. New York: Verso, 1989.

Spicer, Edward H. *Cycles of Conquest: The Impact of Spain, Mexico, and the United States on the Indians of the Southwest, 1533–1960*. Tucson: University of Arizona Press, 1962.

——. *The Yaquis: A Cultural History*. Tucson: University of Arizona Press, 1980.

Spurr, David. *The Rhetoric of Empire: Colonial Discourse in Journalism, Travel Writing, and Imperial Administration*. Durham, NC: Duke University Press, 1993.

Stange, Maren, ed. *Paul Strand: Essays on His Life and Work*. New York: Aperture, 1990.

Starr, Kevin. *Americans and the California Dream, 1850–1915*. New York: Oxford University Press, 1973.

——. *Inventing the Dream: California through the Progressive Era*. New York: Oxford University Press, 1985.

——. *Material Dreams: Southern California through the 1920s*. New York: Oxford University Press, 1990.

Steiner, Michael, and Clarence Mondale, eds. *Region and Regionalism in the United States*. New York: Garland, 1988.

Steiner, Michael, and David M. Wrobel, eds. *Many Wests: Place, Culture, and Regional Identity*. Lawrence: University Press of Kansas, 1993.

Stevens, Wallace. *The Collected Poems of Wallace Stevens*. New York: Alfred A. Knopf, 1989.

——. *Opus Posthumous*. Ed. Milton J. Bates. New York: Vintage Books, 1990.

Stevenson, Matilda Cox. "The Sia." In *Eleventh Annual Printing of the Bureau of Ethnology, 1889–90*. Washington, DC: U.S. Government Printing Office, 1894. 3–157.

Stieglitz, Alfred. *Camera Work: The Complete Illustrations, 1903–1917*. New York: Taschen, 1997.

Stineman, Esther Lanigan. *Mary Austin: Song of a Maverick*. New Haven, CT: Yale University Press, 1989.

Stocking, George, Jr. *The Ethnographer's Magic and Other Essays in the History of Anthropology*. Madison: University of Wisconsin Press, 1992.

——. *Race, Culture and Evolution*. Chicago: University of Chicago Press, 1982.

——, ed. *Observers Observed*. Madison: University of Wisconsin Press, 1983.

Strand, Paul. "The Art Motive in Photography." *British Journal of Photography* 70 (5 October 1923).

——. "Photography and the New God." *Broom* 3 (November 1922): 252–58.

——. "What Was '291'?" Typescript. Yale Collection of American Literature, Beinecke Rare Book and Manuacript Library, Yale University.

Sundquist, Eric. "Realism and Regionalism." In *Columbia Literary History of the United States*. Ed. Emory Elliott. New York: Columbia University Press, 1988. 501–24.

Swann, Brian. *Song of the Sky: Versions of Native American Song-Poems*. Amherst: University of Massachusetts Press, 1985.

——, ed. *On the Translation of Native American Literatures*. Washington, DC: Smithsonian Institution Press, 1992.

Szarkowski, John. *Photography Until Now*. New York: Museum of Modern Art, 1989.

Takaki, Ronald. *A Different Mirror: A History of Multicultural America*. Boston: Little, Brown, 1993.

Talayesva, Don C. *Sun Chief: The Autobiography of a Hopi Indian*. Ed. Leo W. Simmons. New Haven, CT: Yale University Press, 1942.

Tapahonso, Luci. *Blue Horses Rush In*. Tucson: University of Arizona Press, 1997.

Tatum, Stephen. "The Problem of the 'Popular' in the New Western History." *Arizona Quarterly* 53, no. 2 (1997): 153–90.

Taylor, J. Golden, ed. *A Literary History of the American West*. Fort Worth: Texas Christian University Press, 1987.

Teague, David. *The Southwest in American Literature and Art*. Tucson: University of Arizona Press, 1997.

Tedlock, Barbara. *The Beautiful and the Dangerous: Encounters with the Zuni Indians*. New York: Viking Penguin, 1992.

Tedlock, Dennis. *Finding the Center: Narrative Poetry of the Zuni Indians*. New York: Dial Press, 1972.

———. *The Spoken Word and the Work of Interpretation*. 1972. Repr. Philadelphia: University of Pennsylvania Press, 1978.

Thomas, F. Richard, ed. *Literary Admirers of Alfred Stieglitz*. Carbondale: Southern Illinois University Press, 1983.

Tompkins, Jane. *West of Everything: The Inner Life of Westerns*. New York: Oxford University Press, 1992.

Torgovnick, Marianna. *Gone Primitive: Savage Intellect, Modern Lives*. Chicago: University of Chicago Press, 1990.

———. *Primitive Passions: Men, Women, and the Quest for Ecstasy*. New York: Alfred A. Knopf, 1997.

Trachtenberg, Alan. *The Incorporation of America: Culture and Society in the Gilded Age*. New York: Hill and Wang, 1982.

———. *Reading American Photographs: Images as History. Mathew Brady to Walker Evans*. New York: Hill and Wang, 1989.

———, ed. *Classic Essays on Photography*. New Haven, CT: Leete's Island Books, 1980.

Traugott, Joseph, Anna Secco, and Mario Materassi. *La terra incantata dei Pueblo: Fotographie di Charles F. Lummis, 1888–1905*. Treviso, Italy: Vianello, 1991.

Trilling, Lionel. *Sincerity and Authenticity*. Cambridge, MA: Harvard University Pres, 1971.

Turner, Frederick Jackson. "Contributions of the West to American Democracy." *Atlantic Monthly* 91 (January 1903): 83–96.

———. *Frontier and Section: Selected Essays of Frederick Jackson Turner*. Englewood Cliffs, NJ: Prentice-Hall, 1961.

———. "The Problem of the West." *Atlantic Monthly* 78 (September 1896): 289–97.

———. *The Significance of the Frontier in American History*. Ed. Harold P. Simonson. New York: Frederick Ungar, 1963.

Turner, John Kenneth. *Barbarous Mexico*. 1910. Repr. Austin: University of Texas Press, 1969.

Turner, Victor W., and Edward M. Bruner, eds. *The Anthropology of Experience*. Chicago: University of Illinois Press, 1986.

Truman, Major Ben C. *History of the World's Fair*. Philadelphia: Standard Publishing Company, 1893.

Twain, Mark. *Roughing It*. 1872. Repr. Ed. Hamlin Hill. New York: Penguin Books, 1981.

Underhill, Ruth. *Autobiography of a Papago Woman*. Memoirs of the American Anthropological Society, no. 46. Menasha, WI: The Society, 1936.

Urgo, Joseph R. *Willa Cather and the Myth of American Migration*. Chicago: University of Illinois Press, 1995.

Vásquez, Josefina Zoraida, and Lorenzo Meyer. *The United States and Mexico*. Chicago: University of Chicago Press, 1985.

Vélez-Ibáñez, Carlos. *Border Visions: Mexican Cultures of the Southwestern United States.* Tucson: University of Arizona Press, 1996.

Venuti, Lawrence, ed. *The Translation Studies Reader.* London and New York: Routledge, 2000.

Wallerstein, Emmanuel. *Geopolitics and Geoculture.* New York: Cambridge University Press, 1991.

Walton, Eda Lou. *Dawn Boy: Blackfoot and Navajo Songs.* New York: E. P. Dutton, 1926.

Warner, Charles Dudley. "The Heart of the Desert." *Harper's* 82 (February 1891): 392–412.

Waters, Frank. *Masked Gods: Navajo and Pueblo Ceremonialism.* Albuquerque: University of New Mexico Press, 1950.

Webb, William, and Robert A. Weinstein. *Dwellers at the Source: Southwestern Indian Photographs of A. C. Vroman, 1895–1904.* Albuquerque: University of New Mexico Press, 1973.

Weber, Max. *Economy and Society.* Ed. Guenther Roth and Claus Wittich. Berkeley: University of California Press, 1978.

——. *From Max Weber: Essays in Sociology.* Trans. and ed. H. H. Gerth and C. Wright Mills. New York: Oxford University Press, 1946.

Weigle, Marta. "From Desert to Disney World." *Journal of Anthropological Research* 45 (1989): 115–37.

——. *The Penitentes of the Southwest.* Santa Fe, NM: Ancient City Press, 1970.

——. "Southwest Lures: Innocence Detoured, Incensed, Determined." *Journal of the Southwest* 32, no. 4 (1990): 499–540.

——, ed. *Women of New Mexico: Depression Era Images.* Santa Fe, NM: Ancient City Press, 1993.

Weigle, Marta, and Kyle Fiore. *Santa Fe and Taos: The Writer's Era, 1916–1941.* Santa Fe, NM: Ancient City Press, 1982.

Weigle, Marta, and Peter White, eds. *The Lore of New Mexico.* Albuquerque: University of New Mexico Press, 1988.

Welsch, Roger L. *Tall-Tale Postcards: A Pictorial History.* South Brunswick, NJ: A. S. Barnes, 1976.

White, Richard. *"It's Your Misfortune and None of My Own": A New History of the American West.* Norman: University of Oklahoma Press, 1991.

Whiting, Lilian. *The Land of Enchantment: From Pike's Peak to the Pacific.* Boston: Little, Brown, 1906.

Wiebe, Robert H. *The Search for Order, 1877–1920.* New York: Hill and Wang, 1967.

Williams, Raymond. *The Country and the City.* New York: Oxford University Press, 1973.

——. *The Politics of Modernism.* New York: Verso, 1987.

——. *Writing in Society*. London: Verso, 1983.

Wilson, Chris. *The Myth of Santa Fe: Creating a Modern Regional Tradition*. Albuquerque: University of New Mexico Press, 1997.

Wolf, Daniel, ed. *The American Space: Meaning in Nineteenth-Century Landscape Photography*. Middletown, CT: Wesleyan University Press, 1983.

Womack, Craig. *Red on Red: Native American Literary Separatism*. Minneapolis: University of Minnesota Press, 1999.

Woodress, James. *Willa Cather: A Literary Life*. Lincoln: University of Nebraska Press, 1987.

Work, James C., ed. *Prose and Poetry of the American West*. Lincoln: University of Nebraska Press, 1990.

Yates, Steven A., ed. *The Essential Landscape: The New Mexican Photographic Survey*. Albuquerque: University of New Mexico Press, 1985.

Yava, Albert. *Big Falling Snow: A Tewa-Hopi Indian's Life and Times*. Ed. Harold Courlander. New York: Crown, 1978.

Zelinsky, Wilbur. *The Cultural Geography of the United States*. Englewood Cliffs, NJ: Prentice-Hall, 1973.

Zepeda, Ofelia. *Ocean Power: Poems from the Desert*. Tucson: University of Arizona Press, 1995.

Zolbrod, Paul. *Diné bahane': The Navajo Creation Story*. Albuquerque: University of New Mexico Press, 1984.

——. "On the Multicultural Frontier with Washington Matthews." *Journal of the Southwest* 40, no. 1 (1998): 67–86.

——. *Reading the Voice: Native American Oral Poetry on the Page*. Salt Lake City: University of Utah Press, 1995.

Zolbrod, Paul, and Roseann Sandoval Willink. *Weaving a World: Textiles and the Navajo Way of Seeing*. Santa Fe: Museum of New Mexico Press, 1996.

Index

Barnes, Nellie, 126

Bashford, Herbert, 112

Basso, Keith, 175

Benjamin, Walter, xix, 15, 91, 93, 95, 98, 105. Works: "Little History of Photography," 67–69, 74–75, 77, 91–92; "The Task of the Translator," 16, 128; "The Work of Art in the Age of Mechanical Reproduction," 68, 99. *See also* modernism; photography

Bierstadt, Albert, 70

Blue Horses Rush In (Tapahonso), 24

Boas, Franz, 13–15, 123–26, 128; and translation, 176n. 64

borderlands, xxi–xxii, 36, 38, 58–61, 63; and frontier, 58. *See also* formula Western

Bourdieu, Pierre, 39; and habitus, 12, 178n. 29; and literary field, 178n. 18; and trajectory, 169n. 8

Broder, Patricia, 78

Brodhead, Richard, xiv, 41, 147

Buell, Lawrence, 114, 166

Bureau of American Ethnology, 14, 16

Burlin, Natalie Curtis, 126, 135

Bynner, Witter, 118, 122

Cabeza de Vaca, Álvar Núñez, xxi, xxiv

Camera Work (Stieglitz), 95, 119

Canyon de Chelly, 88, *88–90*, 91, 99, 153

Carlin, Deborah, 139

Castro, Michael, 127

Cather, Willa, xvii, xix–xx, 66, 118, 137–64; and aesthetic equilibrium, 160–61, 163; and antimodernism, xx, 140; and artifacts, 151; critical reception of, 138–39, 142, 152,

153–55; and desert, 155, 158; and duality, 138–39, 143–44, 146; and imaginative possession, 137, 153; and Charles Lummis, 34; as modernist, 163–64; as regionalist, 141, 145, 163; and revelation of place, xix–xx, 137–38, 141, 144–45, 159; and sensation, 151; and sublime, 155, 158–59; as tourist, 149; travels of, 140. Works: *Death Comes for the Archbishop,* xix, 138–40, 146, 148, 149, 153–63; "The Enchanted Bluff," 145; *My Ántonia,* 139, 142–46, 150–51; *Not Under Forty,* 138; "The Novel Demeublé," 138; *O Pioneers!* 139, 141–44; "Prairie Spring," 141; *The Professor's House,* xix, 34, 138, 140, 146, 148, 150, 152, 163; *The Song of The Lark,* xix, 139–40, 146, 148, 150–52, 158, 163; *Willa Cather in Europe,* 137; *Willa Cather on Writing,* 138, 149, 151, 162, 164

Cawelti, John, 54

Ceremony (Silko), 134

Chaco Canyon, 13

Chesnutt, Charles, 41, 147

Cheyfitz, Eric, 106

Chicago Exposition (1893), 74

Chippewas, songs of, 127

Chiricahuas, 79

Clifford, James, xxii, 12, 23, 126

Coles, Robert, 102

Collier, John, 97

Conn, Steven, 14

Cooper, James Fenimore, 65, 124, 155

Coronado, Francisco Vásquez de, 140

corrido, 37

Cronyn, George, 127

Curtis, Edward S., xix, 66, 85–86,

autonomy, 90–91, 128, 137; and aura, 67–69; and disenchantment, 69, 105, 148; and high culture, 67–69, 117; and masculinity, 91; and mass culture, 37, 107; and mysticism, 96, 122; and primitivism, 118, 120–21; as re-enchantment, 153, 162; and translation, 187n. 57; and urbanism, 138. *See also* antimodernism

modernity: antinomies of, xiii; and disenchantment, 45; and dislocation, xiii, 33, 118; and region, xiv–xv

Momaday, Scott, 134

Monsen, Frederick, 85, 86

Mooney, James, 127

Moran, Thomas, 70

Morgan, J. Pierpont, 85

Mormons, 42, 48–50. *See also* formula Western, Mormons in

Muir, John, xix, 3, 112, 184n. 15, 185n. 18

Mumford, Lewis, xv

Murray, David, 29

Museum of New Mexico, 30

Myrick, David, 170n. 22

Native American autobiography, 125–26

Native American literature: *Blue Horses Rush In* (Tapahonso), 24; *Ceremony* (Silko), 34; *Gardens in the Dunes* (Silko), xiii; *House Made of Dawn* (Momaday), 134; *Ocean Power* (Zepeda), 135–36

Native American oral tradition: inaccessibility of, 14; translation of, 14–15, 29–30, 187n. 57; volume of, 15. Works: "Coyote and Cicada Woman" (Hopi), 175n. 58;

"The Coyote and the Locust," 24–26; Creation Myth (Kato), 133; Creation Story (Navajo), xx; *Diné bahane'* (Navajo), 16; "Grandmother Spider" (Navajo), 27–28; "Night Chant" (Navajo), 15–16, 161; "Song of Victory" (Paiute), 133; "Young Man's Song," 133

Native Americans. *See* names of individual groups; Native American autobiography; Native American literature; Native American oral tradition; photography, Southwestern, Native American portraiture

Navajos (Diné), 38, 76, 80, 81, 86, 118, 127, 153, 160; conception of wind, 161

New Western History, 4, 36

"Night Chant" (Navajo), 15–16, 161

North American Indian, The (Curtis), 85

O'Brien, Sharon, 139

O'Keeffe, Georgia, 92, 96, 97, 118, 166

Oles, James, 60

Ortiz, Alfonso, 13

Ortiz, Simon, xxiii

O'Sullivan, Timothy, 83, 88, 89, *90*

Otis, Harrison Gray, 18

Our National Parks (Muir), 112

Padget, Martin, 4, 174n. 43

Paiutes, xiii

Papagos. *See* Tohono O'odham

Paredes, Américo, 37

Parker, Robert, 28

Parsons, Elsie Clews, 13, 18–19, 124, 125, 172n. 27

Pasadena Eight, xix, 68, 75, 181n. 17

About the Author

AUDREY GOODMAN graduated from Princeton University and earned her doctorate in English and comparative literature from Columbia University. Since 1997, she has been assistant professor of American literature at Georgia State University. Her published work includes articles on Willa Cather in *Arizona Quarterly* and on amateur ethnography in *Journal of the Southwest*. She lives in Atlanta with her husband, David, and daughter, Ruth.